TEACHING AND LEARNING
IN CITY SCHOOLS

PSYCHOSOCIAL STUDIES IN EDUCATION

From the Research Division, Bank Street College of Education

EDITOR: BARBARA BIBER

ASSOCIATE EDITOR: DORIS WALLACE

1. The Psychological Impact of School Experience:
A Comparative Study of Nine-Year-Old Children in Contrasting Schools
by Patricia Minuchin, Barbara Biber, Edna Shapiro, and Herbert Zimiles

2. Teaching and Learning in City Schools: A Comparative Study
by Eleanor Burke Leacock

TEACHING AND LEARNING IN CITY SCHOOLS
A Comparative Study

Eleanor Burke Leacock

Basic Books, Inc., Publishers NEW YORK LONDON

PREFACE

This study of elementary school classrooms was contributed to by members of various disciplines. However, the majority of the research team were anthropologists, and it is from the science of social anthropology that the theoretical framework of the study was most explicitly drawn. This meant that children's *education* was seen as inseparable from the broader process of their *socialization*, and, in turn, that their socialization by the school was viewed as inextricably bound up with the social system, of which both schools and children are part, and with the status of the class and color groupings to which different children belong. Furthermore, the assumptions about what is important and desirable for children, as well as the goals being conveyed to them in the course of their schooling, were considered to be crucial to the socialization process; it was understood that these assumptions and goals (often loosely encompassed by the term "values") are transmitted to children by implication and indirection at least as often as by direct exhortation.

However, the study is not of socialization as such but of teaching seen in the context of socialization. It is a study of classrooms, pupils, and teachers, and the researchers never lost sight of the fact that teaching involves its own body of theory and technology. Yet this technology, as learned by teachers during their training, is translated into practice within an institutional structure that has many other than strictly educational functions—including not only its general socialization function but also its custodial function of caring for young children much of the day and its political and economic functions of providing livelihood for many as well as power and influence for a few. Therefore, the process of education was understood to involve the interplay among the functional requirements of the socialization process, the structural features of the school system, and the specific technology of teaching as understood by teachers.

In one sense, it is individual teachers who do or do not succeed in teaching children. However, teachers do not act as free agents but are governed both directly and indirectly by the system of which they are a part. The gross inequalities of schools for different groups of children and the obvious inadequacies of the educational system have been much publicized and well-documented of late. It is not my intent in this book simply to underscore the criticism that much about our educational system is geared to miseducation. My intent is rather to present in some detail how it is that hard-working and, on the whole, well-meaning teachers come to play the active role they do in this process of miseducation. Along with the rest of the study team, I am much indebted to the good will of the teachers whose classrooms we were enabled to visit during the course of the study, and my hope is to afford useful insights to the many teachers like them who would like to see their efforts meet with greater success. My desire is also to add to the understanding of parents and others who are trying to find a new approach to the improvement of education for children.

I have not wished to overburden the reader with the details of what goes into research such as this and have, perhaps, made it sound rather too smooth and simple. However, the following pages represent the efforts of eleven people who worked intensively with the study, along with others who advised and assisted in various ways. Together the researchers discussed, argued, experimented, made false starts and started again in their attempts to collect the most meaningful observational and interview materials on classrooms and to sort from them those which seemed most germane to understanding what and why the study children probably were and were not learning, A glance at the "Outline for the Characterization of a Classroom," included in the Appendices, will give the interested reader some notion of how much organization and comparative analysis of materials was carried out before the areas which appeared to be the more significant were selected for more intensive analysis.

In writing this report of a study, I am first and foremost indebted to the "team." They were: from the field of anthropology, Sylvia Knopf Polgar, Rosa Graham, Robert Harrison, Lisa Redfield Peattie, and Eleanor Wenkart Smollett; from education, Phyllis Gunther and Sema Brainin; and from psychology, Julius Trubowitz, Anne Gordon, and Raya Wudowsky. At every step in the working out of the study, from preliminary formulations to the final analysis of the material and criticisms and suggestions on this report, the research was assisted by Barbara Biber, formerly Director of Research, now Distinguished Research Scholar at the Bank Street College of Education and Principal Investigator of the Schools and Mental Health Program; and by Charlotte Winsor, formerly Director of Graduate Programs, now Distinguished Teacher Education Specialist and a co-investigator of the program. The Schools and Mental Health Program of the Bank Street College of Education, of which this study was a part, was made possible by the sponsorship and support of the National Institute of Mental Health (Grant No. 3M–9135).

For advice at various stages in the study I am indebted to senior members of the Bank Street College staff, notably Martin Kohn (psychology), Donald Horton (sociology), and Elizabeth Gilkeson and Annette Frank Shapiro (education). For valuable assistance during the later stages of completing the study, as well as for editorial assistance on this report, I am grateful to Doris Wallace of the Bank Street College administrative staff. I am also grateful to the many members of the secretarial staff of the College who helped along the way, but I particularly wish to express my appreciation for the able helpfulness of Carol Carr, Ruth Kolbe, Margaret Newman, and William Bryan (who was then studying for his degree in psychology).

To all children in our schools, and particularly to the children who are poor and black and most cheated by our schools, this book is dedicated.

May 1969   E. L.
Polytechnic Institute of Brooklyn

EDITOR'S PREFACE

PSYCHOSOCIAL STUDIES IN EDUCATION
From the Research Division, Bank Street College of Education

There are times when ideas converge, generate new directions for thought, and stimulate change in programs for research and action. Sometimes this happens to an individual; sometimes—as is the case in the work to be reported in this series—to a group of co-workers; and occasionally this happens to a larger body-politic, as is true at the time of this writing of the war against poverty. The formulation and funding, in the 1950's, of the studies reported in this series was made possible because of the convergence of three lines of thought in education and mental health.

Progressive thinkers in education had conceptualized a new role for the school and had been trying it out for several decades. This model inaugurated radical changes in practice based on the central tenet that education is a primary force in shaping the whole person—his life of feeling as well as his mind, his power to create as well as to adjust, his inner equilibrium and his outer effectiveness. Inevitably, this model included goals for influencing personality. In addition to developing intellectual power, these schools considered themselves responsible for fostering such aspects of development as self-understanding, relatedness to people, motivated interaction with the environment, and personal qualities such as curiosity, spontaneity, and resilience. It was an image of optimal human functioning derived from psychodynamic theories of personality development, which favored humanist values in the individual's interaction with his world and saw the school, in the perspective of John Dewey, as a vital instrument by which to accomplish these goals for people and for society.

National concern about mental illness had begun to spread its ideo-
logical wings at the same time. By the 1950's, the term "health" in the
mental health movement was no longer a euphemism in the designation
of a whole field of activity. The focus had shifted from exclusive concern
with mental illness as a disease to a concern with goals for healthy human
functioning. In 1958 Marie Jahoda defined the "Current Concepts of Positive Mental Health" as part of the work of the Joint Commission on Mental
Illness and Health, established by the Congressional Mental Health Study
Act in 1955. As a result, what for a long time had been a vague, somewhat
evangelistic concept of mental health was elevated to a condition of
theoretical clarity and applied usefulness. Jahoda's roster of criteria for
individual functioning was based on a review of the work of personality
theorists and clinicians. It was congruent, to an impressive degree, with
the goals that had been formulated by the educators. While this congru-
ence added strength and a measure of validity to each position, little might
have emerged to influence research and programming had not a third
line of thought become increasingly prominent at the same time.

The third convergent line of thinking originated in the field of public
health, where programs of prevention had proved effective in the control
of physical disorders. The adoption of the concept of primary prevention
in the mental health field stimulated new thinking. Whereas the focus had
previously been on psychotherapy for the individual, the target now became the relative psychological health of large sectors of the population.
Social institutions such as the family and the school became the program
locale, and their psychological condition became the programming focus.
The rationale was that changes in the modes of functioning of social institutions would bring about such significant elevation of basic ego strength
in the general population that vulnerability to the various forms of stress
and deprivation associated with the onset of mental disorders would be
significantly reduced. On the one hand, there was no hard evidence that
positive mental health was specifically preventive of mental disorders
and little expectation that the complex relation between health and illness
in the psychological field would lend itself to easy unraveling. On the
other hand, there was the view that what was needed were programs
based on the best available knowledge—from theory and clinical experience—as to the significant etiological forces operating at a community
level and activities to ameliorate long-term noxious influences.

These three forceful lines of thought were running in a common
channel: the model of a school that took upon itself the extended goal of
optimal individual functioning; a concept of positive mental health that
was regarded as deserving of a position in the orbit of preventive psy-

chiatry; and a new public momentum toward investment in change in social institutions as a feasible approach to the nation-wide problems of mental health and illness. The school was obviously an important candidate for such investment. The National Institute of Mental Health was ready to support programs working toward change in education in these directions, and in 1958 the Bank Street College of Education was granted support by NIMH to plan a program of research and action on the basis of its prior experience in preschool and elementary education and school consultation that was congruent with concepts of positive mental health.

The choices of what kind of study and which lines of activity to undertake were not altogether open-ended nor exploratory in the sense that one takes a first try at a vaguely perceived problem. At Bank Street College of Education, prior formulations had been made of the nature of educational impact on developmental processes and of the strategies for effecting change in public schools. These formulations provided the frame of reference for what was envisaged and finally undertaken as a comprehensive program. They can be briefly stated:

First, the quality of experience in school has a differential influence on all phases of development during the years of childhood. Knowledge of the interaction between cognitive and affective realms of functioning makes exclusive attention to intellectual skills an archaic and impractical goal for education. Instead, the competence of the child, which it is the school's responsibility to foster, must be broadly conceived in terms of ego strength, that is, the effective interaction of the individual with the work, the people, and the problems of his environment. This calls on the school to elevate its own competence to support simultaneously the growth of the cognitive functions represented in symbolizing, reasoning, problem solving, and ordering information, and the personality processes related to feelings of self-worth and realization, potential for relating to people, autonomy and creativity, the capacity for emotional investment, and the building of a separate identity.

Second, the potency of school influence can best be understood through detailed study of the internal processes of the classroom. The unique pattern of learning experience and interpersonal relations that characterizes each classroom is a product of complex forces not always open to direct observation nor completely to be subsumed under the academic categories of traditional schooling. The teacher's concept of education and her professional mastery of teaching methods interact with her personality, her motivation, and her own development and orientation as a person. The product is a particular kind of teacher-child relationship which, in turn, becomes the vehicle of a particular kind of teaching-learning process. In addition, the flexibility of the teacher's perceptions of the children as members of a social class, her own values for productive living, and her attitudes toward the probability of the movement of the individual in the society, have a direct influence in the way she uses her professional skills with different populations of children. It is the ferment of these several forces—professional competence, the teacher as a person, and the less visible system of values through which her behavior is screened—that constitutes the dynamic processes of learning and socialization in the classroom.

Furthermore, the teacher and the classroom are at the end of a line of other complex and delimiting educational and social forces that, directly and indirectly, act to establish boundaries for possible change in the fundamental educative process. Each school is a society within itself, with a dominant system of values, a pervasive ideology, and a characteristic network of interrelations between children and teachers, teachers and administrators, school people and parents, school people and other professionals, and between school people and the official and unofficial representatives of the community. Any efforts at altering the nature of classroom processes echo and rebound throughout this network. It follows that programs of change aimed at intra-classroom processes are likely to have lasting value only if there is a clear understanding of all these forces and practical wisdom in taking them into account. A prior need, therefore, is to have a more differentiated knowledge of how the "organized complexity" of a school operates as a sub-society within a larger system.

Finally, the promotion of positive mental health in a school cannot be treated as though it were an additional piece of subject matter, concerned with interpersonal relations, to be added to the curriculum. It involves, rather, the infusion of mental health principles into the educative process at all levels—to the way knowledge is transmitted as much as to the transmission of values implicit in the nature of the teacher-child relationship; to the evaluation of new teaching techniques and devices as much as to the reconception of a learning climate. To be consistent with the concept of primary prevention, consultation services to schools need to follow psychoeducational theory and practice as distinct from the clinically-oriented functions, derived from a mental illness model, that are necessary to detection and treatment of incipient disorders.

The Schools and Mental Health program took two directions: research and action. In the research studies, this opportunity was used to put empirically derived postulates, such as the above, through systematic test and observation, to confirm them as far as they could be confirmed, and to differentiate, revise, and raise new questions where prior assumptions proved equivocal. The first two books in this series, *The Psychological Impact of School Experience* and *Teaching and Learning in City Schools*, report two studies of this kind. The first study, which had begun before the program was launched, explores the basic question: Does a school, perceived in its particularity as a life environment, affect the psychological development of children—their thinking prowess and style, self-knowledge, interpersonal perception, and emerging value systems—in predictable ways? The schools selected and studied contrasted widely in their educational ideology. Their orientation toward child development and the purposes of education ranged from the "modern," meaning the integration of developmental-dynamic thinking into the life of the school, to the "traditional," meaning adherence to goals of academic excellence and formal institutional procedures. The children studied were middle class, at a common stage of development, in fourth-grade classrooms. In general, findings of this study support the premise that the quality of schooling, ideologically defined, has a differential effect on development.

It is pertinent to the essential inquiry concerning the role of the school in relation to the concept of primary prevention that, when the modern ideology was integrated into the total functioning of the school, it did indeed support such elements of healthy personality as clearer knowledge of and greater connectedness with the self, a sense of autonomy in relation to adults as immediate authorities or as prototypes of future roles, and the children's deep involvement in their lives as children. The study also shows that these effects do not operate uniformly for boys and girls, for all personalities, or in all contexts. It therefore points the way to further questions and other studies.

The study to be reported in the second book of the series, *Teaching and Learning in City Schools*, made a different attack on the problem of learning and socialization. Here, the schools selected did not vary in educational ideology, practices, and climate. They were approximately similar in these respects and fairly typical of schools in urban centers in that they were all within the traditional range of the "modern-traditional" continuum as we had conceptualized it. They were characterized by didactic teaching, minimal exploration and initiation by the children, little probing for personal or intellectual meaning, and strong adherence to established curriculum and external symbols of success. Yet, not all classrooms in traditional schools have the same impact on the children. In this study, the child population, rather than the total school milieu, was varied, to include low-income Negro and white classes and middle-income Negro and white classes at second- and fifth-grade levels. The primary interest in this study was to test and examine further the premise that the teacher reflects the dominant values of a society in subtle ways and that teaching and learning in the public schools is compounded by stereotyped attitudes toward low-income and minority group children. In order to understand the complex pattern characteristic of classroom life for each of the child populations—the images of themselves and their futures being shaped for them, the resolution they had to make of the conflicting values to which they were exposed—information was gathered from three perspectives: observations in the classrooms, interviews with the teachers, and brief sessions with the children.

These two studies support and complement each other. The basic coherence, within a school, of educational ideology, value sytem, interpersonal styles, and images projected upon the children, showed itself as a major socializing force in both studies. In the first, the milieu created by a traditional authority was shown to be restrictive with respect to the development of personally expressive styles of response and self-relevant images of what the future might hold for these middle-class children. The second study explored the ways in which a traditional educational ideology was related to materialistic values and discriminatory stereotyped attitudes. The result for lower-income and especially for black lower-income children was a more serious restriction, not only of their intellectual development, but also of avenues for the expression of responsibility and initiative, thus impairing their chances for self-realization through occupational achievement. Instead, these children were being led toward identifying with fixed societal roles that are associated with low ceilings of accomplishment and recognition.

The two studies reflected the methodological approach of the program as a whole. The data were gathered inside schools and classrooms, in the "natural habitat" of children and teachers, after appropriate liaison and practical, cooperative arrangements had been made and formal permission secured. Both studies dealt with a complex influence variable— the school in one, the classroom in the other—and both invested heavily in a detailed analysis of the configuration of school as an environment. Both studies had the benefit of interdisciplinary thinking, as distinct from interdisciplinary team operations. The social anthropologists who took part in these studies worked with educational dimensions as an intrinsic part of their purview of attitudes and value formation in school and classroom; and the psychologists and educators paid major attention to the school's functioning as an institution in their purview of the multiple determinants of educational impact. This approach—to include sociological as well as psychological and educational thinking—was a goal of the program and reflected its alliance with the public health point of view as well as a theoretical kinship with ecological thinking.

The second direction of the program concerned the action phase, which will be reported later in this series. It involved two interrelated field projects in a small suburban school system. One of these was a sociological study of the school system and its interrelations with the surrounding community. The sociologists who undertook this study acted as participant observers. The other field project was a program of psychoeducational consultation in an elementary school within the system in which the change process invoked by the consultation was studied.

The superintendent and a few principals welcomed a change process program oriented toward the application of positive mental health principles to elementary education. The small system, the presence of a number of people in the schools and on the local Board who had kindred goals, and the relative quiescence of this educational scene as a whole, made it feasible to take a different approach from that of the other studies, namely, to work inside a school and a school system where, as educators and sociologists, we could study the processes and problems as participants and participant observers respectively. The members of the two disciplines carved out separate spheres of activity while sustaining continuous communication about the central question of how the basic structural-functional conflicts and problems of a school system, orginating within the system itself or in its relationship to the community, affect school personnel at all levels and, in the end, condition the specific nature of the teaching-learning process in the classroom.

The sociological study will offer a model for analyzing the dynamics of a school system, for understanding the interplay of forces which develop and maintain the system's own internal movements and directions of change—movements to which programs for planned change that enter, invited or uninvited, from elsewhere in the community or the educational world, must somehow be adjusted if they are to become viable. The study examines the relations of the school system to the most important of the external systems with which it is connected: the state, the professional associations, the wider educational world, and the local community. The sometimes conflicting, sometimes convergent values, ideologies, and expectations that come from these external systems are shown to be reconciled in various ways within the school system itself. Demands for expansion and improvement of the system are seen to be developed by the professional staff from the logic of their own professional ideology as well as from the internal needs of the organization and are supported at long range by the professional associations. The study describes how these demands are modified and compromised in the endless conflicts and negotiations with and between the several competing groups constituting the local community—whose financial and political cooperation with each other and with the professional educators are needed to keep the school system going. In order to examine more closely how system properties and processes affect the educational process through their influence upon principals, teachers, and children, the sociologists also made a detailed study of the administrative operation and range of teaching styles in one school in this system.

Ideally, this analysis of the system's functioning should have been available as background to instituting the program of planned change through psychoeducational consultation in another school in the same system. For practical reasons, however, both parts of the field program had to be conducted concurrently.

The consultation project followed a set of principles which had been derived from similar work in the public schools. The designation *psychoeducational* accented the main features of the method. The consultants were educators, experienced in a child development approach to education, and skilled in putting psychological aspects of behavior to the service of the teaching function. The consultants established a role with the participating teachers as non-evaluating co-educators who shared the teachers' knowledge of the children and classrooms. The consultation with the teachers was carried on in group sessions, backed up by regular classroom observations and individual discussions. Open discussion about educational matters of immediate concern to the teachers was the medium through which the consultants worked toward the goals of sensitizing the teachers to more differentiated perceptions of the children, and toward freeing them to attempt newer and more flexible curriculum ideas and practices. They tried to create an atmosphere that allowed for the expression of strong feeling and conflicting opinion without allowing the affect to become the focus of the work. While the relationship included affective interchange, the objective position of the educational consultants was not sacrificed. Thus, the consultants enlisted the gains of a dynamic group process without deflecting the activity into one of group therapy. The focus of this part of the program was not to demonstrate effects but rather to engage in concurrent analysis of the process of change, to study the points of resistance and reinforcement experienced by teachers and consultants as old attitudes and techniques were slowly relinquished for new ones. The analysis traces a gradual shift, on the part of most of the teachers, from a behavior trait typology to a child development perspective and a measure of progress as the teachers moved away from a well-meaning standardized didacticism toward a motivated, involved educational transaction between themselves and the children.

In the decade that has passed between the beginning of this program in psychosocial studies in education and this reporting of its major aspects, the two fields to which it has greatest relevance—education and mental health—have arrived at a condition of magnificent turbulence. There is magnificence in the widespread arousal of conscience, at last, concerning the faults in our social institutions and the tragic human waste for which they are responsible. The turbulence has many components, among them, the undifferentiated rejection of past theory and practice in favor of poorly defined innovation with unrealistic promise of rapid remedy, the presence of social forces that cannot wait for trial and assessment of new plans and programs, and a demand for fantastic flexibility on the part of professionals to alter their role identities radically on the shaky presumption that the new roles will indeed serve the new goals effectively.

In education the major upsurge has been on the front of intellectual mastery, with tremendous investment, corporate and scholarly, in programs focused on cognitive skills, new instructional techniques, and modes of learning that involve a discovery route for the child. Though there has been great gain in this ferment about teaching and learning, the dominant vision falls far short of the expanded concept of the role of the school to foster intellectual competence and simultaneously to support the personality processes that mediate the individual's effectiveness in the world of ideas, work, and people.

The field of mental health has burst its former boundaries and is generally considered to be in a state of "revolution," or, as Charles Hersch recently described it, in a "discontent explosion." Skepticism of established psychotherapeutic theory and method, combined with awareness that the population in greatest need is being served least adequately, has led to a major investment of professional energies and federal funding in the primary prevention approach. There is a new set of criteria for individual mental health and new priorities for social planning. Increasing the individual's intellectual and social effectiveness is expected to yield the strength necessary to cope with conflict and anxiety. Social institutions rather than the clinic are seen as the carriers of mental health in the way their internal functions are processed. A major portion of mental health expertise is to be invested in performing consultant and supporting services to the staffs of these institutions, who are in direct relation to the recipients of educational, remedial, and healing functions.

The basic perspective of the school in relation to mental health that governed the choices to be made in our program had a visionary component at the time it was initiated. However, because of the evolutionary shift in the tenets and strategies of the mental health movement, its perspective has since become dominant in the steps being taken to meet the crisis of poverty and to elevate the basic health of the whole population. It is prominent, for example, in the recommendations to be made by the Joint Commission on Mental Health of Children. Thus, the immediate relevance of these studies is greater now than was anticipated in 1958. It will still be a long time and many studies away before the complex and multiple problems we face are resolved. Our knowledge about how primary institutions influence human development is still in an early stage and as yet there are only preliminary guidelines for modifying their impact. It is hoped, however, that the studies to be reported in this series will be useful in the search for solutions that are based on an ecological perception of the school as an institution and that keep the interplay of individual-psychological and social-institutional forces at the center of the vision in planning for change.

The Schools and Mental Health program at Bank Street College of Education was guided in its planning by a Program Policy Board which consisted of the following people: Barbara Biber, Ph.D., Principal Investigator; Elizabeth Gilkeson and Charlotte B. Winsor, Co-Investigators; Viola Bernard, M.D., Donald Horton, Ph.D., Martin Kohn, Ph.D., and John H. Niemeyer. The program benefited greatly from the experienced guidance of this group.

We wish to thank Dr. Leonard J. Duhl, then with the National Institute of Mental Health, for his active and stimulating support.

Finally, I should like to acknowledge our great debt to Joseph M. Bobbitt. As Associate Director of the National Institute of Mental Health, Dr. Bobbitt vitalized our connection with the agency supporting our work, and his unflagging encouragement, confidence, and generosity were a valuable source of support throughout the program.

New York 　　　　　　　　　　　　　　　　　　　　　BARBARA BIBER
April 1969

CONTENTS

LIST OF TABLES

TEACHING AND LEARNING
IN CITY SCHOOLS

CHAPTER

1

INTRODUCTION

There have been many periods when education has been a subject for dispute, and when serious educational questions have been used as political footballs, with criticisms, challenges, and panaceas flung from all sides. Nonetheless, at no previous time have the schools been so dramatically catapulted into the forefront of the political and social scene as at present. To many of those involved in the massive insistence upon far-reaching reforms in our national life, equal education, as one means of achieving equal employment opportunity, is seen as critical.

The event which first focused on the central position of education was the 1954 Supreme Court decision that "with all deliberate speed" schools should become completely desegregated. On the one hand, this reaffirmation of equal opportunity as a cardinal democratic ideal gave added impetus to the demand of Negroes for equality in all respects. On the other hand, the brutality accompanying the outright refusal on the part of committed segregationists to making this principle a reality, coupled with the even more disturbing, profound, obscure, and complicated resistance to change, have revealed more clearly than ever the contradiction inherent in "our way of life." The dismal failure to enact the principle of equal opportunity, once it had been so clearly restated with added legal reinforcement, posed a sharp challenge to America's claim of moral leadership. Therefore, each evidence of progress—or lack of progress—in equalization of educational opportunity takes on a significance even beyond the immediate issue.

At the same time that resistance to school integration was deeply shaking America's moral position, the appearance of Sputnik on the international scene marked the end of her claim to technological leadership. The reaction on the part of some was extreme, so important a component of pride in being American has technological superiority become, and so committed are many to the idea that maintaining this strategic advantage in a struggle for power is necessary for our very survival. An immediate response was to turn the spotlight on the schools—why are standards so low that we have not produced scientists of a caliber to outstrip all others?

Thus a whole series of pressures have been let loose on the schools, as strong as they have been contradictory. On the international scene fear and angry outrage followed Sputnik (the ambivalent admiration and respect of the less ethnocentrically oriented was quieter and called for no counter measures). Meanwhile, on the national scene, anger, bitterness and disillusionment on the part of Negroes were increasing, along with fear and hate on the part of strongly pro-segregationist white Americans, and concern, ambivalence, and embarrassment on the part of pro-integration white people. All of these reactions reflect different interests and group investments which have been expressed in contrasting programmatic demands, requests, or suggestions for educational change.

The issue of desegregation and concern for raising levels of school performance have both brought into sharp focus the fact that, not just Negro children, but children from lower-income families in general are unequally educated in our schools, and that profound revision is called for in our entire educational system. The broad insistence that education be made equally good for all, however, directly contradicts the louder insistence that performance, particularly in the physical sciences, be stepped up through more concentration on the "talented" students. It seems that voices cry in vain that there need be no basic contradiction here, that given a little time, the fullest educational possibilities for every child create the only climate in which even the more gifted can develop their full potential. The immediate pressure for results is too strong, and as each local politician thinks ahead to election time and reflects his thinking into administrative hierarchies, all kinds of half measures are adopted in the harassed attempt to please everybody at least a little. Ineffective stabs at desegregation combine with the stepping up of "fast" and "special" classes; new methods of teaching, especially in mathematics, follow one another with startling rapidity; various programs locate and advance "talented" Negro children in order to have at least token representation of Negroes in the "better" high schools and colleges; elementary school administrators in desperation pass the buck to the community and cry: Without fundamental changes in poor and segregated neighborhoods, with bad housing and high rates of unemployment, how can the schools change?

There are programs, plans, and experiments. There are also workshops, conferences, and seminars. Serious educators and ambitious bandwagon hoppers rub shoulders as each partial solution suggested raises a host of further problems to be resolved. Some programs are conducted at the college level to raise the standards of Negro colleges, on the one hand, or to enable Negro students to enter predominantly white colleges by revising discriminatory admissions and testing practices, on the other. High school curricula are evaluated and re-evaluated; films, programmed learning, and new teaching methods are worked on. Meanwhile, in a few instances pioneering projects take on the goal of revamping entire communities as well as the schools within them.

At the elementary school level, a basic difference in approach toward educational reform has appeared. Some emphasize that cultural barriers between the school and the home for children in lower-income neighborhoods—styles of language and experience which are in conflict with styles met and valued at school—are responsible for their lower school performance.[1] The suggested solution is different teaching materials and teaching methods built on the particular strengths of working-class children. Others point out that this can be used as a further rationale for unequal education, and insist that schools in middle- and lower-income neighborhoods be equalized along all lines—plant and equipment, level of materials, degree of utilization, and experience of teachers. Negro and other minority groups throw out the challenge: If you cannot or will not educate our children, we will—let us run our own schools! [2]

Withal, the stubborn fact is that of hundreds of thousands of schools, a mere handful have been touched. Gross inequalities in schools do not merely remain; in many cases they are increased. By and large, the double-track system has been strengthened, not weakened; the "special" schools have become more special, the rest are little changed, and ineffective, token integration here and there soothes guilty consciences. The educational budget is, as always, barely adequate for the maintenance of present standards, much less for their improvement. And the assessment of what these standards signify in relation to *real* learning, to autonomous, creative thinking, is still a rarity, a luxury, and unrelated to decisions which are made about schools.

Schools and Society

There is talk of revolution in the schools in the face of deep-seated resistance to any basic change, and there is concern with solving a problem in the face of reluctance to face the nature of its origins. For the simple and unfortunate fact of the matter is that our educational institution, as the socializing institution second only to the family, is primarily geared, from a sociological point of view, to maintaining and reinforcing the social-economic structure of our society. Schools are the means through which children are prepared to fit rungs on the occupational ladder more or less equivalent to those occupied by their parents; they are the means by which children are trained and selected for higher education and hence higher status, not primarily on the basis of ability, but on the basis of their family's position in society.[3] Thus, true education, particularly at the elementary level, can become in many ways almost irrelevant rather than the main functional aim of the school. *Real* teaching can be the exception. Just as studies have revealed the way in which, paradoxically, curing the sick can become peripheral to the main purpose of much hospital routine, so one can document the way in which institutionalized resistance to real educational reforms comes from established hierarchies whose primary function is self-perpetuation rather than education.

One major contribution of John Dewey to the field of education was making the point that children learn through experience, and on this principle he based his social philosophy of education.[4] The history of subsequent events is well known—the changing school atmosphere (to which Dewey's contribution was both a response and a directive), the experimentation with radically different forms of school life, the filtering down of a broader understanding of the total role of school experience to children. The distortions of Dewey's theories are also well known. There was the pendulum swing toward "peer group relations" at the expense of tough-minded intellectual challenge, a pendulum swing meshing with the new emphasis on "popularity" as a measure of success, itself flowing from the rapid expansion of occupational roles calling for styles and attitudes of the "other-directed organization man." Also, in place of genuine intellectual stimulation the concept has often been that learning should be "fun," a concept Dewey spoke of as "humoring the interest," the "sure result [of which] is to substitute caprice and whim for genuine interest." [5]

Deweyan principles can be applied not only to the question of how to develop an atmosphere for learning, but also to the question, what is happening to the one-third of our children who are not mastering school materials? We know what they are *not* learning in the way of certain formal knowledge and skills, but all day long at school what *are* they learning? To a considerable extent *children are learning through their school experience not to learn what is being presented as the substantive content of the curriculum.*

The assumption that these children have been so stunted by poverty and deprivation that they are unequipped to learn must be true of many individual children who have been undermined and demoralized beyond full repair, and who need and should have individual support and help. However, it is hardly true of one-third of our children. No one has assessed the ability these children acquire, such as coping skills essential to their early independence, facility in the use of money through going to the store, or the geographic orientation that follows their management of neighborhood life. Nor has anyone evaluated the vast amount of factual knowledge they control and manipulate. As a guess, one would suggest that they know a great deal about sports, such as the stars and scores of the baseball world and data on boxing and wrestling. They know makes of cars year by year and understand innovations in body design and mechanical features. Their learning also includes space lore, Western lore, and science fiction. Much of the last, as presented on TV, may be fiction, but let us not forget, so is the moralistic mythology about life which is generally presented in the classroom and confused with knowledge—the myth Otto Klineberg has referred to as "life is fun in a smiling, fair-skinned world." [6] Whether what these children learn is "true" is not as relevant here as that they do learn, but outside the formal educational system.

Central to the study that this book will describe was the question: What is actually being taught, being conveyed, to children, in its total-ity, insofar as we can discover it, in classrooms which represent major social-economic groupings in an urban center? The aim was not simply to add another blow to the general criticism of the schools, but to de-scribe the reality into which change is to be introduced. Hopefully, it will be of help to teachers, with the real, albeit limited, desire to help at least certain children in a classroom to have a clearer perception of how, even with the best will in the world and the application of consid-erable skill, they unwittingly help perpetuate a system of inequalities. The study revealed how teachers can pass on to children in myriad ways the message: "This is your station in society; act, perform, talk, *learn* according to it and no more." Paradoxically, even the way in which well-intentioned teachers hold up to the lower-income child an image of the middle-class person he should aspire to become can serve the same purpose. It undermines the child's self-confidence by denying him acceptance and respect for what he and his family are, and by presenting him with a largely unobtainable goal as the only valid crite-rion for what he should be, a goal, moreover, primarily defined in terms of material acquisition, rather than the satisfaction resulting from intel-lectual mastery of himself and his surroundings.

Previous studies show the way in which the structure of the school system, as it articulates with the community, sets the framework within which children are in large measure inducted into different styles of adult life. In a school in a middle-class suburban neighborhood, such as that dealt with by Seeley, Sim, and Loosley in *Crestwood Heights*,[7] there may be a considerable feeling of insecurity and competitiveness among parents about their children's eventual access to the higher rungs of the status ladder, but their achievement of at least the middle rungs is on the whole secure. When comparing such a school with one in a lower-income Negro neighborhood in a large city, such as that studied by Martin Deutsch,[8] it is clear that there are discontinuous characteristics with no overlap. This is true even though there is a range of variation within each type of school along, for example, a criterion such as "traditional-progressive" teaching style. The standards and goals set by schools for children and attitudes toward school in relation to the rest of their life are different. There are consistent differences in attitudes toward the parents, arising from the fact that, in the case of a school such as that described by Seeley, Sim, and Loosley, the parents "outrank" the teachers, socially speaking, while in schools such as that described by Deutsch, the reverse is true; and there are differences in the way the school structures entry into adult life via junior high and high school.

Patricia Sexton, in *Education and Income*,[9] documented these and related differences for one large city school system, and James Conant's *Slums and Suburbs*[10] dramatically underscored how widespread these differences are. Conant, however, left the schools too ready an excuse for not tackling the problem of change. To see how totally an institutional shortcoming is woven into the fabric of society as a whole is necessary for laying the foundation for a realistic view of what changes can be introduced and how. All too often, however, it can be used as an excuse for passivity, a passivity we can ill afford, as attested to by such accounts as Nat Hentoff's *Our Children Are Dying*[11] and Jonathan Kozol's *Death at an Early Age*.[12]

Design of the Present Study

The present study takes a somewhat different direction. Not prepared to accept the view that children's ability to learn is significantly impaired at the point at which they enter school (if one is speaking of *true* learning), the study has addressed itself to the examination of what is being imparted to children in ordinary, city school classrooms, and to what the specific differences are among classrooms which represent Negro and white, middle- and lower-income, groups. The study probes into how and what children are learning in school, in order to arrive at a fuller understanding of what aspects of classroom life are most significant for their intellectual growth and understanding. Its purpose is to yield greater insight into the processes of teaching and learning, in the context of observing ways in which children are being socialized, inducted, so to speak, into various roles in American society.

Therefore, after a preliminary review of the literature and visits to some dozen public and private schools, four schools were chosen for study to represent major divisions of American society along the lines of income and racial identification. On the basis of demographic data on school composition and census material on family incomes, schools were selected in four neighborhoods: lower-income Negro, lower-income white, middle-income Negro, and middle-income white.[13] A second and a fifth grade in each school were picked for study—the second to represent a younger group where school routines were already established, and the fifth as an older group, but not so directly oriented toward junior high as the sixth.

In all the study schools classes were "homogeneously" grouped, primarily on the basis of reading performance in the early grades. It was decided to study "middle," rather than either "fast" or "slow" classes. Where there were several middle classes in a grade, the principal selected a regular teacher who had been with the school for at least a few years and who was sufficiently assured not to be unnerved by classroom observation. Although the teachers varied as to age, length of time in teaching, and approach, they were all capable, "better than average" teachers who were reasonably satisfied with their appointments and well suited to school standards and expectations. They were all women. Six had been trained in New York City, and two had been trained in Chicago and Cleveland, respectively.

The size and composition of the eight study classrooms were as follows:

		Boys	Girls	Total [14]
I	Lower-income Negro			
	Second grade	14	16	30
	Fifth grade	13	17	30
II	Lower-income white			
	Second grade	17	11	28
	Fifth grade	18	16	34
III	Middle-income Negro			
	Second grade	19	17	36
	Fifth grade	20	20	40
IV	Middle-income white			
	Second grade	16	16	32
	Fifth grade	22	16	38

In the lower-income Negro school, there were four white children and one Puerto Rican child in the second grade and one white boy in the fifth grade. In the middle-income Negro school, there were one Puerto Rican child and one white child in the second grade and two white children in the fifth grade. In the lower-income white school, there were two Negro children (a boy and a girl) in the second grade and one Negro boy in the fifth grade.

All the classes were observed during the winter and spring of the year, from February to May, after classroom routines were well established but well before the end of the term. Data were collected through observations of classroom proceedings and interviews with the teachers and the children.

Since several studies have demonstrated a high reliability for the analysis of teacher performance from relatively short periods of classroom observation, it was decided to collect observational data in three intensively utilized periods of one and one-half hours each.[15] To assure fullness and detail in the running records, two observers recorded in the classroom: one concentrated on the teacher and the children with whom she was immediately interacting, and the other focused on the children. Both observers recorded the time at the beginning and end of transitions, interruptions, disciplinary episodes, and any other slightly unusual incidents, so that the two accounts could be coordinated and written up as one, with teacher, children, and observers' comments and explanatory remarks separated into different columns on a page.

The first two observation periods, which were given over to running records, were selected to cover reading, social studies, and mathematics for each class. Additional activities generally observed were recess, "milk and cookies," and "news" or "show and tell." The teacher-observer attempted to record, within the context of ongoing classroom activities, as much of the teacher's verbatim evaluative, disciplinary, and motivating statements as possible, the general content and specific techniques of her teaching, and all names of the children she called on, referred to, or signaled. Teacher-observers also recorded the correctness or incorrectness of a child's reply to the teacher and generally noted classroom reactions to specific teacher actions that the child-observer might not catch. In recording the tone and manner of the teacher, there was a serious attempt to aim for that impossibility demanded by objective observation, that is, a vocabulary which is rich and descriptive without being permeated with interpretive judgments.

The child-observer tried to record as much of the quality and atmosphere of the class as possible in terms of child-child interactions, degree of attentiveness, content of elaborated or initiated statements by the children, the behavior of a child after a significant interaction with the teacher was closed, and the reactions of other children. Both observers had a seating plan before them in order to enable them to identify each child by name.

The third observation period was given over to more selective recording, including thumbnail sketches of each child and on-the-spot scoring of various classroom atmosphere dimensions. All members of the research staff but the teacher-interviewer had the benefit of some classroom observation. The teacher-interviewer was excepted so that she could make certain judgments about the classroom independent of those based on the observation, which was desirable in the preliminary stages of analysis. The research team was well aware that the presence of observers in a classroom may "tone down" certain behavior on the part of the teacher and children or may stimulate disruptive behavior by the latter. However, the fact that each teacher was presumably attempting *to do her best as she saw it* did not obscure those characteristics of the classroom which were being analyzed, but, if anything, enabled them to come through more sharply. In the interview each teacher was given a chance to elaborate on any problems she might feel were caused by the observation situation.

Two interviews with the teacher were held in the classroom after school hours or at the teacher's home, according to her preference and that of the principal. The interviews were taped, with the teacher's consent. The first interview preceded the observations, and pertained to the weekly schedule, use of the room, textbooks and other materials, establishment of routines and rules, and descriptions of the children and their backgrounds. The second interview was held after the observations, and it followed up the children and classroom management techniques in greater detail; in addition, it covered the curriculum and some aspects of the school organization and the teacher's own background and training. Each interview lasted about two hours. The questions were somewhat structured but open-ended enough to allow the teacher to elaborate upon her particular concerns and beliefs, so that, in addition to objective information about the classroom, a picture of the teacher's attitudes toward the children and her relationship to them could emerge.

Each school principal was interviewed prior to meeting the teachers. Information was gathered on the school plant, the student population, the neighborhood, the principal's emphasis with regard to curriculum, school rules and routines, and administrative procedures. Although relatively brief, this interview was important, first, for the verification of the school as fitting the sample requirements and, second, to give a picture of the general atmosphere within which a teacher was working and of the kinds of demands made upon her.

Finally, a short questionnaire was individually administered to each child in the classrooms observed. For the second grades, the interviews were conducted during the span of a single school day. Each child was interviewed for ten to fifteen minutes by one of two interviewers. Usually two rooms were set aside for the purpose, but sometimes space limitations forced the two interviewers to work in the same room. In one school, the principal insisted that she or the teacher be in the room, a factor taken into consideration in the analysis. All interviews except those in this school were taped. At the end of each interview, while waiting for the next child, the interviewer jotted down some ratings and a brief description of the child and the nature of his response.

As a preliminary to the interview, a letter was sent to each child's parents, via the child, telling them about the interview and requesting permission for their child to participate. No child was interviewed without permission, but the rate of parental acceptance was high. Of 126 second-grade children, 108 were interviewed, and most of those not interviewed were absent. Only two of the 108 children found difficulty in responding to the questions. The rest responded to almost every question, and many of the answers were quite full. For the fifth-grade children, a more complete set of answers was obtained although this involved the risk of "contamination." An interviewer returned the following day to interview those who had been absent, thereby reducing the number of non-respondents to only ten out of a total of 142 children. The interview, though short, was carefully constructed on the basis of trial runs. It elicited direct replies from children to questions about classroom procedures, their teacher, and their peers; in a short time a surprisingly large amount of behavioral and attitudinal information was gathered, from which inferences could be drawn about the children's attitudes toward school and learning.

Three methods were used for analyzing the data: evaluation or ratings, quantification or counting, and collation of "key" or significant incidents. In working through to a better understanding of classroom life, constant assessment was made as to how each method could be employed most meaningfully. Ratings represent the weighing and balancing of different factors on the part of trained and sensitive observers, yet they yield the *end results* of educated judgment. They do not reveal *processes* (nor, really, do statistically determined relations among such ratings, though these may suggest valuable clues to important relationships that should be explored). Descriptive incidents illuminate processes, give examples of those things being weighed and assessed, yet they are selective and can overemphasize one aspect of a situation, distorting the totality. The coding and counting of statements or incidents is one way of helping to correct this, but in and of itself it is not sufficient. Before knowing what is significant to count, one would have to be at the end, not the beginning, of a study such as this one. Further, counting reveals normative demands made upon the children. To the extent that doing the right things is important, there is positive affect attached to them. However, a single emotionally charged incident, rather than a series of routine ones, may carry greater value impact and define, not just what one is expected *to do*, but what one *should really care about*. A final problem is that, whatever the precise method being used, the final outcome can go no further than the understanding of the researchers. Therefore, one consideration in bringing together the research team was that it should, insofar as possible, contribute different points of view from varied experiences—the viewpoint of the teacher as well as the researcher, the more individual orientation of the psychologist as well as the group orientation of the anthropologist, the empathy and understanding of Negro, white, man, and woman.

The Theoretical Framework of the Study

The precise form of the analysis in a given instance depended upon the conceptual framework within which the society and culture of the classroom were viewed. The initial problem to be resolved in a study of teaching and learning as broad cultural processes is how to deal with the complexity of individual growth and development within a social context. One is tempted either to emphasize the context, and think of it basically as a mold into which individuals are pressed, or to emphasize the individual and see the social system as essentially a sum total of individual psycho-biologically motivated entities. Clearly, neither is adequate for full understanding. The problem is how to deal with given institutional settings as arbitrary cutoff points in an historical or developmental process, by which social institutions are shaping people at the same time as people are shaping social institutions—that is, how to conceptualize the way in which institutions achieve and maintain their functional relation to the total society through building and reinforcing habitual actions and attendant attitudes of the very people who, as they operate within them, are changing the institutions by expressing in their actions and thoughts unresolved problems within the institutions themselves or conflicts between them and other parts of society.

Seen in concrete classroom terms, such problems arise as: How do we deal with the fact that the same classroom has different effects on different children? Also, what is the carry-over from classroom to classroom as a child proceeds through school? Clearly, we cannot view classrooms along simple quantitative bi-polar dimensions and assess their effects on children's growth as good or bad, restrictive or supportive, or conducive to mental health or not. Rather, the classroom must be viewed as providing a framework within which children make choices about their actions and evaluate them. The significant fact is that different classrooms *pattern in different ways the alternatives from which a child can choose.* Choices may seem infinitely variable, but, in fact, the making of one choice *limits the alternatives available for subsequent choices.* To take an obvious example, the decision of a talented child and his parents to continue or not continue with the child's rigorous practice on the violin is final; if not pursued early, the alternative cannot be chosen later. Less obvious are the subtle ways in which this principle operates without our awareness. Owing to the nature of social patterning, certain choices impel a child in one direction or another without his knowledge.

When a quick and curious child who is from a lower-income home and is going to an inadequate school is compared with a similar child who is entering a good school in a middle-income neighborhood, one can see that the same choice—to be a good student and ply the teacher with questions—presents each child with different alternatives. Despite the great variations among teachers, it is more likely that in the middle-class school the child's curiosity and questions will be responded to attentively and will help him gain a certain standing among his peers, albeit with a measure of ambivalence. The road to success in high school and college is clear. In a lower-class school, such questioning is more likely to be passed by, or even categorized as "smart alecky" and difficult by the teacher, and it may appear to the child's peers that he is trying to "butter up the teacher." The child has difficulty achieving satisfaction, and his alternatives are either to withdraw or to become rebellious as an outlet for his intellectual energy. When examining the school as an institution, consistently patterned alternatives such as these may be defined. Which alternative an individual will choose will, of course, follow from the accidents of his particular life history and the ways in which his home, community, and school life interrelate. For instance, whether or when a lively and curious child comes upon a really interested teacher could be crucial for determining the direction which his intellectual energies might take.

In short, the method of analysis employed attempts to avoid a unitary concept of cultural patterning and cultural norms. The classroom is viewed as defining *patterned behavioral and attitudinal alternatives* for children. These, in turn, are seen as relating to patterns of conformity to and deviance from culturally "desirable" norms. Deviations themselves are patterned, and supposedly deviant roles, such as not learning, can become widespread, institutionalized, and as intrinsic to social structure as supposedly dominant norms. Most nonconforming behavior does not follow from lack of ability to adjust but is built into the social structure as integrally as "acceptable" behavior. The well-defined mores of street-gang life, which children in particular areas may accept due to pressures *for*, not against, conformity, aptly illustrate this point.

Goals presented to children in the classroom are likewise not unitary but involve alternative responses to basic cultural themes or concerns. These alternative responses, along with the formally stated and accepted goals themselves, are presented to children by the teacher. They are presented through what and how the teacher actually rewards and punishes, through which children are favored and which disfavored, and through the way the learning situation is structured. In other words, they are transmitted *covertly*, or indirectly, and not *overtly*, or directly. A teacher makes overt statements about what should and should not be done, and at the same time she imparts covert or indirect cues to the children as to what behavior is actually valued or expected. There need be no hypocrisy involved here, and teachers, like parents, are largely unaware of their full role in this socialization process. Our society is committed to many formal goals and ideals which are discrepant with social realities, as embodied in the cynical but accurate homily, "it isn't what you know but who you know" that leads to success. Children learn a complicated mixture of co-operative and competitive techniques. They learn to respect certain ideals and principles, while at the same time acquiring practical knowledge of when these should be applied and when they should not. Further, they are taught to have a commitment to the notion of equal opportunity along with a realistic recognition that it is one's position in the status structure that makes all the difference.

In other words, a social "know-how" is imparted in the classroom. Children learn what adults have already learned, that they must constantly deal with contradictions between overtly stated and actually accepted goals and standards, as well as between accepted goals and standards and objectively observable social conditions. To do this without serious personal costs is not easy. Confronted with contradictions between the goals set for them and the objective conditions that are at odds with these goals, children are in danger of becoming demoralized either by seeing their own shortcomings as being responsible for their difficulties, or by seeing the objective world as being so limiting that they feel powerless to cope with it. In order to develop a sound sense of his own identity and the basis for meaningfully relating to work and to fellow students, an individual must achieve an understanding of where difficulties lie—whether in himself or in the situation—so that he can define for himself those areas in which he must modify his own behavior and conform and those areas in which he must search actively for possible ways of changing the environment. In Marie Jahoda's discussion of positive mental health, she questions the notion of adaptation as a one-way process. She writes, ". . . there is no need to regard hard reality as unchangeable and only the individual as modifiable. Adaptation implies that a workable arrangement between reality and the individual can be achieved by modifications of either or both through individual initiative." [16]

In order to assess the complex set of interacting processes through which children in school are now being taught, or, more correctly, socialized, it is necessary to describe an image of what schools should be. Though quite utopian, this image is necessary to complete our conceptual framework. Schools should impart to children both the feeling and the actuality of competence and mastery, involving technical skills as well as an understanding of the world as a composite of social and natural processes which invite individual and collective adaptation and intervention. Further, children should grow up with an understanding of themselves as being basically similar to others, an understanding balanced with a feeling and respect for the nature and importance of differences, both from individual to individual and from group to group. Schools must present the basis for such understanding in curriculum content, as well as by furnishing the atmosphere for reinforcing this understanding. In other words, *this understanding is best enacted in the classroom* so that children can *directly experience* the satisfaction of intellectual challenge and mastery and the enjoyment of working with and learning from others.

This image of what schools should be raises a series of questions about the ways in which different components of good education are being reinforced or undermined in the classroom, and it provides a baseline for assessing the relative strengths and weaknesses of the classroom as a whole. We may see a pleasant "supportive" atmosphere rendered ineffective by the accompaniment of an inadequate demand for mastery of necessary skills. Or we may observe what seems to be a generally good curriculum underlaid with such a weight of moralizing that its potential for objective understanding is lost. Or a mediocre curriculum may be presented by a teacher who fundamentally respects the children and their ideas and leaves the situation open enough so that they can raise questions and sense the importance of asking a good question as opposed to just knowing a pat answer. Throughout the study there has been an attempt to define the goals for learning and behavior presented to various groups of children and the choices for response implied for them in the classroom context. Hopefully, the results can contribute meaningfully to the inquiry as to what institutional changes can and must be made if more teachers are really to teach in our schools and more children are really to learn.

The following chapters attempt to construct a picture of what is being conveyed to children in the classroom and how it is translated. Chapters 2 and 3 focus on the curriculum, and Chapters 4 and 5 pertain to styles and techniques of classroom management. Some of the major contrasts between schools in different neighborhoods which are brought out by the analysis of teaching practices in eight classrooms are reviewed and developed in Chapter 6. This is followed in Chapter 7 by a discussion of the children's attitudes as revealed in the interviews. The general conclusions drawn from the study and some of their implications for educational innovations are discussed in Chapter 8.

NOTES

1. The presentation of this viewpoint is critically summarized in E. Fuchs, "Education and the Culture of Poverty," in T. Weaver and A. Magid, eds., *Interdisciplinary Perspectives on Poverty* (San Francisco: Chandler, 1969).
2. This development is summarized and evaluated in M. D. Fantini, "Discussion, Implementing Equal Educational Opportunity," *Harvard Educational Review*, XXXVIII (1968), 160–175.
3. See, for example, the discussion in W. L. Warner, M. Meeker, and K. Eells, *Social Class in America* (New York: Harper and Brothers, 1960), pp. 24–28. Also R. Havighurst and B. Neugarten, *Society and Education* (Boston: Allyn and Bacon, 1962), pp. 230, 239–240.
4. J. Dewey, *Lectures in the Philosophy of Education, 1899* (New York: Random House, 1968).
5. J. Dewey, "My Pedagogic Creed," reprinted in M. S. Dworkin, ed., *Dewey on Education*, Classics in Education, No. 3 (New York: Bureau of Publications, Teachers College, Columbia University, 1959), p. 29.
6. O. Klineberg, "Life Is Fun in a Smiling, Fair-Skinned World," *Saturday Review of Literature* (February 16, 1963).
7. J. R. Seeley, R. A. Sim, and E. W. Loosley, *Crestwood Heights* (New York: Basic Books, 1956).
8. M. Deutsch, "Minority Group and Class Status as Related to Social and Personality Factors in Scholastic Achievement," *Society for Applied Anthropology Monograph*, No. 2 (1960).
9. New York: Viking Press, 1961. Sexton has summarized other major works in this area in *The American School, A Sociological Analysis* (Englewood Cliffs, N.J.: Prentice-Hall, 1967), pp. 54–57.
10. New York: McGraw-Hill, 1961.
11. New York: Viking Press, 1966.
12. New York: Houghton Mifflin, 1967.
13. For more detailed information, see Chapter 6.
14. The smaller class size in schools I and II was due to a policy, established by the school system in 1958, which limited the size of classes in lower-income schools. Unfortunately, many such schools, as a result, had to go on double session.
15. Withall found that the characteristic style of all a teacher's statements

taken in any two-hour period matched that drawn from much longer periods [J. Withall, "Assessment of the Social-Emotional Climates Experienced by a Group of Seventh-Graders as They Moved from Class to Class," in A. P. Coladarci, ed., *Educational Psychology* (New York: Dryden Press, 1955), pp. 193–205]. Beecher wrote that in his study scores made after two observations of teacher performance, as broken down into many detailed dimensions, were not substantially revised after a third observation period [D. E. Beecher, *The Evaluation of Teaching* (Syracuse, N.Y.: Syracuse University Press, 1949)]. In the School Experience Study conducted at Bank Street College of Education [P. Minuchin, B. Biber, E. Shapiro, and H. Zimiles, *The Psychological Impact of School Experience* (New York: Basic Books, 1969)], a "first impression" of study classrooms was written after the initial visits. Subsequent systematic observations, while greatly amplifying the "first impressions," did not contradict them.

16. M. Jahoda, *Current Concepts of Positive Mental Health* (New York: Basic Books, 1958), p. 60.

CHAPTER

2

THE PRACTICE OF
TEACHING

When we turn to an analysis of teaching as it is practiced in the urban classroom, we face not only the inequalities among schools, but also the drabness of the curriculum in most of them. Yet it is with an apology that we say this. This report was made possible through the toleration and good will of the women whose classes we observed, and who talked to us freely about their attitudes toward teaching and toward the children with whom they were working. If the discussion that follows seems to be an indictment of their efforts, we must again emphasize that the responsibility for poor education cannot be laid at the door of the individual teacher, any more than poverty is the responsibility of the individual family. The teachers we observed were all experienced, hardworking, and capable people who were trying to do their best for the children in their classrooms within the limits of their training and situations.

It is not within the province of our present study to define the limits of the teaching situation in detail, but the general form is clear and involves various social, economic, and political considerations. First, perhaps, are the deficiencies in teacher training, where the failure to translate educational theory into concrete and applicable teaching practice has become a matter of increasing concern.[1] Second is the perennial problem of budgetary limitations. Both school and community are only too constantly aware of inadequacies in sheer space and educational materials, a problem compounded in schools in low-income areas which receive a smaller share of the budget per child.[2]

A third problem for the teacher is that of political "loyalty," which is so narrowly defined that she is constantly fearful of allowing classroom discussion to supersede its limits. Patriotism is seen as unqualified defense of the status quo, allowing of no inquiry with an eye to a better future. Mercer and Carr write of the threat to the school constituted by people who "equate loyalty with conformity, democracy with a fixed set of beliefs."

> To them democracy is a static thing, a *fait accompli*; they impugn the loyalty of those who dissent, raise questions, or otherwise refuse to be cast in a mold. Some of these "superpatriots" are sincere and conscientious but uninformed persons; others serve groups whose vested interests are endangered by free inquiry. Their efforts result in book purges, loyalty oaths, curriculum restrictions, and other too familiar interferences with freedom to teach and freedom to learn.[3]

Rodehaver, Axtell, and Gross write of the pernicious effects of such interferences upon teachers in elementary and secondary schools, more of whom, "for various reasons . . . tend to delimit their freedom when pressure is brought to bear than seems to be the case with those in the colleges and universities." [4]

Fourth among the problems confronting teachers is the unfortunate fact that the bureaucratic functioning of administrative bodies has far more to do with the programming of education than with educational theory. From the time Weber first defined bureaucratic functioning, it has become increasingly clear that the latent function of protecting and expanding an institution for its own sake often contradicts the stated or manifest function of that institution.[5] Kimball points to the elementary schoolteacher's position on the receiving end of the decision-making process in the educational hierarchy and her heavy custodial responsibilities for children as factors which seriously impair her teaching function.[6] From the teacher's immediate point of view, she experiences the everyday realities of the too-large and underequipped classroom, in which coping with the practicalities of classroom discipline and routines, administrative details, continual small emergencies, and the individual problems of the few children who demand special time and energy mean that there is many a day in which she feels she is hardly able to begin to *teach*. In sum, it is only a most unusual person who can surmount the limits of the educational system. The researcher must always bear this in mind, lest, after spending a few days in a classroom, he harks back to the frustrations of his own early school experiences and focuses too sharply and critically on the teacher herself as she imparts the rigidities, superficialities, the mannerisms of classroom life and of a system for which she is not responsible.

Our purpose in the present chapter is not so much to underscore inadequacies in the educational system as to clarify their nature through analyzing what teachers are trying to achieve in their classrooms. One aspect of the study was an intensive exploration of teaching concepts and processes based on observation and interview data. As described in Chapter 1, running records of the classroom were taken simultaneously by two observers, one concentrating on the teacher and one on the children. The teacher was interviewed at length, once before and once after the observations. The interview dealt with her curriculum, her methods of teaching, her goals in each subject area, and her general goals for the class. The interview was open-ended enough to allow the teacher to expand freely on her ideas and interests.

The classroom observations were examined in detail by a team, including teachers and teacher supervisors as well as the researchers, while the teacher interviews were analyzed independently. Categories for the analysis of material were the following: (1) the nature and clarity of the teacher's teaching concept, particularly with regard to the integration and development of curriculum content; (2) the depth, richness, and variety of the curriculum content; (3) the style of learning and thought being encouraged in the classroom; (4) the value content of classroom materials; and (5) the relation of curriculum content to the children's experiences.[7]

Nature and Clarity of Teaching Concepts

The teachers were asked several questions in the course of the interviews which allowed them to elaborate on their concepts of the learning and teaching process and what they saw themselves as trying to do in the classroom. No teacher limited herself to a traditional "three R" approach to education. All saw themselves, to be sure, as conveying certain skills and knowledge to children, that is, teaching reading and writing, arithmetic, and some preliminary knowledge about the physical and social world around them, but they all elaborated on their socializing function. This was seen in terms of manners, discipline, values, social awareness, or style of life.

Elaborations on the intellectual implications of teaching subject matter were rare. None was made by the second-grade teachers, and very few by the fifth-grade teachers. Almost wholly lacking was an understanding that through conveying basic skills and rudimentary knowledge, one is actually teaching a way of thinking, a way of looking at objective data and conceptualizing about them. Their training had not brought to life for these teachers the idea that one can and should build early the foundation for children to search out the realities that lie behind everyday events and outward appearances. Missing was a unified approach as to how each subject and skill being taught could help develop a child's intellect and lay the basis for an assessing, weighing, curious, and even excited view of the world as a totality to be explored, understood, and, to a degree, changed. Not only was the understanding of how to do this lacking, but also the notion that it should be done at all. A teacher armed with such understanding tries to relate what she is teaching in one subject area to that of another, thus maximizing classroom possibilities for seeing relationships, for locating different avenues by which to approach the same reality. She attempts to present her curriculum in such a way as to lay the basis for consideration, for independent exploration. She plans projects and activities according to the principle that understanding is developed through participation and experience. This ideal is admittedly almost impossible to achieve in the average urban classroom, yet one can observe teachers who are clearly aiming for it.

The one second-grade teacher (classroom IV–2)[8] who attempted to discuss the "integration" of her curriculum with the children's experiences revealed the superficiality of her understanding. She saw "integration" as relating activities primarily to manners and behavior, rather than as forming a basis for building concepts and developing ideas.

> Even taking attendance becomes a mass project. No matter what we do in the classroom, it has to do with some area we are working on in the day. At the present time our unit is planting. . . . Actually this is integrated, or correlated with good manners and self-control and learning how to live with 32 plants and learning how to care for plants. When the plants have fully grown, we shall write invitations to our second-grade classes inviting them to our little flower show. We'll be able to talk to the children when they come in, so it's written composition with the letter, and oral composition to talk to the little people who come in to see the show. Each week we write a paragraph telling the progress of the show—how we have to nurture the seeds and the type of soil, the need of things that are necessary to make a healthy plant grow and we're watching. . . . That gives them all kinds of experiences. Actually I credit this new educational system. I think it is very good because years ago you set up little seeds in boxes and you'd say nothing about them and the children would hardly know that they were there. . . .

Another second-grade teacher (classroom II–2) spoke of bringing her curriculum down "to the experiential level," and "trying to bring everything into relationship with things that [children] know," to "make it clearer to them." She said of her social studies program, "What I'm trying to do is to give them an understanding of the things around them and their relationship and interrelationship between people and their surroundings." Discussing cookie distribution, she said:

> First of all, it demands experience which I want them all to have. They learn how to give change and even these poor children who are not good at math . . . know how to give change. They usually come with a nickel or sometimes a dime. . . . Usually it's change of a nickel or a dime, a math experience.

However, when she expanded on how relating curriculum to experience contributed to the development of concepts—and she used the word "concepts" specifically—she shifted from an emphasis on intellectual mastery to ethical or moral mastery:

> In teaching the children to get along together, and cooperation, if it is during Brotherhood Week, I would say, "Is that brotherhood?" and they understand what brotherhood is. In citizenship, we talk about

being a good citizen. If they are pledging the flag and they are not standing right, or if they are playing instead of pledging, I'll say, "Is that citizenship?" We'll discuss what showing they are proud of their country means. They have a slight understanding of these broad concepts. Of course they know that it's each one's responsibility to help his neighbor. We include days like Brotherhood Week and United Nations Day in the curriculum. We would discuss it—the concepts— and carry it down from the broader concepts to how we can have brotherhood in our class. . . .

This teacher spoke fully and capably about her curriculum and was concerned about keeping abreast of educational theory. In the classroom, she was observed to handle the children extremely well. She knew how to arouse their interest by referring to personal experiences, by humor and playfulness, by encouragement, and by supportive use of partial answers. Yet she was limited in her attempts to develop the children's ability to conceptualize by her tendency to equate *concepts* with social or ethical *precepts*.

The confusion between the intellectual and the moral is, however, no individual shortcoming. The overemphasis on social "adjustment" as a task of the school and the equation of "adjustment" with good manners, popularity, and the expression of or nominal adherence to conventional aphorisms are writ so large in educational institutions generally that one can hardly expect to find it otherwise at the elementary school level. Furthermore, as has already been suggested, these educational "errors" are not entirely happenstance. Although they may stifle the intellect, they do lead to relative "success" on most rungs of the occupational ladder.[9] Thus, although there has been some qualification of the emphasis on the social adjustment of school children, and although greater attention is being given to intellectual development as such, there has been no real disentangling of morality and intellect. There has been no real clarification of the fact that improving a "climate for learning" means more than nurturing a receptive classroom atmosphere. It means the full use of personal and social experiences as well as school-improvised ones for building intellectual mastery and curiosity. The sheer heterogeneity of children's backgrounds means that personal experiences can be successfully incorporated into the curriculum only within the framework of a broadly humanistic attitude—they can never be meaningfully integrated into classroom discussions and projects within narrowly moralistic or judgmental confines.

One second-grade teacher (classroom III–2) was very clear and organized in her understanding of what she wanted to impart to the children and the steps by which she planned to achieve her goals. From her interview, it was clear that she saw teaching as a one-way process (from herself to the children). Her view of working with children emphasized demonstration through her own discussion, rather than the development of their ability to apply skills to new problems or relate new ideas to previous experiences. As observed in the classroom, she was highly able in conveying skills and knowledge but uninterested in working with the children's own concepts. She developed ideas, but only through herself, and she relied on the intensity of her delivery and the skill of her own performance to transmit interest to the children. When describing the teaching of creative writing, she referred to "forcing" the children's thoughts in order to teach them how to put several sentences together that related to one idea. In story-writing the teacher's approach, relying purely on exposition rather than building on the positive features of the children's compositions was strongly evidenced.

During the reading lesson, the same teacher was concerned that the children give some thought to the content of the story and that they conceptualize the "problem" (or dilemma) a child faces who must make a choice as to whether to save his money and go to a circus later, or to go immediately to a dog and pony show which is passing through:

> While the children are waiting to begin, T says, "I want everybody to think about the story." A few hands go up and T repeats, "Don't raise your hands, think. . . . Janice is thinking about it. The other children will be here in a minute. I want you to think about the problem that John Day had."
>
> When the other children return to the classroom, T says, "For those who just walked in, we are going to think of the problem John Day had. . . . Arthur, do you want to tell us of John Day's problem?"
>
> Arthur stands and (as might be expected of a second-grader) begins to tell the story of John Day, who was going to go to the circus, and then there was a dog and pony show . . . T interrupts, "Yes, but you're telling the story. What was the *problem?*" She repeats her point, persuasively, trying to get the children to think of the concept of a problem, but she does not involve them in a query about dilemmas they themselves may have faced.
>
> Another child answers at some length, getting closer to the problem of John's choice. T answers, "That's part of it," and the child sits down with a little air of disappointment.
>
> Peter is called on and talks at length about John's difficulty in mak-

ing a choice, though not pinpointing the notion of problem as such. T says, "Yes, it was very tempting," and she restates John's problem, talking at some length about the little dog and pony show. The children remain attentive. Her exposition is full and clear. She then addresses the class again, "The dog and pony show didn't have what?"

Here T has a specific answer in mind, and several children attempt to answer without hitting upon it. "What is exciting about a *real* circus?" T asks, and Morris, called on unexpectedly, falters, "Animals." T points out the small show had them too. She calls on Sarah, who says, "Elephants." T says, "Yes, and they are something special."

T questions the children further; then, with an expressive face, she repeats the story, speaking clearly, quickly, and with emphasis.

As we have indicated, this episode shows little understanding of how to utilize the children's own thinking in building toward the point the teacher wishes to convey. Yet this was a generally good teacher. She knew how to hold the children's interest and maintained a high level of performance. She was straightforward, impartial, and respectful with the children, and she was sincerely interested in seeing them achieve. She knew how to work slowly and patiently with individuals in an effort to draw them from an incorrect to a correct answer. As aforesaid, she was clear about what she wanted to accomplish with her classroom and how she was going to do it. Her failure, from the viewpoint of optimum learning, lay in the fact that her concept of teaching included no recognition of how to involve the children more actively in the learning process. When she spoke of discussion, it was as "a good exercise of the mind," which helped the children correct their speech patterns and learn how to express themselves.

Two of the fifth-grade teachers stressed the importance of involving the children's ideas and experiences as fully as possible in their lessons. One of them (classroom III–5) said that as she interwove history and geography in her social studies program, making "America grow from the seaboard to the west," any elaboration came "from the children's own wishes." She had found the children to be "amazingly well traveled," since many had visited grandparents in other states. "Some of them spend entire summers in a country setting. Therefore, you don't have to build a concept of the difference between city and country living. . . . *You* don't have to do it," since the traveled children help the others learn. "For those who are uninitiated, the others do it because they've had the experience. They relate an experience with, 'Oh yes, when I did so and so,' which is quite fine." This was helpful, she said, in relation to geography and reading and for understanding other people, places, and times. "Television is not a bad help either," she continued. "They do get misinformation, you find, but you don't have to build some of the concepts you formerly would have had to." When discussing her mathematics program, this teacher recounted an instance in which a child brought up an advanced arithmetic problem. Feeling he was ready to handle it, she took advantage of the contribution to explain it. She went on to say that a few days later she would go through it again, "step by step, building it up just as I did before, for the benefit of those people who didn't get it with one run through. . . ."

This teacher appeared in the classroom as a highly skilled technician, knowing how to structure a discussion well, accepting, adding, building on what the children contributed. However, upon analysis it became apparent that, with the exception of mathematics, there was no real possibility for exploring new channels the children might introduce. All was brought back to a predetermined series of points the teacher wished to make. In addition, her teaching suffered from a subtle moralizing and the avoidance of touchy issues. In social studies she had written two subjects for discussion on the board, while a record on Abraham Lincoln was being played: "problems—as a young man" and "evidence—of future greatness." In discussing these topics, the children twice tried to raise the question of slavery. Each time, the teacher sloughed it over. She had in mind for the first, the death of Ann Rutledge. For the second, she stressed Lincoln's sense of responsibility and his command of the English language, as evidenced by the Gettysburg Address, with the obvious implication that the children should watch their own language. Here it was not just the teacher but the content of the record being played that was superficial and sentimental. As evidence of Lincoln's greatness, the record told of an instance when he supposedly helped a pig that was stuck in some mud. Instead of using Lincoln's Gettysburg Address to underline a moral on speech, what a *real* lesson could be built on the question: Why was the address, known as one of the most beautiful pieces of political writing in English, not a success when it was first given? Yet this is not the kind of question considered appropriate to elementary school.

This teacher said she would like to see less "teacher domination" of the classroom and mentioned the difficulties of leading a successful discussion with forty eleven-year-olds. She said it would be different if she could take ten or twelve children and sit around a table or in a semicircle informally and casually, and in "a very unteacherish, one-of-the-group manner," say something, but in this case "you have to really get in there and roll up your sleeves and go." She had tried more pupil participation in running the lesson and had found "you have to get back and take it over." With such a large group, you needed "to pull in the reins."

Finally, in her interview, the teacher indicated a fundamentally moralistic, rather than intellectual or scientific, approach to subject matter (which unfortunately permeates our entire educational system). She spoke of the opportunities in reading and social studies for discussions "where the emphasis is placed on character, or the biography of the person, or of groups of people, such as frontier people, what qualities they had to have, and so on . . ." and then concluded with the ultimate purpose of the discussion: ". . . then you can bring it back into the personal without making it look as if you're preaching." Here, then, is a teacher who is capably imparting to her pupils necessary skills and knowledge but who almost certainly has never had the question raised to her, "How does one search out the full meaning curriculum materials might hold for the *intellectual* development of children?" For example, the teacher might have considered what a challenge it could be for the children to examine more generally the needs of pioneer life in terms of the physical environment. Further, she had long since learned, presumably, to steer clear of "controversial" areas. In the one instance where she picked up a child's question and built something new on it, it was in a "safe" area of specific fact—the date of Lincoln's death. Here the teacher took time to work with the question, fully developing the notion of how to estimate a date on the basis of facts already known.

The other fifth-grade teacher (classroom II–5), referred to as attempting to involve the children actively in the learning process, spoke seriously and thoughtfully both about her own limitations and those imposed by inadequate resources. She referred to the constant challenge of making the curriculum meaningful to the children, of the ingenuity needed to involve something the children bring up or some item they bring in. Mathematics was her favorite subject, and she spoke of the difficulty of bridging the gap between the theoretical and practical: "I find that that is the hardest thing for most people, getting to be able to apply the theoretical mathematics to an actual situation." Trips, she stated, should be carefully planned to be worthwhile, and they require a lot of work. The teacher should go first and know what she wants to point out, and the children should have an idea of what they are going to see. It is difficult to write a plan book, she said, because one does not know what the children may raise. She found social studies difficult to teach and found it hard to use the committee structure, nor was she sure "the children are in most cases ready." These problems were further aggravated by limited materials. This was especially true ". . . if your room is not equipped with source material."

> I find it very hard to get or be enthusiastic about committees and to give them proper background for it when I can't give them the information. And you can't even go to the library unless you are scheduled for the library.[10] To have a committee with just one book doesn't seem right either.

The children liked social studies, she continued, and enjoyed the books they read, asking good questions. She tried to be inventive about finding items from papers and magazines to bring in, or "someone will bring a book from home and I will have a report given from it."

This teacher's reading program was also hampered, she pointed out, by limited books. She would have liked to make reading interesting by having enough books so that everyone could read a part from a play. "I would need about ten copies, or at least one for every character, but I haven't been able to find anything like that in the school. . . . I wish we could do more of the plays where they actually read from the book."

In a mathematics session and a report on a science project, this teacher was clearly attempting to teach the children to evaluate material thoughtfully and reason out answers. In social studies, the teacher handled factual questions in a lesson on the Gold Rush competently: What was a forty-niner? How long did it take to get to California? How was gold actually discovered? By what route was the gold brought back? The session moved along easily and pleasantly. The teacher was friendly, supportive, humorous; she allowed the children freedom to enlarge on their own experiences, which they did, often at length, bringing up personal items such as movies they had seen, and so forth. The teacher did likewise. When the children wandered too far from the point, they were pleasantly brought back. They were quite involved, looking up answers in the text and reading appropriate passages. In other ways, as she herself pointed out, the teacher's limitations were revealed. The interchange was fundamentally conversational, with no real depth or development of ideas. When there was an answer in the book, the teacher failed to deepen the subject; at other times, when she apparently could not handle a subject raised, she cut it off. At no time was there presented the broad vista of a spreading country, inhabited by village Indians, where now Hollywood, shipping companies, airplane factories thrive. There was no insight into the realities of life in a frontier mining town, and there were no such questions as the impact of the Gold Rush on the opening up of the West. Yet it was apparent that this was not due to an inadequacy in knowledge or ability but in understanding—in *training* in what could be done.

It is hardly a new or surprising thought that teachers are limited in their ability successfully to direct their curriculum activities toward revealing the essences, or processes, of the physical and social world—the real meaning of an integrated curriculum.[11] They have not been taught the fundamental principles of mathematics, social studies, and the physical sciences to the degree necessary to convey their essentials to children at different age levels. Indeed, to expect such an all-encompassing mastery would be an extraordinary demand to make of most people, one that is not even made of the college professor. Yet this is a question we are hardly prepared to face. The problem of training teachers is usually conceived as teaching them how to translate complicated materials of the type now learned in college into terms children can understand, while in fact this involves a knowledge of fundamental scientific principles which is far beyond that generally achieved by college graduates. Even in graduate schools, as in elementary schools, the curriculum is still disparate bodies of data. At best there may be a routine survey of different approaches to or theories about a given subject matter, and it is almost by accident that more thoughtful individuals stumble onto deeper questions that are the true meat of the subject. The recent concern with science teaching is directed toward making this less a matter of accident and more a conscious design. However, until more imaginative and courageous revisions than yet envisaged are made in our educational system, pupils at all levels will basically be learning to parrot a series of rules and formulas.

Since this is so, it is no wonder that some teachers—and some parents also—long for the "good old days" when one was secure in the emphasis on factual knowledge. One of the fifth-grade teachers (classroom I–5) expressed her own feelings of inadequacy along these lines, saying that the social studies program as conceived today is "so all encompassing." When she was young, they had "specifics"—history was one thing and geography another. "Today it is all meshed in some way. I feel that teachers, including myself, get lost in this big maze, not knowing what to leave out, what to draw in." She said there is little interest in dates today, yet she feels "dates should be a part." "This date to remember—1619–1621—gives you some sort of background—something to hold on to." She spoke enviously of a parochial school where the children were given "very definite things to look for, to find out, to know and to memorize." She said, "I think the social studies program is too large and not enough specifics are given to us. I feel that the children are not getting it, and, in the end, they will be the ones who are losing out."

This teacher's dilemma illustrates the widespread confusion about educational techniques that followed the misinterpretation and cheapening of Dewey's attacks on established educational practices, making teachers cynical about new methods and uncertain about what to teach. This fifth-grade teacher went on to emphasize the importance of explicitness: "I do so and so. . . . This happens next. . . . I divide. . . . I multiply. . . . I bring down. . . ." Were the children's concept of numbers more advanced, she said, she might work on estimation and the like with them and teach them by both the old and new methods—though one is not supposed to; however, with these children she finds herself most successful with "the very old-fashioned method that you and I were taught." Small wonder, considering the present uncertainty about the teaching of mathematics, where the simple fact is that an intellectual grasp of conceptual content in this area is the concern of professional mathematicians and philosophers.[12]

Depth, Richness, and Variety of Curriculum

The various categories under which the curriculum was analyzed turned out to be so interdependent that our previous discussion has already implied the limitations upon "depth" and "richness" which were observed. Achieving "depth" of content clearly involves the intellectual mastery and teaching skills already alluded to. While all the teachers who were observed gave thought to enriching their curricula through planning projects, taking trips tied in with particular subjects, and so forth, it was at a superficial level, and they did not know how to help the children explore the essential meaning of such experiences.

In the schools with higher standards for performance, there was more content to the curriculum, but it was "richer" only in the sense that sheer quantity enriches. The classrooms showing the greatest variety of materials were those to which children brought things from well-off homes in a middle-income white neighborhood. Here the teachers in both second and fifth grades allowed time for reporting on such materials, and the children eagerly brought and shared news clippings, scrapbook projects, models, books from outside libraries, and so forth, and conveyed to each other their enthusiasm and interest. Needless to say, this dependence on well-equipped homes for materials that enrich the classroom contributes heavily to the second-rate educational experience for children who come from homes without spare money to spend on such materials.

However, such materials are not necessarily taken advantage of in those schools which serve children from more economically secure backgrounds. The teachers' questions and level of dealing with the students in the study classrooms were either perfunctory or "sweet" and "supportive," rather than intellectually stimulating, as the following episode from a fifth-grade classroom shows:

> As the observers arrive, Mary is in front of the room, giving a report on a news item about schools, with which the teacher apparently disagrees. The teacher says they say that about the schools, but many people who know a good deal more could have something else to say. . . . We don't take just one reporter's view. . . . We don't read just one book on a subject.
> Lucy proffers some possible explanation, and T replies, "They're just making a study. I wouldn't say yes or no till I heard all the facts. Wouldn't you do the same? Would you take one person's word?"
> Charles goes up to the teacher. She says, "Well, we won't go into that. . . . It's not considered nice. It's not legal. . . ."
> Ronald goes up to the teacher to tell her something, and T says to tell the class. He says, "We were talking about plants, and I told the teacher I could bring in some moss." T asks, "Where does it grow?" Ronald replies, "In my backyard; there are a lot of rocks and moss and stuff." T replies, "Do you like to touch it? It always makes me feel as if it were velvet." She indicates it is time to stop reporting and check math homework.
> Gerald goes up with a book on missiles, starts to talk about it. T

says, to cut him off, "Is that from our library? Aren't you lucky to have such a good library? Show your book, too, Alice."

Alice has a book on Einstein. She says, "He is a great scientist, a genius." T says, "Yes, a great man." During this, Mary is in the back putting up the clippings she has brought. Gerald is still showing his book, explaining the different pictures. T says, "If you're interested in missiles, you might like this, but . . ." She is eager for this to end. "All right, show them one or two or we won't have time for our arithmetic. . . . Just one or two, dear."

Gerald goes right on, without any sign of slowing down. When he does, Charles is back at the front, with a book he says is "on the Soviet Union—on missiles and Sputnik." He says he got the book from the library, "The First Book of the Soviet Union." He shows a picture of Sputnik, points out "where the dog goes."

T asks, "Did you read any of it?" Charles answers, "Yes." T: "Does it tell what the children do?" Charles says, "That comes later." He talks about Rasputin. "This man Rasputin was a good doctor. He was premier of Russia many years ago. . . . They gave him some poison, but he didn't die. Finally they shot him . . ."

T interrupts, "Very good dear, thank you. Even though we don't agree with the way they live, it's good for us to know about it. . . . Who is in charge of arithmetic homework?" Ronald is back in front of the room, telling of a Russian space man in a mental hospital.

T says, "All right. . . . Mary, you are doing a good job, but you can finish later." (Mary is monitor for arithmetic homework this week.) Ronald says, "Albert Einstein wasn't very smart in grade school." T replies, "That is encouraging, isn't it?" This is sarcastically said; then, more seriously, "But though he was quiet and didn't talk much, I think he was doing a great deal of what . . . ?"

The answer comes from the class, "Thinking." Mary is now in front of the class, and starts asking for answers on the arithmetic homework.

This record illustrates both the opportunity given to the children to exchange their experiences, and the failure of the teacher to use these experiences to develop the children's thinking.

In another fifth-grade classroom (I–5), the children's interest and enthusiasm were woefully cheated by the paltry level of the school curriculum. In a science lesson children are given seeds to plant. They have done this before, as evidenced by the plant table in the back of the room, and they clearly enjoy the activity. However, as a lesson in science, it would not pass muster at any level of age or presumed learning ability.

T passes out seeds to the front seats of each row, explaining that she is going to let each group plant something. "You may get out of the seats and gather around the front desk of your group, nicely." The children move to the front with a convivial, but reasonably subdued, hubbub.

T pours dirt into a pan for Group 3. Mark calls in a plaintive voice, "Mrs. __, come over here. . . ." T brings the sack of dirt to Group 2, says to Mark, "You go to plant with them." She moves to Group 1. Aside from quiet directives to each group, there has been no discussion or introduction of the project.

Richard enters, asks, "What are we doing?" He goes over to Peter, then joins his group. T goes from one group to the next distributing seeds, gives quiet directives on planting, smiles, involves herself in no discussion. She tells Mark to get something out of her desk drawer. He rummages first in the lower, then in the upper. A girl comes over to help him. They find what they are looking for, tongue depressors to label the plant boxes with.

The children are actively and noisily discussing the planting. They kid, saying how they are doing it, dividing up the work with humor, discussion, and little argument. Group 3 is noisier than the other two. The noise level on the whole is not high, partly due to the large room.

Lucy goes up and speaks to the teacher, who is working at her desk. The teacher says, "Yes." Lucy corrects something on the board, dances back to T, then changes it in her book. There is movement in the room as the children water the boxes, label them, and carry them to the back, where, on the "science table," there are many other plants, labeled. Some skip animatedly; some walk bouncily. They look to see how the other plants are doing.

T announces what Group 1 has planted, and then the others. She says, "Suppose Group 3 puts their tray in the closet and see what happens if there is no light."

There are little cries, "In the *closet*!" T repeats the directive, says, "All right, back to your seats," and sharply, "One, two." The children return to their seats and a girl gives out towels for them to wipe their hands.

T is sitting at the front of the room. She says again, "We're going to use Group 3's seeds as an experiment to watch the seeds and report." "All right, let me see Donald in his seat. Let me see Patty in her seat. Make sure you do your homework tonight. . . ."

The children obviously knew well what would happen, and their response, rather than interest, was disappointment. The "experiment" was thus transformed from a learning experience into a punishment. Although this project was not at a fifth-grade level in the first place, there could at least have been some discussion about photosynthesis and plant growth that would suggest "experimenting" with different conditions. Further, preparation for the fact that the plants would grow a little before dying could open up discussion of stored energy.

Unfortunately, the level of teaching that this incident illustrates pervaded this classroom, and it is little wonder that it was the most apathetic of those observed. Nonetheless, as the incident shows, the children responded eagerly, showing considerable initiative, to a chance for participation. In a later chapter, we shall return to this classroom, with a summary of its total character.

Style of Learning and Thought Encouraged in the Classroom

On the basis of studying teachers and their training, Sarason, Davidson, and Blatt write, "The more we get into the problem, the more we become convinced [that] most teachers teach in a way reflecting the concept that education consists primarily of what we put into children rather than what we can get out of them." [13] They go on to show how largely this concept of teaching derives from the style in which the teachers themselves were trained, and they document with interview material the frustration of teacher trainees who were not being given the understanding of how to translate general principles of child growth and learning into concrete and practical terms of teaching technique.[14] As we observed in classrooms, we were witnessing the same phenomenon in teachers who might try to formulate a notion of teaching as "getting something out of a child" but had no understanding of what this means or how to act upon it.

As part of our analysis of teaching techniques, we tallied all teacher responses to children's statements, answers, or questions, according to whether they "closed" or "opened up" a subject. Responses judged as closing a subject could be accepting, evaluating, or correcting, and included nonverbal responses, such as the teacher turning to another child in response to an incorrect statement. Teacher responses were judged as opening up a subject if they contained further questions or the seeking out of errors. It was found that closing responses were far more frequent than those which elaborated on the child's responses. In three of the second-grade classrooms, only one in every ten of the teachers' responses opened up a subject, and in the fourth second-grade classroom about one in five was of this kind.[15] In the fifth grades, all classrooms hovered around the one-in-five proportion.[16]

Both the content and number of curriculum interchanges entered into the evaluation of the teachers observed. Many of the recorded responses were superficial, and almost all were isolated, that is, not contributing to a sequence of ideas aimed at really exploring a subject. However, even a superficial "opening-up" mode of teacher response at least allows for some further development of a child's thought. We found that it occurred remarkably little, although many of the lessons observed were of the type that specifically called for it. By far, the largest proportion of the observations was taken up by: (1) reports by the children in social studies and current events, generally accompanied by comments and questions from the teacher, and sometimes from the children; (2) social studies discussion led by the teacher and involving the whole classroom; (3) work on methods of problem solving in arithmetic; and (4) discussion of workbook questions on reading, or other discussion of story content. Sarason and his colleagues mention the classroom emphasis on determining whether a child knows a correct answer, rather than on involving him in the process of finding or elaborating it,[17] and they go on to show how this parallels methods of teacher training. Our observation of teachers who, as we have said, were all good teachers by their schools' standards and self-assured in the handling of their teaching tasks, affords a further confirmation of Sarason's assessment.

The picture of a good teacher that emerges from the literature is one who uses different modes of student involvement appropriate to the various subject areas as she develops her curriculum content. She combines a measure of good, effective drill or practice in skills with relatively structured training in systematic thinking and problem solving and with quite unstructured sessions which allow for the possibility of adventurous thinking or exploration of subjective experience. She is able consciously to shift from one to another style, according to the subject matter or in response to something that has been introduced by a child. Thus, mastery of phonetic principles and facility in handling numbers would involve practice, repetition, or, in short, drill; workbook questions are often so couched as to open up possibilities for practice in problem solving, while some discussions or taking the parts of different characters in reading a story might precipitate a shift into the third or more exploratory mode of pupil involvement.

The best teachers[18] in the classrooms observed, which included the eight in the core study and some dozen others visited during the formulation of the research design, fell loosely into two categories: those who emphasized drill and training in skills and involved the children in thinking through problems in mathematics and science; and those who allowed enough leeway in discussions and group projects, picked up enough of what the children contributed, and covered enough material to enable the children to become directly involved with the material. Teachers in the first group tended to overstructure discussion and limit free expression of ideas; those in the second tended to be careless about factual material, to slight systematic acquisition of skills and knowledge, and to keep discussion at too "conversational" a level. The poorest teachers among those we observed handled all modes ineffectively, with little good drill, confused attempts to involve the children in thinking problems through, and no real leeway for discussion; some, as a slight improvement, at least allowed the children to present and talk about materials, albeit without meaningful follow-through.

PROBLEM SOLVING AND NUMBER PRACTICE IN MATHEMATICS

The area of practice in numbers affords examples of successful and unsuccessful drilling sessions. Some were simple "old-fashioned" drills, and others were attempts to interest the children and enliven the session through creating concrete contexts for an exercise. The issue in the pages that follow is not "old" versus "new" methods of teaching mathematics, but the degree of command a teacher has over whatever technique she is using.

A fifth-grade teacher (classroom III–5) spoke of combining drill in various forms with the rest of her lesson and spoke of the children as enjoying it and of the necessity for such practice, even in a fifth grade, since she is "carrying the residue of the 'we didn't get it' of the prior grades." The children, she said, need training in rapid recall of simple addition, subtraction, and multiplication. As observed in the classroom, they did gain satisfaction from the short, rapid, and generally successful answering of questions from the multiplication table.

> T says, "Let's see how alert we are. . . ." She tells the children to get their pencils and papers ready, saying, "We are going to review because some people in our class are new. . . ." She gives questions from the 8 table very fast, skipping around, and the children write the answers. She then calls for answers, nodding at the children, who reply with great rapidity. T says, "Would you like to try another?"

> There is a chorus of yesses. . . . T then calls from the 10 table, the whole lasting four minutes.

In the second-grade classrooms, teachers often combined "number experience" with practical examples where it might be applied. A highly successful session observed in one of the pilot-study second grades used a "card shop," or rack, well marked and attractive, with ten rows of cards, each numbered (1 to 10) and grouped according to a clearly defined type—Christmas, Birthday, Valentine, etc. Using the buying of cards, the teacher drilled in addition, then subtraction (How much more did certain cards cost than others?), multiplication (How much would a given number of a certain type of card cost?), and division (With so much money, how many of such and such a card could one buy?). The entire session was simple and clear; it proceeded quickly and held the children's attention. The teacher then introduced the idea of a sale, either 1, 2, or 3 cents. When she mentioned a 3-cent sale, which reduced the cards by 3 cents, all hands flew up at the challenge, with exclamations of pleasure. The resulting price of each card was then asked, and decisions made as to what to do with cards that were already 3 cents and less. This allowed for multiple problems, "These are 2 for a penny; how many can you buy for 10 cents?" At this question, the children began to have difficulty. The teacher explained the reasoning involved, but the pace slowed, the children's attention began to drift, and the teacher closed the session.

Another second-grade teacher (classroom I-2) called 9 children to the front of the room and asked others to group them in different combinations, which she wrote on the board. The problem became to locate the missing combinations. At the end, the list read: 5 and 4, 7 and 2, 8 and 1, 6 and 3, 4 and 5, 1 and 8, 3 and 6, and a child discovered the missing 2 and 7. Although the lesson held the interest of the children as it proceeded, it became cumbersome, with such elaboration of the circumstances that relatively little "number experience" occupied the ten minutes that the episode lasted. The teacher then shifted to another technique:

> T tells a "story" about lending another T in school some books, using names the children know. She calls on a child to impersonate a teacher, and borrow 3 books from her stack of 9. "After I gave Mrs. ___ 3 books, how many do I have left?" She asks further questions, saying, "Who can tell me this story?" and receives the answer, "9 take away 4 is 5," etc.

T then shifts, "Remember one day we had breakfast in school and we brought spoons." She picks up plastic spoons and holds them up, asking how many she has left. There are 9. The children then impersonate teachers borrowing spoons according to the teacher's questions, and she writes the different combinations of 9 minus . . . on the board. (At this juncture the problem of having a boy impersonate a woman teacher arises and remains unresolved.)

T then shifts to plates, and finally says, "We have one story left; we'll do it with envelopes. Who'd like to tell me how many envelopes?" She then recapitulates the combinations they have done, and has the children repeat them in unison.

In this lesson, over twenty minutes was spent drilling in the various combinations that add up to 9, in terms of both addition and subtraction. Each of sixteen number combinations were covered once and were repeated in unison by the children. The time was spent pleasantly but it was hardly an effective drill session. Nor was it a real exercise in problem solving. It lay somewhere in between as "number experience," pleasantly, capably, and imaginatively carried out, in keeping with curriculum directives, but lacking any quality of serious intellectual challenge. It was far more successful, however, than a session observed in another classroom, where a well-meant attempt to "integrate" a mathematics lesson with an ongoing class activity, a flower show, resulted in hopeless confusion. The teacher (classroom IV-2) introduced the lesson by talking about a flower show that the children were planning, and she wrote the names of flowers on the board. She mentioned the small pots of seedlings on the window sill and table, asked about watering them, and discussed how they should be grouped. She spoke of having a flower show so the children "can learn."

T then says, when things go into a museum, they are put in . . . She pauses for a word, then says, "I'm thinking of a word beginning with 'o.'" Someone responds "order." T says, "That's right," and a child says they should put the plants in alphabetical order. T suggests they could be put in order of height, short and tall. She then asks how she can arrange discs on a magna board so they will have 10 plants. She asks for an arrangement for 10, and elicits the suggestion, 4 and 6. T gathers some of the pots from the window sill, and puts them on a table near her desk. The children watch with interest.

T discusses 6 and 4, and talks about having 6 marigolds and 4 morning glories. She says she wants the children to "make believe the discs are plants," and asks for an arrangement to show 6 marigolds and 4 morning glories. A child goes to the board, works slowly arranging the discs in two groups, and T asks for the children to arrange their discs at their desks. She calls Joan to "tell a story." Joan says, "I have 6 marigolds and 4 morning glories; how many pots do I have?" She calls on Patricia, who answers, "2." T puts 4 of the 10 pots on her desk, and says to Patricia, "Here's a dear little flower, just beginning to sprout. Come and count them, Patricia."

Patricia comes slowly, with a look of concentration. T puts her arm around her and says, "Touch each of them." Patricia counts 6. T then says, "Come over here" (to the other 4 on her desk), "I want you to put your finger on them too." Patricia counts out 4 and looks at T.

There is inattention and mild talking developing in the classroom. T tries to explain that 6 pots of one flower and 4 of another make 10. T asks Joan, still at the board, to put her hands around the 4 marigolds on the magna board, saying, "While Patricia counts marigolds on the desk, Joan is counting discs on the board." The class is relatively quiet (in sufferance, not interest). There is scattered whispering. Patricia recounts the flowers.

T continues, saying 6 morning glories and 4 marigolds are what? She asks the children to count discs at their desks. They do so in unison, the 6 and the 4. T says, "I wonder how many plants altogether?" The class is unresponsive; no one answers. T asks Gerald, who does not respond. She goes over to his desk counting with him, and has the class count the discs from 1 to 10. She asks Gerald, "How many?" He does not answer. She then asks Gerald to go to the front of the room with Patricia, and count the pots. After this count, Gerald says, "10." T then asks him to go to the board and count the discs. He repeats 10.

T says, "Thank you, children, you did a lovely job," with relief in her voice. "Count 6 and 4 discs and tell me how many I have altogether." A child answers "10." T calls on Ann to tell the story, and helps her, "6 and 4 are . . ." Ann says, "10." T says, "I'm going to call on one more boy to tell the story of the marigolds." She directs Lester first to the marigolds, then the morning glories, pulling him from one set of pots to another, asking him how many flowers. She asks one more boy to repeat the operation, telling him to touch the pots, not the leaves. She finally says, "Tomorrow we are going to play another game. . . . Do you like games, Ronald?" Ronald does not reply. The children are noisy.

T has the children put their discs away, telling them to keep saying to themselves that 6 and 4 are 10. . . .

In this session, twenty-five minutes were spent working with one number combination, $6 + 4 = 10$, yet the teacher's inept attempt to make the exercise meaningful and enjoyable led only to puzzlement. The episode exemplifies, with unfortunate clarity, the confusion that can result when new concepts of mathematics teaching are not adequately spelled out to teachers. However, this teacher did not, like the teacher mentioned above, admit to confusion. She said she liked the "new program." "You take each number and you just tear it apart limb from limb," she said. "Whereas, years ago, the old program went on further . . . they weren't learning the concrete fashion. . . . Now everything is concrete, and they know exactly what they're seeing and counting, and the value of the ones within the tens, and tens within the hundreds. They're constantly being made aware of this, which is very good. . . ."

The point is not to favor a return to "old-fashioned" practice in speedy repetition of factual knowledge in place of teaching techniques that explore operations like $6 + 4 = 10$ and relate them to the children's thinking and experience. It is rather that well-meant but inadequate attempts to involve children in thinking about numbers through manipulation of objects can become superficial or confusing. What is worse is that it can become a substitute for real exercises in thinking, problem solving, sorting and weighing of information, and reasoning from less adequate to more adequate formulations or solutions.

It is noteworthy that the teacher who was most clear in her presentation of problem solving in arithmetic was the fifth-grade teacher (classroom III-5) who also emphasized straight drill and had a lively, quick, and challenging way of making factual material readily available to her pupils. This teacher interrupted a discussion to take up a child's question about a date and, saying, "Let us estimate . . . ," introduced in clear detail ideas of proof, verification, and evidence in relation to the problem. In her mathematics session, she demonstrated that there were different ways to do a problem and that the "better" are usually done only because they are shorter. She introduced her lesson with some drill to warm the children up and then wrote a problem on the board:

> In the school paper, Jane has a column 3 inches wide. She wants a ½ inch margin on the left. How many inches are left in the column?

The teacher called on different children to count by fractions of 2, in two ways, then to read the problem, then to restate it in arithmetical terms. What, she asked, was the main operation in the problem? What was the answer? How was it arrived at?

> T then asks, "How shall we estimate that answer? Does anyone object?" Ronald gives an alternative way of arriving at the same solution,

with quite a developed statement. T asks, "Of the two people who gave you answers, whom would you accept?" Ruth chooses the first. T asks why, and Ruth replies that his way was shorter than Ronald's. T says, "Yes, though what Ronald did wasn't wrong." She calls Edward to the board to write out the operation. . . .

The teacher then involved the children in writing and/or describing various ways that ½ could be subtracted from 3. One changed the 3 to %, subtracted ½, and reduced the answer; another changed the 3 to 2 and ⅔. One worked with the 3 as a whole, doing the operation in his head, and one took 1 from 3, and then ½ from that, subsequently adding the other half back on! The teacher accepted and developed each of these methods and then pointed out the way it was "usually done," though the other ways were "right and showed good thinking." The session, including the drill, lasted about a half hour.

Attempts by some other teachers to involve children in analyzing mathematical processes were less successful due to a weak command of techniques for carrying out the intent. In another fifth-grade classroom (I-5), the teacher asked for answers to the problem: "Pencils cost 2 for 5 cents. If you buy 6 pencils, how much will they cost?" After a few failures, a child answered 15 cents. The teacher asked him to put it on the board, and when he remained uncertain what to do, she called on another child, Peter, to "help." Peter wrote $5 \times 3 = 15$. The teacher asked why he picked 3, and he explained. Then the teacher diagrammed on the board 3 sets of 2 pencils each, with a 5 under each. She asked about buying 8 pencils, received the correct answer, 20 cents, which the child wrote on the board as $5 \times 4 = 20$. The teacher asked, "Why did you put the 4 there? Show us in a picture," and the child drew 4 sets of 2 pencils each. She then questioned further, trying to elicit from the children that they were illustrating the step of dividing the number of pencils that cost the unit price into the total number of pencils wanted. She never explained this, however, and the children, confused by her questions, kept repeating the diagram on the board.

William draws 2 sets of 2 rulers, placing 25 under each and writing:

$$\frac{25}{\times 2}$$

T asks, "What was your first step?" William, doubtfully, "Multiplying?" T: "What was your *first* step?" William: "Divide?" T: "I didn't see anywhere that you are dividing."

She said no more than this, asked another child to come to the board. This child uncertainly, carefully, looking at the teacher for her reaction, again drew 2 sets of rulers. The teacher pointed out that this was what William had done, and called another child, who stood, puzzled, alongside William.

> T: "There are 4 rulers, right? How many sets of 2?" The children answer, 2. T: "Right . . ." She fails to explain her point. The children leave the board, still puzzled. T, to another child (presumably to call him to attention), "Do you understand, John?" John says yes. T: "All right, then let's do some." She gives further problems, such as, "Gummed stickers cost 12 for 54 cents. How much will 36 cost?"

The teacher here ran into the difficulty of how to analyze a problem that was so simple that the children could do it in their heads without knowing precisely what they were doing. She emphasized that they should learn the process, that "some of you got the answer, but you didn't know *how* you got it." However, by failing to make the process clear, she could only undermine their assurance about figuring correctly in the first place. The same teacher, in social studies, spoke of the children doing research, but she allowed only twenty minutes at the end of a morning to finish up a report that was due the next day, and the only source available to the children was their textbook. Like the "experiment" with plants grown without light (previously referred to), the notions of process and research were mentioned but given no real embodiment.

On occasion a misplaced cuteness perverted a possibility for conceptualization—a teacher who said that "let's" was the way you say "let us" when you're tired, or another who told the children to look for the little word in "tired," meaning the structurally and semantically unrelated word "red." Another problem observed was an inappropriate assumption of logic where it did not exist—spelling was such a pitfall. The fifth-grade teacher who was very good at conveying the processes involved in mathematics lost her class in confusion when attempting to explain the logic of certain spelling rules, despite the fact that English is so hopelessly inconsistent. One could better build a session on the multiple ways the same sound can be spelled, thereby making clear to the children the arbitrariness of English spelling and the importance of sheer memory and familiarity with words.[19]

CONTENT AND CONCEPTS IN THE SOCIAL SCIENCES

In areas involving social content, social studies itself, reading, and news or current-events reports, the emphasis on interjecting a moral into the lesson, albeit subtly, was often seen to hinder a true search for meaning. The evasion of controversial subjects, the tendency to keep discussion on a "nice" and essentially conversational level, and the lack of training in how to deal with the theoretical content of behavioral science materials all contributed to the absence of a problem-solving approach in this area. The Panel on Educational Research and Development speaks of the "irrelevance, hypocrisy, and misplaced emphasis [which] destroy the value of many of . . . [the] efforts [to improve social studies]."

> What the child needs is a growing knowledge of who he is, what kind of world he is living in, how his future role in this world may be shaped, and how he may help shape it. This is a matter for self-scrutiny, honest, and careful observation. It is not a matter for didactic oversimplification.[20] [Also,] there are fears that when . . . [social studies] courses of communism or of Russia, or, domestically, of poverty or race relations or other controversial subjects [are taught], public pressure will impose upon the schools materials which are so bland or oversimplified as to be useless.[21]

This last has, of course, been a matter of concern in relation to teaching social studies for some time. Over a decade ago, toward the beginning of the "cold war," Henry Steele Commager addressed himself to the current definition of "loyalty," writing as follows:

> It is, above all, conformity. It is the uncritical and unquestioning acceptance of America as it is—the political institutions, the economic practices. It rejects inquiry into the race question or socialized medicine, or public housing, or into the wisdom and validity of our foreign policy. It regards as particularly heinous any challenge to what is called "the system of private enterprise," identifying that system with Americanism. It abandons evolution, repudiates the once popular concept of progress, and regards America as a finished product, perfect and complete.[22]

Disturbed by the increasingly restrictive effect on education of an insistence on this type of "loyalty," the Board of Directors of the National Council for the Social Studies approved an official statement of the Committee on Academic Freedom, published in 1953, that students have a right "to study and discuss significant moral, scientific, social, economic, and political issues, . . . to have access to a variety of publications and materials that relate to issues studied in class, . . . to study and discuss all sides of the issue in an atmosphere where there can be a give and take on ideas without loss of personal dignity, . . . [and] to teach and express an opinion or hold values that may be different from those of other members of the class and from those of the teacher." [23] Although the statement was written with higher education in mind, it is appropriate to all levels of teaching.[24] For instance, the same ideas are implied in another context in Charlotte Winsor's summary statement of what good elementary school teaching calls for in this area:

> We must strive to avoid dilution of important ideas and ideals for children's learning. We need to find strength in independent thinking as we teach. . . . As teachers, we need not only the directives of program and content, but the directives of courage and knowledge. Most of all we need the admonition to seek further knowledge and understanding of our own world. . . . It is only as teachers under-stand their world as well as their children that they can develop a climate of discovery. . . .[25]

The realities of classroom life observed were, needless to say, far from this ideal. Instead of inquiry, questioning, exploring the signifi-cance of various happenings, teaching, by and large, involved a repeti-tion of events and search for predetermined interpretations of these events, drawn from the children through the medium of a question-answer interchange or "discussion." Committee projects were perfunc-tory and suffered, in the ill-equipped schools, from lack of varied source materials. In "discussions," honest, eager questions of significance—such as questions or comments about slavery, some aspects of our econ-omy, the Soviet Union, or a current political event—were either ig-nored, said to be beside the point, or otherwise cursorily disposed of.

Whereas there is much emphasis on discussion as a teaching device, there is little training in how discussions can be effectively led. Instead of being used to open up possibilities for children to explore the world, discussion tends to become a way of directing their thinking into "proper" channels. One could argue that as long as a child is learning no more than $2 \times 2 = 4$ and Columbus discovered America in 1492, his own private thinking, while scarcely stimulated, is at least not invaded. When, instead, he is asked to imagine how Columbus and his sailors might have *felt* sailing outward into the unknown, the question can —and should—open up a vista enabling him to think about the meaning of Columbus' voyage more sharply. However, such questions are generally asked directively, thereby teaching children how *they are supposed to feel* that Columbus felt and thus how they themselves are supposed to feel in comparable situations.

In the best of discussions some of this will take place, since people are (and need to be) sensitized to moving toward the understanding and position of others. However, there is the fine point at which sensitivity can cease to be a means for enabling children to live with others empathically while they feel themselves out as individuals, and instead can become used to encourage them to submerge their individuality in the interest of a safe conformity. Philosophers, poets, and psychologists alike bemoan the degree to which this latter is widespread in our society, while most teachers pursue with dedication the use of social studies and other discussion to inculcate in children the virtues of a standardized conformity and loyalty. True curiosity is all too often off limits. Riesman, Glazer, and Denny speak of the "socialization of taste and interest" which is taught in the modern classroom, with the teacher, as opinion leader, conveying to the children that "what matters is not their industry or learning as such but their adjustment in the group, their cooperation, their [carefully stylized and limited] initiative and leadership." The real demand on the children is that they be "nice," and they are thus "supposed to learn democracy by underplaying the skills of intellect and overplaying the skills of gregariousness and amiability." [26] Calitri expands on the implications the moral standards set for children in the classroom have for their self-respect. He writes:

> We defeat them with our assault of honesty, goodness, integrity, bravery, and courage as the qualifications of humanity, setting up for them images of excellence which are impossible of imitation. This we have managed for all youth . . .
>
> We hold forth such values in an almost uncompromising fashion, pretending that these lie behind the precepts which any fine American must follow. . . . We are telling them further that they are not worthy to be in the world as we see it . . .
>
> I have no intention of demeaning either our country's heroes or the values of our society and culture. . . . I do intend to point out that, if we are to have any success in our educational exchange with youth, then our share must be the honesty of things as they are. [27]

Here, indeed, the teacher is beset with a difficult problem, for she cannot easily surmount her culture. However, from observations in our classrooms, we see that there is considerable variation in the extent to which a teacher either values the individual thoughts and ideas of her students or constantly interjects her own tastes and attitudes. Take, for example, a teacher (classroom IV–5) who involved the children in thinking about "going west" and followed discussion of the dangers met by the pioneers with the question, "Last week we had someone going into the unknown—there were dangers attached to that. Who am I thinking of?" There is a chorus of "Shepherd." So far so good, but the teacher then asked what attributes spacemen have to have which are the same as the pioneers. After a wrong start with the answer "supplies," she begins to draw the answers she wants. "Courage—yes, *that's the boy. . . .* Yes, loyalty, yes, he went for his country. . . . Yes, self-confidence, and besides self-confidence, he had to have self . . . ?" The answer comes from the class, "Reliance." "Yes," said the teacher, "was mommy there to tell him what to do? . . . It was the same thing with the other pioneers . . ." and she moved to another part of the lesson.

This teacher, with her rather casual interjection of behavioral directives in place of intellectual content, fell somewhere in between the most and the least moralizing teachers we observed. The teacher (classroom IV–2) who stressed most heavily the importance of the moral lesson said to the interviewer that she explained to the children that "they are going to become good citizens of the United States, and be helpful to their country," though now their task was to "respect each other" for which "all the opportunities in the class are provided for them." She continued, "You've got to drill that into them constantly to make them understand that that is part of their being good citizens." Fair enough, except for the fact that her concept of "good citizenship" was, essentially, agreement with her own particular political leanings. She reprimanded a child for bringing in Primary Day material, stating, "Please do not bring in any material related to politics." She took the papers away and went on to say that in the class "current events" but not "politics" was discussed.

However, after disallowing formal discussion of current political issues, the teacher proceeded to interject her own viewpoint into a spelling lesson. In reference to the word "great," the teacher said tomorrow they would talk of great men, but today she wanted the name of "just one great man." A child volunteered the name, apparently, of the teacher's own candidate in a past campaign, for she responded with, "I am so glad you named him. All the children who were going to name him, raise their hands." Most hands went up, and the teacher said, "Isn't that wonderful?" The children glowed with pleasure at her approval.

Occasional contradictions of this type are hard to avoid, but when they represent a style that permeates the teaching atmosphere, then systematic thinking is indeed being systematically discouraged! Unfortunately, from our observations, we have to agree with Jules Henry's caustic comment: "Nowadays, in America, there is much talk about teaching children to think. In five years of observation in American schools, however, we have found very little behavior that tends in this direction. . . ." [28]

We have discussed ways in which a moralistic approach to content in addition to inadequate training in teaching techniques contribute to the failure to encourage systematic thinking. A third impediment has also been mentioned, an emphasis on the correctness of an answer rather than on the process of arriving at it. The Panel on Educational Research and Development speaks of the new "discovery methods" of teaching, where "the chief activating element . . . is the 'teasing value' of uncertainty—presentation of issues that are conjectural, rather than the laying out of hard, dry, finished facts," which "act as a natural stimulant to the impulse to discover on one's own. . . ." [29] Sarason and his colleagues, writing from the viewpoint of teacher training, pinpoint, as key to fostering this impulse to discover, the development of an atmosphere in which a child can say, "I don't know," without feeling it a sign of stupidity or inferiority, so that he is able "to reflect upon and give verbal expression to his *own* ideas [italics theirs] or methods of problem solution without undue concern about what others consider to be the 'right' answer." "There is probably no more crucial factor in productive learning and thinking," they write, "than when the recognition that one does not know or understand something is followed by the quest for knowledge and understanding. . . ." [30]

In a later chapter we shall give variations in the study teachers' evaluations of children's answers. For the present, we might say that the general emphasis on the answer itself, the fact that "ours is a culture in which it is not easy for the individual to say 'I don't know.'" [31] the vulnerability of children to the desire to please the teacher, and the prevalent interjection of a moral into a lesson all contribute to the universal practice, in discussion, of second-guessing the teacher. This is parodied by rhetorical questions, with the children singing out the correct answer in unison. The effect is exaggerated when the question is misunderstood. For example, take the incident:

TEACHER: Do we need this?
CLASS, in chorus: Ye-e-e-es.
TEACHER, with slight displeasure: *Do* we?
CLASS, with equal certitude: No-o-o.

EXPLORATORY THINKING IN THE CLASSROOM

We have suggested above that one can define three primary modes of teaching—that which gives practice in skills and factual knowledge, that which develops the ability to think systematically, and that which encourages free-floating, adventurous thinking and exploration of subjective experience. Learning and discovery involve all three. However, there has been the tendency, associated with arguments about "progressive" versus "old-fashioned" teaching, to pit one against another as more or less preferable. Generally lacking is an awareness of the differences among the three modes and their appropriateness in varying proportions to different curriculum areas. Capable teachers among those in our study either emphasized the skill and systematic thinking areas, allowing little leeway for exploratory thinking, or favored a discussion technique likely to be overcasual about factual accuracy and to encourage unfocused responses rather than serious thought. Discussion moved back and forth between the "systematic" and "exploratory" areas, developing almost accidentally, and usually not taken advantage of by the teacher. Further, the purpose of discussion was seldom seen as involving the children in developing their own thinking, instead of manipulating them into reflecting the teacher's thinking. "I ask the leading question to get the answer that I want," said a teacher when discussing "experience charts." "As we are discussing, I will put down the main thoughts of what I want to go down on the chart. They enjoy that. They like to talk. They enjoy discussion. . . ."

In this instance, the teacher is confusing the notion of discussion with the rigorous technique of preparing a reading chart which calls for limited vocabulary and sentence structure. In a true discussion there must be the possibility of raising new or different ideas and formulations and expressing varying individual responses and preferences. In the following interchange, a teacher in one of the pilot-study classrooms realized herself the inappropriateness of pressing too hard for a specific word to describe what could only be a variety of individual responses. She was seeking for a particular word with which to introduce a spelling lesson. Having just closed a poetry session, she said:

> T: You read poetry for your . . . ?
> CHILD: Enjoyment.
> T: What else?
> ANOTHER CHILD: Entertainment.
> T: Yes, another word?
> MARCIA: Recreation.
> T: Yes, but what does it make you feel?
> ROGER: Good.
> T: Yes, it's good for you, and don't you also read it for *pleasure*?
>   T writes the word "pleasure" on the board, and says, somewhat apologetically, "I wanted to get my own word in."

The subjects where teachers felt children should have independence for expression of their own ideas were, appropriately, painting and writing. Some gave careful attention to these areas. In one second-grade classroom an easel was in constant use, for the children took turns to paint a full hour at a time. The teacher in this classroom took time during formal art sessions to let the children tell what they saw in their own and in each other's paintings, and she accepted their answers without evaluation. Another teacher spoke of using situations when the class was keyed up emotionally to have the children write about how they felt. A third had an envelope into which children could put poems they had written. From time to time the teacher would select some to share with the class.

Other teachers, however, made no attempt to encourage individual expression. One said in her interview, "My class doesn't do very much creative writing. They aren't too capable. I tried it twice, and it was fair. But before the term ends, I would like to try it again. . . ." [32] Another took no advantage of a good opportunity she herself had created for expression of individual feelings. The children reported to the class on a character they would not like to be in the story they had individually read, and most of them spoke eagerly and at some length. However, instead of free-floating questions or exchange among the children, only the teacher asked questions or made comments, and these were either strictly factual or corrective. In her interview, this teacher said that the children enjoyed their reading but that the stories were not the kind with which they could identify.

This last instance indicates a major problem in allowing leeway for exploratory thinking, the consistent practice of structuring the learning situation as between the teacher and each child. During our observations of the classrooms there was virtually no opening up of real possibilities for interchange among the children themselves which could enable them to build on one another's thinking. Where children questioned each other on a committee report, it was highly structured, following the teacher-child pattern, and questions were of a factual or critical nature. In one class where we observed extensive license taken by the children to discuss a point among themselves, it was an argument over the correctness of a particular answer.

It could be argued that this is just as well, given a climate in which both curriculum content and discussion techniques are so commonly seen as affording the opportunity to inculcate manners, attitudes, and habits into children. What is supposed to be encouragement of independent exploration can become no more than manipulation when its purpose is seen to be obtaining the "proper" answer. It is not only teacher training that perpetuates this mistaken conception. Workbook questions of the multiple-choice type reinforce the tendency to teach the proper ideas to have rather than encourage the ability to know and describe personal perceptions. As an example, consider a second-grade child who became most upset when a workbook answer brought forth laughter at her expense from the rest of the class, as well as criticism from the teacher. The problem was to select items which had a "swishing" sound. The child checked, "correctly," a taffeta skirt and waves lapping on a beach, and then, "incorrectly," coal being dumped. Coal being hard and solid should not, clearly, "swish," but, as the child explained, "When you hear coal being dumped way down the street, it *does* have a swishing sound." She was being taught, in essence, to deny her own correct perception in favor of a formally acceptable answer.

A final example of inappropriately "correcting" a child's perception is taken from a nonstudy school. In this instance, a second-grade class was called on to write poems on "winter," from which some would be selected to be mimeographed in a class bulletin. One poem read:

> Oh, see the snow tinkling down
> Over the sky

So wide, so high
Down, down it falls
Over the hills and mountainside
Over the world wide
Over the glass sheets
In the wide world high

The poem was one of those selected—after the teacher, commenting "It doesn't make sense," had changed the last three lines to read:

Over the wide world
Over the glass sheets
In the wide, wide sky

NOTES

1. S. B. Sarason, K. Davidson, and B. Blatt, *The Preparation of Teachers, An Unstudied Problem in Education* (New York: John Wiley, 1962).
2. Although there has been allocation of considerable funds for experimental programs in lower-income schools, this picture has remained basically unaffected. See also, Patricia Cayo Sexton, *Education and Income* (New York: Viking Press, 1961); and her summary of recent literature, in *The American School, A Sociological Analysis* (Englewood Cliffs, N.J.: Prentice-Hall, 1967), pp. 54–55. According to the United States Office of Education report, *Equality of Educational Opportunity* (Washington, D.C.: U.S. Government Printing Office, 1966), the so-called "Coleman Report," regional variations in unequal school facilities exceed those for racial or ethnic minorities. However, Harold Howe, II, United States Commissioner of Education, writing in *The New York Times Annual Education Review*, January 11, 1967, pointed out that ". . . 'average' is a tricky notion, often concealing more than it conveys. In New York's case, for example, the school district with the highest expenditure per pupil spent almost seven times as much as the district with the lowest. Such inequities . . . characterize every state in the Union. . . . Typically in our schools we spend less on the child who comes to school with a disadvantage and more on the fortunate youngster. . . ."
3. B. E. Mercer and E. R. Carr, *Education and the Social Order* (New York: Rinehart, 1957), p. 489.
4. They go on to say that at times high school teachers "have been told frankly how they should register politically and which candidates to support." In other cases "school boards have fired teachers or refused to offer contracts when the instructor was reported to be teaching con-

troversial questions. The inevitable result . . . gradually brought a curtain of self-censorship into many classrooms . . . felt particularly in the social studies area." During the McCarthy era this became so extreme that as late as 1955, in a newspaper survey, "a significant percentage of instructors indicated that they did not feel free to discuss the implications of the Declaration of Independence or the American Constitution in their classes." M. W. Rodehaver, W. B. Axtell, and R. E. Gross, *The Sociology of the School* (New York: Thomas Y. Crowell, 1957), pp. 237–238.

5. The distinction between "manifest" and "latent" functions was first made explicit by Freud, but the concept was borrowed and reinterpreted by the sociologist Robert Merton, who applied it to institutional functioning. R. K. Merton, *Social Theory and Social Structure* (London: Collier-Macmillan, Free Press of Glencoe, 1964), pp. 60–61.

6. S. Kimball, "An Anthropological View of Social Systems and Learning," in E. Lloyd-Jones and E. M. Westervelt, eds., *Behavioral Science and Guidance, Proposals and Perspectives* (New York: Bureau of Publications, Teachers College, Columbia University, 1963), pp. 28–30.

7. The findings for the first three of these categories are discussed in this chapter; the last two are taken up in Chapter 3. The schedule for the teacher interview and the outline for the analysis of data will be found in the Appendixes. The third source of study data, a child interview, will be discussed later, when the classrooms are looked at from the viewpoint of the children themselves. In addition to direct analysis of interview and observation content, many aspects of the teacher's style of teaching and classroom management were subjected to quantitative analysis.

8. The study schools and grades are referred to by this numbering system (see Chapter 1, p. 10, for the four schools and their assigned numbers).

9. In his stringent criticism of contemporary teaching methods, John Holt writes, "When a child gets right answers by illegitimate means, and gets credit for knowing what he doesn't know, and knows he doesn't know, it does double harm. First, he doesn't learn, his confusions are not cleared up; second, he comes to believe that a combination of bluffing, guessing, mind reading, snatching at clues, and getting answers from other people is what he is supposed to do at school; that this is what school is all about; that nothing else is possible." [*How Children Fail* (New York: Pitman, 1965), p. 146.] The problem goes deeper than the school, for the same techniques with which one can "get along" at school satisfactorily without really mastering what is being taught are rewarded by some measure of success throughout the middle-class occupational world.

10. The school was overcrowded and on triple session.

11. See L. S. Mitchell, *Young Geographers* (New York: Basic Books, 1963).

12. The Panel on Educational Research and Development to the U.S. Com-

missioner of Education wrote the following, for example: "But achieving superior education depends not only on studying more mathematics (if the prospective teacher is to teach mathematics), but also on the parts of mathematics which are studied. A prospective teacher of elementary mathematics may gain more insight by studying elementary mathematics from an advanced point of view than by studying, say, differential equations or even modern algebra." [*Innovation and Experiment in Education*, A Progress Report of the Panel on Educational Research and Development to the U.S. Commissioner of Education, the Director of the National Science Foundation, and the Special Assistant to the President for Science and Technology (Washington, D.C.: U.S. Government Printing Office, March 1964).]

John Holt comments on how much more "there is to this business of 'understanding' arithmetic than meets the eye," and that "there is nothing particularly simple about 'simple' arithmetic." To assume a woman needs to be no more than "nice" and "sympathetic" to teach children to *understand* arithmetic, he states, "is just plain foolish" (Holt, *op. cit.*, p. 83).

13. Sarason, Davidson, and Blatt, *op. cit.*, pp. xi–xii.
14. See Biber, Gilkeson, and Winsor for a discussion of this same topic: B. Biber, E. Gilkeson, and C. Winsor, "Basic Approaches to Mental Health: Teacher Education at Bank Street College," *Personnel and Guidance Journal*, XXXVII (April 1959), 558–568.
15. The actual percentages, during three hours of observation of, in each case, mathematics, language arts, and social studies, plus whatever else chanced to fall within the observation period, were 8, 8, 11, and 22 per cent.
16. Actual percentages were 16, 18, 21, and 23 per cent.
17. Sarason, Davidson, and Blatt, *op. cit.*, pp. 30, 53–54.
18. "Best" according to the judgment of the researchers, teachers, and teacher educators who analyzed and rated the observational records.
19. Reference to the reasons for English inconsistency as compared with consistency in Spanish could be a productive interjection. At what age level could the children enjoy Bernard Shaw's example of how to spell fish: gh as in enou*gh*, o as in w*o*men, ti as in na*ti*on—which gives us "ghoti"?
20. Report of the Panel on Educational Research and Development, *op. cit.*, p. 33.
21. *Ibid.*, p. 42.
22. H. S. Commager, "Who is Loyal to America?" *Harper's Magazine* (September 1947).
23. Official statement of The Committee on Academic Freedom, approved by Board of Directors of National Council for the Social Studies, *Social Education*, xxxvii (May 1953), 217–219.
24. At a National Education Association Conference, professional social

scientists made similar points when they were asked to compare college and university with elementary-school curricula. The gap was probably at its widest in sociology, and the comment was made that sociology must be built on "the spirit of free inquiry and objectivity." The understanding of society as a system cannot help but be undermined "if its teaching is curbed and channeled by the demands of an ideology, even a democratic one." Criticism was expressed of the overidealized view of political life presented in the classroom. The teaching of the belief that men who enter this area of life are "hard-working, benevolent, acting entirely in the interest of the collective welfare," and have "only the finest and most wholesome approach," can only have the consequence of failing to prepare the children for their future, and lead to naïveté, withdrawal, and cyncism. [National Education Association, *The Scholars Look at the Schools*, A Report of the Disciplines Seminar convened at the NEA Center, June 15–17, 1961 (Washington, D.C.: NEA, 1962), pp. 28–29, 42.]

25. C. Winsor, "Social Education of Young Children," in M. Willcockson, ed., *Social Education of Young Children, Kindergarten–Primary Grades,* Curriculum Series, No. 4, 2nd rev. ed. (Washington, D.C.: National Council for Social Studies, 1956).

26. D. Riesman, N. Glazer, and R. Denny, *The Lonely Crowd* (New York: Anchor Books, Doubleday, 1953), pp. 82–84.

27. C. J. Calitri, "The Nature and Values of Culturally Different Youth," in A. Jewett et al., eds., *Improving English Skills of Culturally Different Youth in Large Cities* (Washington, D.C.: U.S. Department of Health, Education, and Welfare, Office of Education, 1964).

28. J. Henry, "A Cross-Cultural Outline of Education," *Current Anthropology,* I, No. 4 (July 1960), 274.

29. Report of the Panel on Educational Research and Development, *op. cit.,* p. 12.

30. Sarason, Davidson, and Blatt, *op. cit.,* pp. 9–10. Holt also analyzes at some length the "answer-centered" strategies, rather than "problem-centered" strategies emphasized at school, the techniques children use to guess or to elicit the right answers from their teachers, and the anxiety engendered for children over the fear that they may not have or get the right answer (J. Holt, *op. cit.,* pp. 24–25, 47–49, 88–90, 146, 151).

31. Sarason, Davidson, and Blatt, *op. cit.,* p. 9.

32. Hopefully, the growing literature on the use of children's writings in the classroom will begin to introduce a new note in teachers' understanding of their use. See, for example, J. Castro, "The Untapped Verbal Fluency of Negro School Children as Observed through Participant Observation," *New York City Education,* I, No. 2 (New York: Office of Educational Publications, 1968); and M. Wolman, "Cultural Factors and Creativity," in S. W. Webster, ed., *The Disadvantaged Learner, Knowing, Under-*

standing, Educating (San Francisco: Chandler, 1966). Herbert Kohl, author of *36 Children,* speaks of the success teachers have had with children of all social backgrounds when exploring language and literature on the basis of their own writings. Such teachers do not share any philosophy of education, nor do they necessarily agree on the most desirable amount of classroom control. Instead, common to their work "is the concern to listen to what the children have to say and the ability to respond to it as honestly as possible, no matter how painful it may be to . . . teacherly prides and preconceptions." H. Kohl, "Children Writing: the Story of an Experiment," *The New York Review of Books* (November 17, 1966), p. 26.

CHAPTER

3

THE CURRICULUM AND THE QUESTION OF VALUES

The term "values" has become common in educational parlance. It is used loosely to refer to what is considered of importance—what is *valued*. It pertains to those group-defined goals and attitudes that constitute powerful sources for individual drives, aspirations, and motivation (or lack of them). Some values are overtly stated and taught. Others are taken for granted and hardly mentioned but are indicated as important indirectly through ways of behaving. Everything a teacher says or does sets goals for the children in her classroom and emphasizes certain behaviors as valued beyond others, or as more stringently taboo than others. A teacher's role in imparting values is particularly significant for she holds the attention of a group for so many hours a day.

Not only do the children focus on her much of the time and on her treatment of others and their responses to her, but they are often placed in the highly charged position of having both teacher and peers focus on them. Children may react negatively to a teacher's "messages"; they may withdraw or rebel, but they cannot help "taking them in" on some level.

Thus the study of a classroom's value content cannot rest with spoken or written statements but must also tease out the meanings implied by the teacher's and children's actions, the goals assumed by her and the children, and the feelings about what is important and what is not that are taken for granted in the course of classroom life. We shall here consider the value the teacher places on learning in her stated goals for the class, in the directives and statements she makes to individual children, and in the interest she shows in their work. We shall also discuss the attitudes she is communicating to the children through her evaluation of their work and through the extent to which she incorporates their contributions into her teaching.[1] Other strongly value-laden aspects of classroom life, such as behavioral requirements, the cause and content of rewards and punishments and their distribution among different children, will be considered under classroom management.

Not only is a teacher, or any adult, unaware of the totality his actions convey to children, but much of his behavior is determined by forces beyond his effective control. The contradictory—and frustrating—position the teacher finds herself in is that, while her function is to educate children, she faces daily classroom realities which make the placing of real value on education difficult, if not impossible. For instance, classroom order and discipline ideally arise from the children's interest in the work they are doing. For the most part, however, the drab content of school curricula plus the size of classrooms and requirements for formal order make it well nigh impossible for the individual interests and abilities of a sizeable majority in the classroom to be aroused and challenged for more than fleeting moments. At best, teachers control the children through humor and the virtuosity of their own performance. More commonly, they clamp down with disciplinary rules, thus overemphasizing behavior at the expense of learning. Further, they appeal to the children's competitive desire to excel or they favor the docile, eager-to-please children rather than the curious and questioning ones. The values conveyed are therefore not those stressing knowledge, thinking, or insight, but those emphasizing as important order and discipline, conformity, pleasing the teacher, quick, competitive performance, and being entertained.

These values are hardly foreign to our culture; they are, in fact, central to it, though seldom overtly stated in the classroom. Children, taking them in, learn that some things are *stated* as important, but that one must learn other goals to act upon if one is to be successful. This discrepancy between the "real" and the "ideal" is an ordinary part of any culture and not in and of itself pernicious, especially if it is a matter of having goals that are one step ahead of practical realities. However, it is always a potential source of trouble. Consider, for example, the distress of a deeply thoughtful child who asks complicated and "odd" questions, thus running the danger of becoming subtly (or sometimes obviously) tagged as a nuisance. Not being a problem to the teacher is, in fact, important, but it is seldom stated as more important than the questions raised by his independent thought. It is therefore difficult for such a child to be clear about his own commitment and the choices he must make.

More serious and pervasive a problem, however, is the teacher's undermining of the stated value of learning by devaluing or undercutting the children themselves. All too often an unsuccessful teacher, feeling she can turn nowhere for insight into her difficulties, will "pass the buck" by questioning the children's ability, either by directly accusing them of being "stupid" or by conveying the same idea in less obvious or even unconscious ways. This is not uncommonly established as a school pattern in low-income areas.[2] A great deal has been said about the "value conflict" posed to working-class children in the "middle-class" school atmosphere, but, as we shall discuss in a later chapter, this oversimplified phrasing ignores the direct devaluing of these children and the message they are constantly receiving—that they are not expected to learn.

Stated Classroom Goals

In their interviews, most of the teachers observed expressed learning goals primarily in terms of mastering different subject areas. Some, however, placed them more broadly. Said one, "I want the children to like to learn. . . . If I can only get them to want to learn and to have a curiosity and to be able to find things for themselves. . . ." Some stressed behavior more than learning as goals for the children, with wide variations in the definition of desirable behavior. In answer to a question about what she felt was most important for her second-grade children to learn, one teacher replied, "To get along with people, to understand people, to recognize people for what they are, and appreciate each one for what he can do. . . ." She went on to say, "Emotionally, to understand one's self. . . . Educationally, to have them develop to the utmost of their ability. . . ." Although she started with "to get along with people," this was, on the whole, a statement oriented toward learning; other goals stated—cleanliness, neatness, not fighting—were not. One teacher said without hesitation that what the children should get from school was, "First of all, discipline. They should know that when an older person talks to them or gives a command that they should respond, that they should listen. . . ." This teacher, as it happened, was not a harsh disciplinarian in the classroom, but her learning goals for the children were low.

From the classroom observations we culled the more goal-oriented or value-laden statements, in which the teacher is explicit about the message she is conveying. Remarks like, "Good, that is really thinking," or "Robert is thinking it over," were straightforward underpinnings of the work situation, implying that a child needs to think something through. There were very few such comments. More commonly, a teacher would call on another child for an answer. Unusual also were statements like, "It's all right if you don't know it; you will by Friday," or "If you made a mistake and know how to correct it, that's also smart," which defined a mistake or lack of knowledge as a prelude to knowledge, rather than sheer failure. Also uncommon were remarks that stressed a child's own learning as helping someone else ("Say what you are doing, please; it helps us"; "If you have a question, please raise it; it may help someone else too") or that pointed to future attainments through learning ("John, Bill, and Terry are going to be scientists").

All such statements were rare. Most of those which placed an importance on learning defined it as pleasing to the teacher, or the mother, or as leading to competitive success ("I like the way you are reading. . . . I'm enjoying it"; "I *love* the way you're working"; "Let's see if we can do three hours' work in an hour so you can go home and tell your mothers you have done a whole day's work. This is what she would most want to hear."). Or remarks might be cute, and hypocritical: "Children are always happy if they have two pages [to work on] and happier if there are three;" or, "I like this page. I wish I had time to sit down and do it. Oh, I wish I had time to sit down and do it." Or, undermining: "Do your homework. . . . You need to read desperately"; "I want to see you working up to your capacity. I haven't seen you do much." Often an emphasis on learning was introduced as a way of enjoining good behavior: "If you turned around and sat straight, you might know the answer"; "Smart boys and girls answer when they are called on, and other smart boys and girls sit up in perfect self-control."

Goals for behavior were most commonly stated as demands or requests for discipline and order and will be dealt with later. They were rarely placed in a context that defined orderly behavior as a background for learning, as in the simple directive, "Don't wave your hands when a child is thinking." Pleasing the teacher was often stressed: "I love your backs," "I'm very proud of quite a number of children," "Let's make me proud of you again." Or competition: "Henry, it is your job to see if you can be the best boy, or is Joseph going to be the best boy?" Or "nice" behavior was stressed for its own sake: "I'm watching all the lovely children who have their hands folded," "I'm going to look for nice reading habits. Let's lock our lips. We have our thumbs where they belong?" "I will choose two lovely children to show their book reports to our visitors. I will only choose two of the nicest people, the two with the best self-control."

That learning was not more commonly stated as a direct goal is not particularly surprising. It is implicit in the existence of schools themselves and could become a hollow echo if constantly reiterated. What is more significant is that learning as a goal is not a more common implication of the varied and quite frequent value-laden statements made by the teacher in the course of the day. This would seem to reflect the realities of classroom life we have referred to, whereby it is the rare teacher who is able to place greater value on learning itself than on the variety of secondary goals she transmits in order to direct and control the children's behavior.

The Teacher's Interest in the Children's Work and the Proportion of Her Remarks Directed to the Curriculum

Another way of looking at the emphasis on learning enacted in the classroom was to consider the proportion of remarks pertaining to the curriculum relative to those addressed to behavior. The total number of remarks that the teacher addressed to the class, or to individual children, in three hours of classroom time that had the intention of eliciting a specific response, an answer, a change in behavior, or shift in work—excluding the exposition or explanation of a particular subject but including the question that usually punctuates its closure—ranged from 187 to 366 in the eight classrooms, or from 6 to 10 per child. The proportion of these remarks which concerned the curriculum itself was 64 or 65 per cent (in three of the eight classrooms), 60 per cent (in two), 48 or 49 per cent (in two), and 44 per cent (in one). The range was from 6.5 to 2.7 per child.

Directly after the observation, each observer rated and described the quality of interest conveyed by the teacher as she responded to children's efforts and looked at their papers. They used a three-point scale: high, medium, and low in each of the three major subjects—reading, mathematics, and social studies. Table 3–1 shows that the trend for the percentage of remarks addressed to the curriculum, as well as their absolute number and especially the number per child, tally with the degree and quality of the teacher's interest in the children's work. The first school listed appears to be an exception to this trend, but this was the accidental result of a fire drill which interrupted and shortened the observation period.

Ratings of the value the teacher places on learning (teacher interest), as judged from the interview, were made independently, on the basis of a five-point scale: very high, high, medium, low, and very low. In all but one class (IV–2) these ratings concurred with observers' ratings and with the proportion of remarks addressed to the curriculum. In classroom IV–2 the problem of rating the value placed on learning *as defined by the teacher* created a problem. The teacher interview report speaks of a "high emphasis" placed on learning but continues, ". . . learning is spoken of in terms which stress good habits of work and work relations. . . ." Thus, as observed in this classroom, the interest in the children's work per se was rated lower than the emphasis on learning as evidenced in the interview, and the quality of the teacher's response to the children was described as "simulated."

An initial assumption of the study was that a high emphasis on learning in a classroom would be balanced by a relatively low emphasis on behavior and vice versa. In two classrooms (III–5 and III–2), a high value was placed on learning along with a marked stress on disciplined,

TABLE 3–1

Curricular Comments and Teacher's Interest

School and Grade	Class Size	Total No. of Teacher Remarks	T's Curricular Remarks			Rating of T Interest		Quality of T Interest*
			No.	% of Total	Average No. per Child	Obs.	Int.	
III–5	40	240	155	65	3.9	HHH	VH	Seemed sincere, albeit as a credit to T
II–5	34	335	217	65	6.4	HHM	H	Seemed sincere
III–2	36	366	234	64	6.5	HHH	H	Seemed sincere, albeit as a credit to T
II–2	28	260	157	60	5.6	MMM	M	Supportive concern for children, more emotional than intellectual
IV–5	38	290	174	60	4.6	MML	M	Personal rather than intellectual
IV–2	32	249	122	49	3.8	MML	H	Simulated
I–2	30	252	122	48	4.1	MMM	L	Simulated, often over-eager, emotional rather than intellectual
I–5	30	187	82	44	2.7	LLL	VL	Laconic, even sarcastic

* *Consensus judgment of research team.*

controlled behavior, although in another (classroom II–5), an emphasis on learning was coupled with the acceptance of considerable talking and moving about among the children. In the four "medium" classrooms, the emphasis on behavior varied; in two (classrooms II–2 and I–2), there was considerable tolerance of movement and noise, while in the other two (classrooms IV–5 and IV–2), there was tolerance by default, so to speak, with the teacher apparently having to accept more than she would have liked. In these two classes, there was considerable stress on goals and values, with statements about loyalty, propriety, piety, self-control, and consideration of others.

In the classroom characterized by a low emphasis on achievement (I–5), the teacher stated in her interview that the main lesson the children should be learning was discipline. However, she was in fact quite permissive, and there was more casual, relaxed, and at times playful movement interwoven easily with other activities in this than any other classroom. In some of the others, movement and noise might rise higher, but only in specific periods, such as during milk and cookies or in transitions from one subject to another, and the teacher would respond with an effort to bring the children under control.

As one might expect, there were marked similarities in classroom atmosphere between the second and fifth grades within the same school.[3] The two highly disciplined classrooms were in school III, the two "moralistic" ones in school IV, and the four classrooms which did not markedly emphasize behavioral norms in schools I and II. We shall explore these similarities within each school in a later chapter.

Modes of Evaluating the Children's Work

One would expect interest and competence mutually to reinforce each other, and we did, in fact, note a general match between a high emphasis on learning and the assessment of a teacher's skill and ability along the lines explored in the previous chapter. Since these tallied with the proportion of remarks the teacher addressed to the curriculum, we questioned whether there might be additional relationships with other measurable features of a teacher's style. The categories we had employed for analyzing a teacher's mode of response to a child's statement or answer were as follows:

1. *Neutral acceptance or affirmation:* Either no answer, or a comment like "yes," "that's it," "right," delivered in a neutral tone.

2. *Positive evaluation:* "Good boy," "very good," "very nice," "that's fine," or more extensive remarks, such as "Good, you're working on it," "Good, now you've proved that." Remarks such as "good," though coded as positive, present a problem in that they may be delivered automatically as virtually neutral acceptance or said with an added emphasis and supportive intent. Positive comments need not only follow correct answers; remarks like "Good, that's part of it," or "Good, you're trying," can follow mistakes.

3. *Negative evaluation:* "You don't know too well . . . ," "Stick to

your topic," "We're not talking about that." Negative evaluations need not only follow mistakes. Teachers can respond to a correct answer with, "That's enough for you" (cutting off discussion), "Make it in the form of a sentence," or "Let's label our answer" (if a cent sign, for example, is left out of a mathematics example).

4. *Correction or completion* of an answer, or *passing on* to another child without comment.

5. *"Opening" responses:* Either following up a correct answer, seeking the errors in an incorrect answer, or affirming and elaborating upon or developing an answer leading to a new question. Most of the responses that had to be coded as "opening" were on a trivial or superficial level. The better "openers" observed were remarks like "Good, how did you arrive at that number?" "Good, show us on the board," or "All right, why do you say that?"

6. *Miscellaneous:* Other or unclear incidents.

From the analysis, certain differences between second- and fifth-grade classrooms are apparent. Routine acceptance of answers turned out to be surprisingly close to three-fifths of all teacher responses in the second grades and two-fifths in fifth grade, with one exception, where it was one-half. Whereas positive evaluations did not run higher for second grades than fifth grades, negative evaluations did run considerably lower. "Opening" responses ran higher for the fifth grades than the second grades, although not as high as one would wish, considering that herein lies the essence of real teaching. As can be seen from Table 3-2, however, no clear trend emerged relating the value placed on learning with a specific mode of teacher response.

These categories were far too unrefined to identify better teaching, although they are of the type that has been widely used in classroom research.[4] "Opening up" responses should be frequent but would have to be further rated according to their depth. As stated, most of the "opening up" responses observed were extremely superficial. Positive evaluation should also be high, one would assume, with a teacher building confidence through rewarding successes. Yet many supposedly positive comments had a saccharine or hypocritical character; their apparent sincerity would have to be rated for a true index of supportiveness. Similarly, negative evaluations of the children's work should be low, one would suppose, and there were indeed classrooms where they

TABLE 3–2

Modes of Teachers' Responses in the Curriculum Area

School and Grade	Rating of T Interest (Obs.)	Neutral Accept- ance (%)	Positive Evalu- ation (%)	Negative Evalu- ation (%)	Correcting, Com- pleting, Passing On (%)	"Opening" Response (%)	Miscel- laneous (%)
III–5	HHH	38	21	7	14	18	2
II–5	HHM	42	13	6	13	21	5
III–2	HHH	64	11	8	7	8	2
II–2	MMM	61	7	0	8	22	1
IV–5	MML	50	14	12	8	16	0
IV–2	MML	60	12	4	9	11	3
I–2	MMM	57	20	2	8	8	4
I–5	LLL	40	7	16	13	23	0

were extremely undermining. Yet in one second grade, strict and demanding, but straightforward and quite respectful negative assessment was coupled with a high demand placed on the children which, although too rigorous to be desirable, was not as undermining as other supposedly more supportive styles.

Tables 3–1 and 3–2, however, indicate that there may be a point at which the proportion of negative evaluations, especially their ratio to positive evaluations, becomes significant. The classroom (I–5) with the lowest rating of teacher interest, lowest proportion of curricular to total statements, and by far the lowest absolute number of curricular remarks and number per child, not only has the highest proportion of negative evaluations, *but it is also the only class in which they outweigh positive evaluations.*[5] The observers felt the teacher undercut the children due to her inadequate skill and training. When unsuccessful in her attempts to help a child work through a problem, she would imply the confusion to be his fault, not her own. She was also the only teacher observed to derogate the learning ability of the class as a whole during the observation period. The following episode illustrates how this teacher would at times translate a child's success into failure:

The teacher has reviewed how to do a certain type of problem, and assigns two. The children work on them at their desks, and Jerry is then called to do the first on the board. He goes up, talking about the problem as he writes it. T asks blunt questions, gives directives. Somehow he says 12 times 3, although on the board he is dividing 36 by 12 correctly. T says, "12 times 3?" Jerry corrects himself, finishes. He forgets to put a cent sign on the answer. T says, "36 stickers will cost? Let's label our answer, please." Jerry adds cents, leaves the board with a big smile.

Although Jerry's main reaction is pleasure at his own success, nonetheless, the teacher has twice seized on a small error and has not acknowledged the final correctness of his answer. The episode continues:

> T recapitulates the process, says, "Do we understand this?" She repeats, then says, "Second one, all right, Peter." Peter, who had his hand up, goes to the board, starts giving the process aloud. He gets stuck and looks to T for help. She questions him. He gets nowhere. T reads the example again. Scattered hands are up. T says, "Emily, do you want to try it?"

The impression of the observers during this session was of a real inability on the part of the teacher to explain or clarify arithmetic examples to the children, but responsibility for the failure is accorded to the children.

> Peter stays at the board as Emily tries, somewhat hesitantly, not speaking. T: "Oooh, I can't hear a sound." She repeats this, then says, "Arlene, do you want to help her—do you want to help them?"

This time the teacher has made no attempt to lead the child through to successful completion of the problem, although the child had originally raised her hand to be called on.

> Arlene goes to the board, does the example efficiently, talking as she writes. The answer is 45. T: "45 what?" Arlene: "45 cents." T: "Show me that it's 45 cents. It doesn't look like 45 cents to me. It looks just like 45." Arlene adds a cent sign.

Again the teacher has emphasized a minor omission and has not acknowledged the competent handling of the problem. In concluding this part of the lesson, she asks a question irrelevant to the problems being done, and leaves it hanging, as another failure.

> T: "Can anybody show me another way of writing 45 cents?" She calls Paula. Paula does not answer. T: "All right, leave it as it is. . . ."

In contrast with this episode is an illustration of the way in which competence and assurance are related to a "positive" approach, taken from classroom II–5. The teacher commonly used the technique of affirmation or elaboration, picking up a child's answer to develop a point. When correcting a wrong answer, she would say things like, "Yes, but . . . ," or, "Oh, I think you are confusing something else with . . . ," in an accepting and noncritical manner. Her "positive evaluations" were usually a straightforward "good," or "very good," with occasional variations like, "Oh, you have it," "You did it," or, "Wonderful." She did not use overstatement or exaggeration like some of the almost saccharine "supportiveness" found in classrooms IV–2 and I–2. Her "negative evaluations" consisted mainly of admonitions to listen and pay attention. She also used humorous chiding. Her "positive" style is illustrated in the following episode from a mathematics lesson:

> T: "Next question . . ." She calls on Bobby, who has trouble. Other children start to answer and coax him. "You're only expending your own knowledge at the expense of the person you're telling," the teacher says to caution another child not to help, and then, "Now, wait, you've been in the same position."
>
> A child comes into the room with a request for monitors. All the children raise their hands eagerly to be picked. "Let's do this fairly. Who is not on the clean-up squad?" T picks some children. There are some complaints. T says, "You can register your complaint later, when we have our meeting." She calls on Murray.
>
> Murray makes a couple of incorrect attempts, then gives the correct answer. He says, "Mrs. ____, you know why I got confused—they all kept telling me." She says, "Some people think they're being helpful when they are really not. Next question, Marjorie."
>
> Marjorie, her hand up, hesitates. T: "Yipes, some people are raising their hands before they really know the answer. I expect you to know the answer when you raise your hand. . . ."
>
> The lesson continues. T calls on Janice, who has difficulty with a problem, making several tries, not seeming disturbed by her wrong answers. T then leads her step by step to the solution, spending several minutes with her, saying, "Yes, now you're getting it," and "Good, fine." She gives her several other examples on the same principle which Janice solves correctly. T says, "Hang on to it for a while. You may forget it, but sometimes one little thing will bring it back."
>
> She asks the class what happens when you sometimes forget how to work out a problem. Murray says, "It comes back again." T elaborates on this, explaining that sometimes we clam up, and our hands get cold and that makes us forget. The lesson continues. "That's what's so interesting about word problems," the teacher says. "You have to read them carefully. . . ."

Another aspect of teaching style which conveys to children whether their learning is or is not of real value involves the incorporation of their experiences and contributions into the teaching process. One of the second-grade teachers (classroom I–2) was warm and supportive with the children, seldom negatively evaluating their work. However, she was concurrently but unwittingly undermining the foundation for their learning for she completely devalued their concrete life experiences. This was a classroom with Negro children from low-income homes and a teacher who stated there was nothing in their backgrounds on which to build learning. In the following episode, she virtually ignores the eager accounts of three children about trains and airplanes, and in one incident "closes" a child's report with a negating, potentially embarrassing, and entirely irrelevant personal question, presumably arising from her own curiosity.

> T talks about fuels, about locomotives using coal, or oil, and then comes back to the fact that airplanes need gas. . . . Larry volunteers information about engineers. He is quite excited and involved with what he is saying. T responds to some of it, but does not incorporate it into the discussion.
>
> She calls on Judy to read. When Judy finishes, she says, "Very nice, Judy. Would someone like to read the next page . . . ? Arthur . . ."
>
> After Arthur finishes reading, T asks, "Have any of you been to the airport?" Many children raise their hands. T asks, "What did you see, Ronald?" Ronald tells a long story about planes landing and taking off. T asks, "Who took you?" Ronald responds, "Day Care." T says, "Very nice," and calls on Louis.
>
> Louis tells about going to the airport. "My uncle went to see the people in the South . . ." he says; "I saw an airplane flying. . . ."
>
> When Louis finishes, T remarks to the children, "You know (stagy pause) I've never been on an airplane." She pauses to let the effect of this sink in, and then continues, "What is something Mrs. ___ is going to do soon?" The class makes no response.

The closure of this episode is particularly interesting because teachers so often feel frustrated and confused by a lack of response such as this, which touches both personal and intellectual areas. However, the incident captures the fact that it can be—in the early grades at least—the mirror image of a teacher's own lack of true response to the children. The above episode contrasts markedly with the middle-income white second grade, where several times the children eagerly and immediately answered the teacher's request to state her tastes or preferences. In this classroom, the teacher responded to the children's proffered experiences with, "Oh, how wonderful," "How lovely," or "Laura, is that you, yourself? I'm the happiest teacher in the world. . . ." Superficial and exaggerated, to be sure, but nonetheless reflecting her acceptance and identification with their activities. Their response was to accept hers.

Such incidents suggest that an emphasis in "value conflict"—"middle" versus "working class" obscures sheer negation of the children by the teacher. To attribute this simply to the teacher's "middle-class values" and adjure her to "accept" the children is to miss the crux of the matter, which is that such negation interferes with the development of a give and take between teacher and children which is essential for the teaching process. Contrast the above episode with the following from another classroom (II–2) also on transportation:

> Alec expands on his previous story, saying his father owns a station wagon truck for the post office. T writes "Mail" on the board, saying, "Oh good, your father drives a mail truck" (not questioning, but rephrasing, the "owns").
> Bobby tells of his father driving a truck that drives other cars. T says, "Oh your father drives a truck that carries new cars. . . ." Bobby explains not that kind of truck. T says, "Oh, a tow truck," writing it down.
> Sam proffers a garbage truck, Edward an army truck. The children chime in freely, hands go up and down. Sometimes T calls on a child, and other times they speak out without being called.
> T discusses trucks and transportation with an easy flow.
> Lucy stands and tells of an experience she had. "When my mother was taking me home on the boat. . . ." She goes on, smiling, seemingly eager to be heard, her eyes sparkling. T says, "Good," and tells her to save the story until they talk of boats. Lucy seems pleased.
> T asks further about trucks. Jerry stands and suggests the truck that carries cars. Sam mentions a dump truck and cement truck. Alex tells a long story about the snow plow on a dump truck. T affirms the answers, continuing the list on the board. . . .

Here the teacher has used the "working-class" knowledge of those whose fathers are truckmen and has easily and naturally incorporated it into the lesson. In fact, the second-grade social studies program on "community helpers" (in use at the time of the study) would have lent itself well to such discussion in a lower-income classroom, where many children have fathers and other relatives who *are* the firemen, policemen, transit workers, sanitation workers, postal clerks, and where the builders, hospital workers, service workers, etc., could readily be included. It is ironic that "community helpers" was often taught at the same time that the life experiences of children whose fathers were these very people was devalued.

Further, the negating of children's experiences interferes with the ability of the teacher to take a child where he is and from there help him build a conceptual approach to the realities around him. It interferes with what is understood to be a primary technique for teaching, that is, "helping the child penetrate experience . . . to the level of relationships [thus] preparing the child to order and deal with his world in terms of his society's logic and perception of reality." [6] Teaching, particularly at the elementary level, necessarily involves constant learning from children how they perceive their world. No matter how much one may have read or studied, this is always something to be learned more fully, even if the children's world is theoretically similar to one's own. Essential to the process is respect—placing a value on the child's present understanding—and this is interfered with when children are from "low-status" families. Ignoring or negating a child's experiences, continually holding up an image of something else, can only lead to teaching as trying to "put something into" the child; it rules out teaching as learning also to "draw something out of" him.

Value Content of the Curriculum Itself: Wall Displays

A teacher conveys any number of messages to the children, some intentionally, some not, by the material displayed on the classroom walls and the extent to which children are involved in its selection and placement. Materials are of three general types: children's work (test papers, drawings, reports, etc.), charts and lists of various sorts, and printed pictures and posters. A teacher usually strikes some balance among the three, although one may see children's own work slighted in favor of a neater display of commercial prints. Some study teachers exhibited only the children's very best work, emphasizing the importance of academic achievement but devaluing the effort of those who may try hard but not reach 100 per cent. In one classroom, this was exaggerated, with names or work of "champs" in the various subjects featured. A less common practice was to post all of a given set of papers, although this posed the opposite problem of placing too little value on effort and achievement. Here again, the teachers usually found a middle ground. In one classroom where a high value was placed on academic achievement, as evidenced in the teacher interview and observation and by the posting of the very best papers in different subjects, the teacher had a space for clippings on current events with the children's added comments. Here everyone who made the extra effort to find and comment on a news item relevant to some aspect of the curriculum could have his or her work displayed. The common practice of exhibiting drawings, often but not necessarily illustrations of science or social studies themes, was another way teachers enabled a wider range of children to find a place on the walls while at the same time maintaining high goals for performance.

Charts of various sorts ranged from straightforward practical directives about subject matter (steps for studying a word, outlines for a book review, etc.) to equally practical and school-related behavioral injunctions (rules for behavior on the bus and during a fire, for handling library books, etc.) to frankly moralistic mottoes and homilies. A chart found in one classroom, which was a type not seen in any other, contained the words of the National Anthem and was posted above the blackboard in the space often occupied by alphabetic script as a model for penmanship. Obviously, in choosing what to feature, a teacher follows the goals she has in mind for the children, although she must to an extent conform to established practices about materials considered suitable. Usually the wall displays tallied closely with goals as stated by the teacher in her interview, although in one instance a strongly moralistic teacher, in both interview and observation, emphasized competition and work achievement in her wall displays rather than the moralistic injunctions one might expect.

A list of monitors or helpers is standard in almost all classrooms. The one classroom in our study in which it did not appear was the one where children's contributions were so devalued in other ways. In this classroom as much, if not more, responsibility was taken by the children as in some of the others where it was formally allocated and recognized. However, instead of a monitor list on the wall, there was a folder containing the names of children eligible to receive free lunch. There was no such folder in the three other classrooms with "free-lunch children." In one fifth grade, formal social participation was emphasized with charts that were not found in the other study classes—a list of Junior Red Cross members, children who had contributed to the Red Cross, children with school savings bank accounts, and children who had paid for *Newstime*. A contrasting message about what is important was conveyed in another class by featuring academic "champs." A more neutral listing, also emphasizing curriculum, was a chart where children could list books they had read; this was found in one class with an individualized reading program and in another as an inducement to explore the library shelves.

Posters, exhibited separately and more or less permanently, in contrast with clippings tacked onto appropriate bulletin boards, usually concerned safety, health, diet, and dentistry. Others were purely decorative—travel posters, flower illustrations, cute pictures of children and the like. Consistent throughout was the exaggerated blondness of the people portrayed—the absence of any dark-skinned people anywhere on the walls. Not only have materials portraying the world as blond long been the most readily available generally, but in addition they have been prepared in great numbers for schools by myriad commercial and special-interest groups.[7] Doubtless teachers have simply used them without giving the matter much thought. If they had, perhaps, considered some deviation from the norm, they might have been deterred by fear of the subtle but always effective raised eyebrow, or supposedly humorous snipe, through which people in our society keep each other "in line." In any case, the only appearance of a dark-skinned person in any of the schools was on a chart entitled, "Slavery and the Civil War." Missing, unhappily, but all too inevitably, was any representation of Frederick Douglass, Harriet Tubman, or Sojourner Truth. The board featured a magazine picture of a plantation, children's compositions, maps, and drawings (one of Lincoln and one of a Negro slave). The value implication was clear—adjurations about "brotherhood" occur regularly every February as formally stated ideals, but the world of success and goal achievement is white.

While no teachers posted original or unusual materials on their walls, some used no commercially prepared illustrations at all. Interestingly, two of the classrooms which most underrated the value of learning utilized more than any of the others random or "cute" illustrations and posters, with no relevance to the curriculum. Both were all-Negro classrooms.

It is a sad commentary that there was no program in this school system to make respectful pictures of dark-skinned people available to all classrooms. Doubtless there were some classrooms at the time of the study where teachers responded to the growing emphasis on racial pride and self-respect among black people and found pictures of Negro statesmen, artists, and men of science and letters to post. It would be interesting to know how widespread such wall displays are today and whether there are any in America's white classrooms. This raises a further question that has profound implications: Are there more than a handful of classrooms where, in place of the depersonalized advertising-type depictions of white people—bland, characterless, and stereotyped —one finds dignified and meaningful portrayals or pictures of *individuals* with the full dimensions of a human being!

Value Content of the Curriculum: Texts

A teacher has some choice with regard to wall displays, but when it comes to texts and workbook materials, on the whole she has nothing to say. Indeed, entire school systems are committed to the use of texts that are now widely considered to be inadequate at best, pernicious at worst. The primary message they have carried has been characterized by the social psychologist Otto Klineberg as "life is fun in a smiling, fair-skinned world." [8] Not only readers, but social studies and history books have distorted reality with the implication that white, "middle-class" suburban America represents the pinnacle of human achievement. They have adhered to and reinforced a profound ethnocentrism, a definition of patriotism whereby one believes in a desirable "we" and an undesirable "they" who are, however (especially in February), as "good as" we are in the sense that they are capable of becoming "like us." The result of this message is ultimately the deindividualizing of people, the depersonalizing of individuals. What starts as a negation of their world for dark-skinned children and for children of blue-collar workers, becomes pernicious, not only for them, but for all children.

A study of twenty-three social studies texts that were being used at the time of the study in three all-Negro schools (one of which fell in our sample) shows how serious were both the omissions in these books and the direct statements they made about other nations and racial and religious minorities. [9] Only one mentioned Africans among the early settlers of America (*Your Country's Story*, Ginn and Company), and "this book virtually ignores the fact in the very next sentence by stating that 'they [the early settlers] all had much the same experiences.' " [10]

Missing from the texts was any mention of the consistent fight for freedom engaged in by the Negro people, or any discussion of the moral and physical injustices of slavery. One book alone briefly mentioned slavery as an evil (*Your Country's Story*). Several books repeated the myth that Negroes were well suited to hard work in the hot sun. For example, in *My Country's Growth* (Webster Publishing Company) one discovered that the Negro people "were not useful in the northern mills and factories . . . [but] on the southern plantations . . . they worked away quite cheerfully." There was no mention of the abolitionist leaders, Negro and white, or of the half million Negroes living as free men at the outbreak of the Civil War. "We found no indication that the word Negro meant anything other than slave," states the report.[11]

The reconstruction period was not mentioned in most texts. One book alone referred to any positive accomplishments of the period with a brief reference to the establishment of a public school system. There was no reference to the twenty-two Negroes who served in Congress, but, rather, statements like, "The slaves had been freed, but most of them didn't know how to use their new liberty" (*Our America*), or "Many of the Negroes who had been given their freedom wandered about and would not work" (*My Country's Growth*). Of the Ku Klux Klan, *Your Country's Story* stated:

> Southern taxpayers became impatient with the general dishonesty and bad management of their state government. Some of the white people decided to organize in societies and bring about a change. . . . The most famous of these secret organizations was a group called the Ku Klux Klan. . . . At first the Ku Klux Klan was used to keep the Negroes, carpetbaggers, and scalawags out of politics. Later, however, some of its members committed serious crimes.[12]

Other minorities were similarly treated. Jews were not mentioned as early settlers of the United States, nor did they more than peripherally figure in the Fascist crimes prior to World War II. One would not surmise from the texts that more Jewish people live in the United States than in any other country. In *Ways of Our Land* (Silver Burdett Company), Jews, Negroes, and Puerto Ricans were not mentioned in a listing of some national minorities that make up the New York City population. Inhabitants of the developing nations were often characterized as "happy," "carefree," "contented," and "used to" poverty. Of the Chinese and Japanese immigrants, *Your Country's Story* stated: "People of these races had, over hundreds of years, become accustomed to eating and wearing less and to needing less shelter than any peoples of the Western races. They could also work longer hours and were willing to do so." [13] The slighting of Africa and the references to American Indians as a strange and exotic people round out the ethnocentric image presented in school textbooks, which implies the industrious success of the Anglo-Saxon as compared with the indolence—albeit pleasant, easygoing, and "happy"—of other peoples.

In the past few years, the distortion of American history through ignoring and falsifying the roles many races and nationalities have played in the building of our country has been raised as a matter of public concern, and some of the most glaringly offensive statements have been or are being cut from new editions of school texts. However, this is far from the total revision that is needed to change the basic image that is presented of the superior successful blond "we" and the poor and unsuccessful darker "they." Moreover, this image has already been strongly underpinned for the school child by the basal reader series, with their blond, blue-eyed suburban families. In virtually all of these, "national, racial, cultural, and ethnic differences are just not presented"; in the few exceptions, they are pictured as remote and "quaint," hardly relevant to today's world.[14] Here, too, there is an awareness of the problem, and lately there have been pioneering ventures in interracially and interculturally oriented readers.[15] However, they cannot become prevalent on school shelves until they are produced in sufficient variety, until the older books literally wear out, and until the commitments to the text of a given publisher are canceled.

Comparison of the content in the readers *Fun with Dick and Jane* and *Our New Friends* with the life circumstances of twenty-eight children from a study school in an all-Negro lower-income neighborhood illustrates the distance between the white textbook family and the reality of their world.[16] Instead of a house set in a lawn, studded with trees and bushes, the children lived in apartment houses or city projects. In the housing projects there was chained-off greenery; around the apartment houses there was no greenery but an occasional tree. In place of the neat and inevitable three-child family, three-quarters of the children had three or more siblings, and one-third had uncles, aunts, grandparents, or boarders included in the household. Much has been written about the role of the mother as the sole parent in the Negro family, *yet this was not the main point of difference in this relatively stable working-class neighborhood.*[17] Four out of every five children interviewed in the study were living with both their mothers and fathers.

Some activities familiar to the children were portrayed in the readers, such as riding on a merry-go-round, and about half were familiar with playing house and playing with blocks, but many activities pictured were not their own. None had flown kites, and almost none played with such elaborate toys as train sets, cooking sets, paint sets, and construction paper. On the other hand, the games commonly played on the city streets, such as a tag, hide and seek, ring around the rosy, loop the loop, etc., were not portrayed in the readers; in their place were unknown games such as "Who Am I?" and "Find the Hidden Object." Less than one-third of the children had pets or had had experiences like the Dick and Jane family of caring for or playing with animals or visiting a farm.

The types of characters that figure in the "stories" and themes of these books reinforce the distance from life, not only for Negro children, but for most working-class children as well. Harriet Robbins writes, with wry humor:

> The study reveals that these 18 preprimers adhere to the traditional preprimer formula: Father, Mother, 2 or 3 children, Dog, Kitten; substantial suburban home, late-model car; fun and togetherness—no distress, no challenge, no excitement. The four-color art accentuates this effect with Mother wearing chic clothes and a vapid smile; Father in a business suit, carrying attaché case or presents, standing on his head or puttering at do-it-yourself activities.[18]

Otto Klineberg writes on the same theme: "Americans in these readers are all quite well-to-do; not exactly wealthy, perhaps, but certainly quite comfortable, to say the least." [19] He, too, describes the comfortable suburban home, with poverty existing only in fairy tales or stories set in a foreign environment, although, even in this case, "everything turns out right before the end."

> Not only is there no poverty, but work seems to be readily available to everybody, and is on the whole not only easy, but "fun." . . . In fact, life in general is fun, filled almost exclusively with friendly, smiling people, including gentle and understanding parents, doting grand-

parents, generous and cooperative neighbors, even warm-hearted strangers. There is an occasional display of anger, but it is usually very transitory. In general, all is peaceful and happy.

In summary, then, life in the United States as it is portrayed in these children's readers is in a general way easy and comfortable, frustrations are rare and usually overcome quite easily, people (all white, mostly blond, and "North European" in origin) are almost invariably kind and generous. There are other kinds of people in the world, but they live in far-off countries or in days gone by; they evidently have no place on the American scene.[20]

Thus the content of school readers can utterly devalue the experiences of Negro and working-class children by erasing them from the world; it poses the problem that in order to accept formal educational goals that involve mastering such material, they must devalue themselves. Further, this is often seen by teachers as the conscious intent of such materials. When asked about the failure of school texts to portray anything familiar to the children in the all-Negro low-income school, the second-grade teacher responded that the children's backgrounds were "so limited that there's very little that you can base a reader on." She felt the content of readers to be good, because "it enriches their experience to read these things and talk about them. Maybe it will give them a few ideas on how they would like to live when they grow older. Maybe it will inspire them to do better." She went on to say, "Books have children with such lovely toys and mother is so sweet, and they have a dog and a cat, and go shopping. They have a real telephone, and a car, and they go to visit grandmother and grandfather who live on a farm. The children enjoy reading these stories, and love to talk about them." Yet these were children, we must interject, who from grade to grade fell increasingly behind in their reading achievement.

However, as already suggested, textbook negation of the world known to working-class and Negro children does a serious disservice, not only to them, but to middle-class white children as well. They are hardly presented with a picture of reality that arms them with the understanding and moral integrity to deal with life as it is. The amiable series of cute incidents through which a "nice" and polite world is presented hardly conveys a positive and meaningful message about what is important.[21] The tendency to solve the problem of biased text content by introducing brown faces into a substantially unchanged context, while something of a positive step (at least in its intent), is certainly no real solution.

How, then, a concerned author of readers may ask, can one deal with "poverty" and "slum life" respectfully and not patronizingly? The answer is not to deal mechanically with poverty (about which we tend, anyway, to have a stereotyped view), but to deal with *people* and people who are written about by authors who can *write*! Mark Twain's *Huckleberry Finn*, for example, is a real person who needs no moral or comment. The message he brings is not that "although poor and different, he is really the same as—or as good as—'we' are." Instead, he is respected for the *individual* he is. Claudia Lewis makes the point that it is not external similarities to their own lives which make possible children's identification with literature, but the degree to which the characters are convincing, understandable, and believable. It is this that makes reading "a *literary* experience for children, stirring the emotions, exciting the feelings." [22] She feels that books "simply are not sufficiently meaningful; they do not offer enough to satisfy the interests and curiosities and capabilities of children today." Nor is it impossible to write real stories for primers if we revise our outworn ideas of how many words a child can master if he is interested. Keeping books at a relatively easy-to-read level does not mean they cannot be adventurous, human, and truly humorous, Lewis writes.

Thus, the problem of content in school readers is far deeper than the portrayal of a uniformly blond physical type in a uniformly suburban setting; it includes bleaching out the mystery of the individual, the pain, wonder, sorrow, hate, love, fear, and courage of living. Following this, how can adjurations to altruism, loyalty, and bravery have other than a hollow ring? The denial of their very existence must impede school learning for Negro and working-class children, but what kind of learning is engendered in middle-class white children when it is coupled with extreme depersonalization? The pernicious and undermining effect on dark-skinned children of a history presented as shaped by white people alone and an environment in which only blond people exist has been pointed out. Less often is it suggested that the presentation of such an illusory world also creates problems for the healthy development of white children. One need but consider the near-psychotic reactions of white adults who are deeply committed to the myth of their superiority when it is shaken and remember the German Nazis in their insane attempt to preserve an illusory world. Here the valuing of one's individual self is even less assured than is suggested by psychologists for burdened Negro children in a white-dominated world. [23]

In relation to history and social studies content, therefore, as with reader content, superficial revisions hardly fill the need. The introduction of Negro history for Negro children, while it is an important step forward, is not the answer. The answer lies rather in the portrayal of American history—black and white, Indian and Oriental—for American children—black and white, Indian and Oriental. History can encompass no less than man's story of striving for a meaningful life for mankind's children, within which the wonder and value of each individual human being must stand supreme.

NOTES

1. These dimensions are derived from the two remaining categories of analysis which were listed in Chapter 2 (p. 23).
2. M. Deutsch, "Minority Group and Class Status as Related to Social and Personality Factors in Scholastic Achievement," *Society for Applied Anthropology Monograph,* No. 2 (1960), 26.
3. In a recent study, the influence of the school as a whole on any one classroom has been fully documented. See Chapters 3, 4, and 16 in P. Minuchin, B. Biber, E. Shapiro, and H. Zimiles, *The Psychological Impact of School Experience* (New York: Basic Books, 1969).
4. In a study of 301 teachers recommended as unusually able, Kraus found great diversity in teacher style, but a similarity in attitude: "Many of the teachers looked upon their classroom experiences as fields for exploration and experimentation, and as opportunities for self-evaluation. The feeling that a teacher's own horizons would expand through the knowledge gleaned from observation of children in action was often expressed. Summing up the attitudes of such teachers, it might well be said that they saw themselves not only as teachers but also as learners." He also found considerable use of children's first-hand experiences, an emphasis on critical thinking, a wide variety of teaching materials, a free interpretation of teaching manuals, and a sense of children's individual needs and abilities [Board of Education of The City of New York, *Skillful Teaching Practices in the Elementary Schools,* Curriculum Bulletin, 1961–1962 Series, No. 12 (1961–1962), pp. 114–115; project directed by Philip E. Kraus].
5. A comparison with the figures given by Bellack *et al.* for high school classes in urban and suburban New York is interesting. Their sample, while including some class spread, apparently does not include many really deprived children. Their categorization of T's "reacting moves" with our parallel categories is as follows:

	%	
Substantive	16.8	(our "corrects and completes" and "opens up")
Rating	46.2	(our "neutral acceptance" and "evaluation")
Procedural	6.9	(included in our "misc.")
Substantive-rating	27.2	
Substantive-procedural	2.9	

Bellack *et al.* comment on the relatively small proportion of substantive reactions and the fact that almost three-quarters of the responses involve rating. The proportion of these which are positive as compared with negative is 4 to 1 (with one-third of the positives equating with our "neutral acceptance" so that "positive" to "negative" in our terms would be more like 5 to 2). They comment, "When the teacher does react negatively to the pupil, he is more inclined to qualify rather than to not admit or to express a distinctly negative reaction. This is true of the teacher's reactions to incongruent pupil responses as well as to congruent pupil responses" [A. A. Bellack, H. M. Kliebard, R. T. Hyman, and F. L. Smith, Jr., *The Language of the Classroom* (New York: Bureau of Publications, Teachers College, Columbia University, 1966), pp. 177– 178, 191]. It would be interesting to compare Bellack's findings to those from some of New York City's "poor" and vocational high schools with high percentages of Negro students and "drop-out" rates, or to differentiate, to the extent that their sample would allow, between teacher's reacting moves in higher- and lower-income classroom situations.

6. B. Biber, "Integration of Mental Health Principles in the School Setting," in G. Caplan, ed., *Prevention of Mental Disorders in Children* (New York: Basic Books, 1961).

7. Dahlke discusses the "vast" amount of such materials made available to schools, writing: "The special interest group advertises and urges its free wares upon the schools. Any issue of the NEA Journal is replete with this type of free offer. . . ." He goes on to give examples of free materials offered by everyone from Wrigley's gum to the Association of American Railroads [H. O. Dahlke, *Values in Culture and Classroom* (New York: Harper and Brothers, 1958), p. 472].

8. O. Klineberg, "Life Is Fun in a Smiling, Fair-Skinned World," *Saturday Review of Literature* (February 16, 1963).

9. "A Report on the Treatment of Minorities in Elementary School Textbooks," prepared for a conference jointly sponsored by the Brower Park Club of the Emma Lazarus Federation of Jewish Women's Clubs and the Brooklyn Branch of the Association for the Study of Negro Life and History (May 1961), mimeographed. This report summarized the books in use in a study school at the time classroom observations were made. Broader as well as more recent studies document the per-

sisting inadequacy of texts used in public schools as well as the inade-
quacy of children's literature generally. See, for example, L. Marcus,
The Treatment of Minorities in Secondary School Textbooks (New
York: Anti-Defamation League of B'nai B'rith, 1961); I. Sloan, *The
Negro in Modern American History Textbooks* (Chicago: American
Federation of Teachers, AFL-CIO, 1966); N. Larrick, "The All-White
World of Children's Books," *Saturday Review of Literature* (Septem-
ber 1965).

10. "A Report on the Treatment of Minorities in Elementary School Text-
    books," *op. cit.*, p. 7.
11. *Ibid.*, p. 8.
12. *Ibid.*, p. 10.
13. *Ibid.*, pp. 12–14.
14. *Ibid.*, p. 16.
15. Bank Street Readers: *In the City* (1965), *People Read* (1965), *Around
    the City* (1966), *Uptown Downtown* (1965), *My City* (1965), *Green
    Light Go* (1966), *City Sidewalks* (1966), *Round the Corner* (1966)
    (New York: Macmillan).
16. Sydelle Sipress, untitled manuscript.
17. Conditions of extreme poverty do often lead to broken homes, but this
    originally well-meaning discovery leads to a destructive stereotype
    when one ignores the broken homes behind the assured status and
    sufficient alimony of a middle-class family. At the time of the study,
    a first-grade class in a white Protestant middle-class parochial school
    found half of its children living with divorced or separated mothers.
18. H. Robbins, "Introduction to a Study of the Preprimers of Six of the
    Leading Basal Readers," Bank Street College of Education Report, p. 2,
    mimeographed. The readers studied were the latest 1962 editions.
19. Klineberg, *op. cit.*
20. *Ibid.*
21. G. Graham speaks of the easy prey that students are to propaganda ap-
    pealing to the defense of the "American way of life." She writes, "The
    cynical, disillusioned, and apathetic attitudes that many Americans hold
    toward political processes are too often the result of the kind of educa-
    tion for citizenship that they have had. They were taught what 'ought
    to be' rather than what 'is.' They learned a general and vague rhetoric
    about American goals and values. They read textbooks which described
    in detail constitutional provisions and which said very little about what
    actually happens in the political arena. . . ." [*The Public School in the
    American Community* (New York: Harper and Row, 1963), p. 93.]
22. C. Lewis, "Children's Books in a Changing Culture," Associates of Bank
    Street College of Education, *Diversity in Our Society, Challenge to the
    Schools* (New York: Bank Street College of Education, 1960), pp. 22–
    26.
23. R. G. Corwin writes: ". . . the underlying meaning of conformity,

the most abhorred meaning implied in the negative connotations of the term [is]: the prominence of external, formal symbols of status. . . . What is significant about externality . . . is the demise of sincerity in human relations. Personal alienation, the absence of meaning in one's social roles, is one manifestation of this insincerity. For the lack of resemblance between a person's true identity and what he pretends to be, implied in the term, leads to emotional withdrawal. The complacency and privatism of many college students symbolizes this emotional withdrawal from life. . . ." [*A Sociology of Education, Emerging Patterns of Class, Status and Power in the Public Schools* (New York: Appleton-Century-Crofts, 1965), p. 98.]

C H A P T E R

4

TECHNIQUES OF
CLASSROOM MANAGEMENT

We have seen that school curricula suffer because general principles about how children learn and should be taught are not sufficiently translated for teachers into the practical terms of urban school reality. This failure to supply teachers with practical means for achieving stated educational goals is even more pronounced when it comes to the area of management, discipline, and "control." By and large, teachers are trained to know general principles of child behavior but are disarmed when it comes to effective methods for welding a classroom of children into a working group. Teachers know they should develop class groups that are, in the words of Bany and Johnson, "cohesive, have good morale, and work cooperatively toward socially desirable goals." They have been taught this is "essential for progress toward curricular learning and other educational aims." [1] However, just how to do this in any but an ideal setting is, to say the least, vague. Moreover, a new teacher soon learns that it is her success in maintaining classroom quiet and order, in the narrow sense, which is first noted and which is apt to be the school administrator's first measure of her performance. Classroom management becomes, not a means to an end, but an end in itself.

While preservice training gives teachers some idea of what classrooms can be like, the observation of an already formed group led by an experienced teacher does not prepare them for their first day with a new and as yet unorganized class. Rather than how to teach the children, how to *manage* them is the primary challenge they experience, and handling children often remains what they feel to be their most difficult task. [2] Here they sink or swim as they develop their particular style of management, building a composite from the school's rules and routines and the children's expectations and readiness to challenge or to comply, on the one hand, and, on the other, the teacher's understanding of children and habitual style of relating to them, her goals and ideals for herself as a teacher in relation to a particular group of children, and her personal assurance. As a new teacher, she may attempt to apply the principles of child psychology she has been taught, but by and large, through trial and error and through learning from other teachers, she will adopt practices for managing her classroom which include only some of the methods she has learned. As the discrepancy becomes clear between the abstract context within which child development and learning are taught and the intractable reality of large and underequipped classrooms, restricted curriculum and materials, and perhaps previously deteriorated expectations on the part of the children for their relations with teachers, the teacher perforce draws from a battery of techniques which would hardly have been marked "A" on her examinations, and which includes threats, cajolery, bribes, warnings, seduction, appeals to competition, physical punishment, divide and rule tactics of various sorts, and so on. If the particular selection and use of the techniques that a teacher develops do not "work" with the children she is teaching and to some degree mesh with general school practices, she will generally try to transfer to what she hopes will be a more congenial situation or may give up teaching altogether.

Bany and Johnson point out that the emphasis of teacher-education programs has been overweighted in relation to the individual, with too little consideration for the group. As the definition of the teacher role has changed—at least ideally—from the disciplinarian to something more like the group leader, teacher knowledge, attitudes, and goals have changed considerably, and there is a strong theoretical commitment to supportive rather than punitive ways of handling children. However, these are phrased in terms of individual children, whereas what teachers are actually working with is a group. "In most instances," Bany and Johnson write, "training programs have overlooked the importance of developing teacher understanding of class group behavior." Whereas "understanding how classroom groups behave and why they behave as they do is increasingly recognized as part of the teacher's needed professional knowledge"; and whereas educators "discuss in theoretical terms the importance to the individual of providing a good group climate" and "stress the values of group participation in planning and in problem solving"; this is not translated into practical methods. "Few attempts are made," they state, "to close the gap between educational theory and actual classroom practice." [3] Thus the teacher is given new goals and high standards for performance, with few practical directives as to how these can be implemented. There is constant emphasis on the philosophy behind the use of group techniques, rather than the psychological principles underlying group behavior; the terms used in method texts are vague and imprecise, and there is no explicit "exposition of relevant psychological knowledge of groups and how such knowledge relates to actual classroom methodology." [4]

Those who have been engaged in research on the classroom feel there has been generally increasing insight into group dynamics, but they are frank about their failure to make this greater understanding applicable to classroom practices. Kounin, Gump, and Ryan discuss their "feelings of inadequacy in trying to help teachers, especially beginning ones, with problems of importance to them," especially discipline. They state that teachers' questions about handling children are "shrugged off with impatience" or "answered with slogans or 'principles,'" and go on to say that "scientific research about the technology and theory of controlling misbehavior in a classroom is either lacking or inadequate." [5] Their own research is concerned with illuminating the complexities of classroom processes and the naïveté of simplistic statements about what one should or should not do. They emphasize the importance of studying what teachers actually *do* and its effects, rather than rating teacher "personality," and they document the variability of children's responses to a teacher action according to their familiarity with her, their particular orientation at the time of the incident, and the status of the particular child with whom she is dealing. They refer to a study that shows children will assess similar teacher acts differently, according to the reaction of the reprimanded children and their status in the classroom.[6]

In an article reviewing studies of "authoritarian" or "teacher-centered" versus "democratic" or "learner-centered" behavior, Anderson also discusses the limitations of research methods that oversimplify classroom realities. The many attempts to test the hypothesis that "democratic" teacher behavior should lead to higher morale and higher productivity among children than "authoritarian" behavior have failed to yield conclusive findings. Anderson attributes this in large part to the inadequate conceptualization of leadership behavior and the structuring of experimental groups in which the "authoritarian" leader has been "unreasonably harsh and austere." He ends by commenting on the lack of classroom materials on the observed effects of teacher style. He writes:

> When a satisfactory body of knowledge *about learning in social situations* is available it will then be possible to describe the behaviors which a teacher can exhibit to achieve a given learning outcome. It seems reasonable to suppose that *leadership styles or teaching methods emanating from knowledge about learning* will have a higher probability of meeting criteria of effectiveness than do *a priori* styles or methods. At least, studies based on two *a priori* styles have not led to consistent or easily interpretable results.[7]

In our study of classroom life we wished to reconsider dimensions of teacher behavior that have commonly been studied in order to maximize the possibility of making comparative statements. More important, however, we wished to deepen our understanding of the intricate process whereby teacher actions reinforce stated goals or undermine some and convey others. On the basis of educational theory and research generally, we decided to organize our observation and teacher interview materials into three main areas.

1. *"Supportiveness":* The teacher's style of evaluation and control in

relation to a "supportive" versus "undermining" continuum, presumably relevant to the building of children's positive feelings about themselves.

2. *Enabling of independence:* The teacher's rules and routines for the classroom in relation to the enabling or restricting of independent action on the children's parts, relevant to their development of an autonomous sense of self.

3. *Leeway for child interaction:* Allowed or enabled by the teacher, as the basis for learning social skills to be directed toward the accomplishment of a task.

We approached each of these dimensions in a number of ways. First, all members of the observer teams independently rated each teacher on a five-point scale, keeping in mind the total feeling tone of the teacher's style and the classroom atmosphere she helped create. Where there were differences in judgment, though these were in no case marked, they were adjudicated. Second, all teacher remarks directed at behavior were coded as positive, negative, or neutral, and a count was made of their distribution in a three-hour period.[8] Third, all teacher actions and statements pertaining to running the classroom were collated under different headings for description and comparison. The headings included: teacher's behavioral directives to the class; noise and movement allowed; handling of transitions and routines like dismissal, milk and cookies, etc.; structuring of the learning situation; assignment of formal responsibilities in the classroom; children's participation in the planning of their day; and allowance for free periods. Physical features of the classroom were also described, such as seating arrangements and availability of equipment and supplies. The data on classroom management, as observed, were paralleled by interview material where the teacher described her goals and practices for handling the children. From both teacher-interviewer and classroom observers, we also had ratings on such characteristics as strictness and consistency of demands upon the children, effectiveness in achieving them, assurance of manner, approachability, and partiality. Ratings on the three broad dimensions of teacher style—supportiveness, enabling of independence, and leeway for child interaction—are given in Table 4–1.

As might be expected, the three variables were highly interdependent. However, there were important differences between classrooms with similar scores due to the complexity of the dimensions. Although

TABLE 4–1

Ratings of Teachers' Management Styles

School and Grade	Sum of T Interview and Obs. Ratings	Supportiveness		Enabling of Independence		Leeway for Child Interaction	
		T Int.	Obs.	T Int.	Obs.	T Int.	Obs.
II–5	25	4	5	4	4	4	4
II–2	24	4	4	4	4	4	4
I–2	23	4	4	4	4	4	3
I–5	18	2	2	2	5	3	4
IV–5	17	2	3	2	4	3	3
III–5	14	2	3	4	1	2	2
IV–2	12	2	3	2	2	1	2
III–2	9	2	2	2	1	1	1

one teacher could be rated as generally more supportive than the others, her style could be supportive in some ways and undermining in others. Similarly, teachers could be rated on an enabling-restricting continuum, but the important question of enabling in what ways and restricting in what ways would be lost. The ambiguity of this dimension is illustrated by the considerable difference in scores on enabling of independence for teacher interview and observation in three of the classrooms. In one instance (classroom III–5) the teacher stressed the need for children to learn independence but was observed to control them strongly; in another (classroom IV–5) she spoke of the importance of control but allowed considerable independence, largely out of inability to control it; in the third (classroom I–5) the teacher expressed little interest in developing the children's ability to function on their own, but in practice she allowed considerable latitude for independent initiative.

Our over-all ratings of supportiveness, the enabling of independence, and allowing leeway for child interaction were not viewed as "findings," but as providing a framework within which to ask further questions. It might be assumed that the classrooms with higher scores would present atmospheres more conducive to learning than the "undermining" and "restrictive" classrooms. From our data, however, we do not arrive at so direct a relation between goals for learning and goals for behavior.

Supportiveness of Teacher's Style

Table 4–2 juxtaposes observer ratings of teacher "supportiveness," given in rank order from high to low, the frequency of positive and negative statements made by a teacher in a three-hour period in both behavioral and curriculum areas, and ratings of teacher interest in the children's work.

As can be seen from Table 4–2, there is no direct relation between the teacher's supportiveness in the area of behavior and the value or emphasis she places on learning as indicated by the ratings of teacher interest. The closer relation which should obtain, according to ideal models of education, is apparently contradicted by practical features of ongoing classroom life in the usual city school. It must be remembered, however, that the classrooms studied were all relatively benign, with reasonably competent teachers. We studied no classroom (although we did visit some) where teacher-student relations had become crystallized in a pitched battle and the goal of learning so intermixed with discipline and compliance that it is a wonder learning took place at all.[9] In such classrooms, the straight quantitative weight of negative statements of all kinds might well be a sufficient index of nonsupportiveness that relates directly to a low goal for learning.

It can be seen that "supportiveness" of teacher style, as rated by observers, shows no consistent relation to proportion of positive-to-negative teacher statements. The specific content of a teacher's statement is always modified in its impact by her general tone and her total style of relating to the children. One teacher can say jovially, as did the teacher rated highest on supportiveness (classroom II–5), "Gerald, do you want to get slit from ear to ear?" and bother Gerald not a whit, while another, with a forbidding look, can reduce a child to nameless fear. "Arthur, sit down and be quiet," can be either a casual, neutrally delivered directive or an ominous warning. Thus, it is extremely difficult to arrive at a method for quantifying or counting elements of a style.

The ratings took into account, not only the specific content of a teacher's statements, but also the feeling tone they conveyed, the appropriateness of her demands in given situations, and the extent to which children were being enabled to fill them.[10] They were, in effect, making an attempt to reduce to a point on a scale the complex totality whereby positive motivations leading to genuine satisfaction are held

TABLE 4-2

Relationship of Teacher's "Supportiveness" to
Positive and Negative Statements in the Classroom

School and Grade	Obs. Rating of "Support- iveness"	Total No. T State- ments	Positive Statements				Negative Statements				Ratio of Positive to Negative Statements %	Teacher Interest*
			Behavior No.	%	Curriculum No.	%	Behavior No.	%	Curriculum No.	%		
II-5	5	335	0	0	27	8	77	23	15	4	30	H
II-2	4	260	11	4	12	5	40	15	0	0	60	M
I-2	4	252	26	10	26	10	42	17	3	1	111	M-L
IV-5	3	290	10	3	28	10	62	21	22	7	46	M
III-5	3	240	4	2	23	14	37	15	11	5	80	H
IV-2	3	249	18	7	20	8	33	13	5	2	100	M
I-5	2	187	0	0	5	3	37	20	15	8	11	L
III-2	2	366	18	5	28	8	40	11	19	5	81	H

* This rating is a composite of the interview and observation ratings given in Table 3-1.

out to a child, as compared with undermining techniques whereby they are motivated through fear of failing or displeasing. *Consensus among the judges was high, yet it did not correlate with anything that could be readily counted in the classroom.* However, this is not the first time a study has found it impossible to deal with the complicated totality of life situations with simple standardized methods of description.[11]

In order to clarify variations in types of supportiveness and relations between supportiveness with regard to curriculum and in the behavior area, we shall consider three fifth-grade classrooms in some detail.

THE FIRST CLASSROOM—NONSUPPORTIVE IN THE CURRICULUM AREA

Whereas counts of coded statements do not, on the whole, yield an index of supportiveness, there may well be a cutoff point. In the previous chapter, we discussed classroom I-5, which shows (in Table 4-2) the lowest proportion of positive-to-negative statements—11 per cent. We pointed out that *this is the only classroom where negative responses in the curriculum area are more common than positive responses,* and that it is also the classroom *with the lowest value placed on curriculum* and *with the lowest number of remarks on curriculum both in toto and per child.* It was also judged to be the poorest fifth grade as far as level of curriculum and teaching methods were concerned. Thus two readily countable features—fewer interchanges about the curriculum and more negative responses on the teacher's part to the children's answers—related to other observed aspects of poor teaching.[12] The low value placed on learning as a goal by the teacher was reflected, interestingly enough, inversely by the children in their interviews.[13] This is the only fifth grade where there was no reference to poor grades or nonpromotion as a punishment!

This teacher's interview suggests that her lack of support in the curriculum area was tied in both with her lack of teaching skill and with the low goals she set for her students. It was she who felt discipline, that is, obeying "commands," to be the main thing the children should learn at school. She was also the only teacher who mentioned work as a punishment:

> One of my pet things has been getting the dictionary and beginning at some part of the alphabet . . . even the thought of it, I think, the dictionary and writing, having to look back and forth, I think to them is tedious. . . .

This teacher enjoyed being thought of as strict, and she was complimented by the principal as a "wonderful disciplinarian." She commented, "I don't expect the children to be angels all the time, but you have to yell at them now and then," and she said she felt the parents liked her though "they might think that I yell too much." She was glad, she said, that a child's mother spanked him when he ran home from school, and continued:

> I feel that a lot of them need the old . . . maybe mothers do not beat their children nowadays. I do not say that this is the answer, but let them know that there is a rod now and then. I know that it did not hurt me any. It gives them respect. . . .

As observed in the classroom, however, this teacher was not as stern as she sounds for she was not very punitive in relation to behavior. A great deal of noise and movement around the room was allowed, and posture and neatness, though referred to occasionally, were not stressed. Orders were given in a calm, quiet voice, with the expectation that the children would obey. They did, but casually and easily. When she felt it necessary, she did bear down sharply and restore order in a loud ringing tone, but on the whole she was lenient and permissive. She smiled with the children, talked casually with them individually and in groups, occasionally put an arm around a girl. She showed the highest count of "neutral interchanges," or conversational interactions, with the children. Negative sanctions in relation to behavior were comparatively low in number.

When she spoke of her control methods, she said she expressed pleasure with good behavior by hugging, smiling, and through her manner of talking. She did not give stars. "I think that yourself—your smile—the way you talk to them, a gentle pat on the shoulder or a little hug now and then—I think with all that they know that you are pleased with their behavior." She spoke of helping a child who was placed in her class because he was having trouble with another teacher:

> I find that working with him and talking with him seems to work, but of course there are times when you have to be positive with him. . . . This has been working so far. . . . I feel that if you will be a friend to these children that they will respond to you and they do for the most part.

In their interviews, the children also referred to writing, "I must not talk," "I must stay in my seat," or, "I must be quiet." They mentioned the changing mood of the teacher when she was pleased—"she acts mightier happier," "she'll be glad," "she starts laughing and claps her hands," or she "smiles at the children," or "just laughs."

A comparison between this classroom and the one (II–5) with the next lowest ratio of positive to negative statements (30 per cent), which nevertheless has a high rating of "supportiveness," illustrates the way in which the teacher's specific style and feeling tone outweigh a simple count of negative statements.

THE SECOND CLASSROOM—THE USE OF HUMOR

The most "supportive" classroom (II–5) as rated by the research team had a higher number and percentage of negative sanctions in relation to behavior than any other, yet these betokened neither greater restrictiveness nor inability to handle children.[14] Instead, they were frequent but rather mild reminders of limits on what was considerable tolerance of noise and movement. The teacher would ignore talking and moving about for a while, then attempt to deal with it indirectly or humorously. She would laugh, kid the children, exclaim "heavens" with mock horror, use exaggerated sternness ("When you are whipped with them"—magazines a boy was reading under his desk—"you won't like it") and occasional sarcasm. When these techniques would fail, her tone would shift from humorous to stern, and if the children still did not heed, she would bring them to attention with loud sharp directives. Thus, she used a bantering technique when she could, but if it did not work, she was not afraid to tangle directly with her pupils.

Her discussion of the children showed both realism and empathy, as well as a characteristically joking style of approaching disciplinary problems:

> I find that most children are very sensitive. I think as they get older . . . they can hide it. I think that these girls probably will too. . . . But I know how they feel because I think I can remember when I felt somewhat the same way, and we all go through it. They get that startled fawn look in their eyes and you feel sorry for them. . . . It is hard with a class full. Some of these little tough eggs get to acting up and it is hard to be nice to all of them. Sometimes you do speak a harsh word to them and you break their little hearts. It's so hard . . .

She had no serious discipline problems, she said, and although she would like "to swat them" once in a while, the children on the whole were nice and fairly well-behaved, with nothing malicious about them.

She preferred to handle situations by leaving the children alone, or by catching a child's eye and giving him a look. She might let him know how she felt by calling on him when she knew he was unprepared. This might be "sneaky," she said, but it was effective in getting a child involved with work again. Sometimes she would raise her voice, but she has never sent a child out of the room.

In their interviews the children do not describe her as "yelling" or "hollering" when annoyed with them, but rather as disapproving or scolding, making them write, "I must not talk," or, "I was bad in class," twenty-five or fifty times (honest though she was trying to be, she did not mention this to the interviewer), excluding them from the group (not the room), or giving them bad marks. Two comments on what she did when pleased show a response to her use of humor: "She starts making jokes," said one child, and, "She fools around with us and makes us happy," said another.

The teacher talked of having the children bring up problems outside of their school work at class meetings, where they discussed everything from "How can I tell my little sister to leave me alone without hurting her feelings?" to "How can I keep from talking in class?" She decried the short day in this triple-session school which did not allow enough time for the children to talk about their out-of-school experiences. One such discussion period was observed. The subject was the weekly allowance, and the children proffered their experiences, arguing, agreeing, kidding, and questioning one another.

As a reward for work well done, the teacher described herself as "putting on a big act to the class," beaming and patting them on the back. She stated her feeling that the best way is never to say anything bad, but to emphasize the desirable things. If work is messy, she hands it back and withholds credit until it is redone, she said. Good work is hung on the bulletin board.

THE THIRD CLASSROOM—THE PROBLEM OF INSINCERITY

A third fifth grade (IV–5), lying midway on the supportive–nonsupportive continuum, introduces other dimensions into the discussion concerning manipulativeness and insincerity and offers a contrast to both the above classrooms. In her interview, the teacher of this grade revealed herself as using her knowledge of children to frighten and manipulate them. She tried to be supportive, she said, and stressed complimenting them to show she was pleased with their work. "I always try to stress the positive, accent the positive," she said and continued:

> Never—well I can't say that I *never* say that I'm not pleased. Sometimes I get angry and say I am not pleased with this kind of paper and I want it rewritten but very often it's penmanship. I'll always find one word and I say this is beautifully written, how about the rest? And it is understood that they'll work on it. It's no use getting myself worn out by saying I don't like this, I don't like that, but that would be destructive, not only for the children but for me. I could never feel as though I were doing a good job if I immediately said, "I don't like anything about you."

However, she spoke of threatening a child (whom we knew to be highly disturbed and insecure) with being put in the "hanging closet," as she referred to it. In another instance she spoke of threatening to call a boy's parents when he teased some girls, although she knew that he was already troubled about his relations with them.

She spoke of checking up on the children's work, being pleased with them, and encouraging them to be involved in committee work even when they were shy. "If the class does not understand the problem, I explain it, maybe to a small group, and then we'll review it together." In the classroom she attempted to restrain annoyance or impatience and express warm supportive motherliness. She beamed, smiled, joked, shushed the children, took them by the arm, or put her arm around their shoulders, calling them "dear" and "darling" and, to temper being really annoyed, "sweetheart." One of the classroom observers commented on the "gap between the sweety utterances and underlying annoyance," explaining, "as she gets more cross and critical, she tries to compensate by saying more 'nice things.'" Her voice was generally quiet and calm, and when she became strained, irritated, or flustered and sharp, she immediately asserted enjoyment and good humor. She was the only teacher in the fifth grades to praise individual children for good behavior (some compliment the group as a whole) and to use a technique more common in the lower grades—that of holding up a child as a model—"Sarah is ready. . . ."

Rather than giving clear directives, this teacher often preferred to cajole a child into obeying: "Lenny, I miss you." "Sweetheart, I want to hear you, but . . ." "Do it later. I want to hear you read. Archie, *darling*, I want to hear you read. . . ." However, when she really wanted order, she referred to rule by code number—"I love those children who obey No. 7 . . ."—or more directly called for No. 7. According to the children's interviews, this was backed up by the threat of being "put on a list," with the implication that one might not be promoted. As observed in the classroom, it was certainly effective. Attempting to assess this superficially supportive manner, with its underlying threat, was difficult and clearly posed the problem that some children can take such behavior casually enough in their stride, whereas others find it menacing. This teacher also undercut a general supportiveness in the curriculum area. She would respond on the whole, positively (albeit superficially) to discussion but would, at times, cut a child off sharply with, "That's enough for you," or, "We won't go into that. . . . It's not considered nice. . . ." Throughout, her supportive manner was superficial and contradicted by semi-veiled threats or subtly deriding directives.

To sum up, the first two of these fifth-grade classrooms (I–5 and II–5) indicate that supportiveness in the curriculum area need not be directly related to supportiveness in the behavior area. In fact, the first classroom documents a type of "permissiveness" which is not so much related to a positive attitude toward children's individuality as to a low value placed on what they do beyond observing minimum requirements for good behavior. The third classroom raised the question, what is the effect of an insincere supportive air?

Enabling of Independent Action

We have mentioned above the ambiguity of "independence" as a single factor. Several second-grade classrooms illustrate this point. In the most controlled one (classroom III–2), the teacher told the interviewer she had not reached her goal in achieving "perfect discipline" although she felt discipline was generally good. She considered monitorial positions quite unimportant although she said they are valued by the children; class officers, she said, head the lines and sit on stage in assembly. She spoke of lining up the children even for discarding milk containers, allowing no other moving around, being bothered if a child got out of his seat during a lesson, not allowing sharpening of pencils for it might break her chain of thought. She spoke of allowing quiet whispering and changing of seats at specified times. She had replaced whispering time during milk and cookies by a session in which she read to the children.

When observed, the learning situation was seen to be even more stringently teacher structured than is usual in public school classrooms, with the teacher either calling down rows or insisting on hands raised, reprimanding speaking out, and limiting the children's participation strictly to answering her questions. Her approach was epitomized by directives for work like: "Don't start before you watch what I do at the board," "There is no reason to do this if you do not do what I do," or, "That isn't the way I wrote it on the board; I want it the same way as it is on the board." In the sewing session, the children were not allowed to choose their own colors but were told, "When you come forward for yours, tell me what your last color was—not the color you want, but your last color. . . ." During sewing, children were allowed to whisper, with the teacher saying, "Now remember the rules. If you whisper that's fine, but whispering means I can't hear you. . . ." This was followed by constant reminders that whispering could be heard, although the children seemed to the observers to be exerting considerable self-control. No carrying out of monitorial duties was observed, except for collecting papers. Even here, they were usually passed to the front of each row. After milk and cookies, children were called by rows to put their empty containers on a tray, having been trained to go around by the back and return by the front. Directives stressed posture, quiet, and staying in one's seat. ("I want everybody's back up straight and nice," "Are we sitting nicely?" "Sit up tall with your back straight.")

Even in this highly controlled classroom there was an area left for independent initiative. Since the demand for quiet, orderly behavior was high, a child had to be resourceful when in trouble, by comparison with a classroom where greater freedom allows for greater dependence on the teacher to solve personal problems. For example, when a child saw her milk seeping out of her lunch box, she nervously but efficiently managed to cope with the situation without attracting the teacher's attention. In evaluating the demands and limitations of different situations, one would have to take such a requirement to solve problems unobtrusively into account, although the negative feeling involved for a child is in contradiction to what is ordinarily implied by the concept "enabling of independent action."

This teacher also placed high demands on the children for independence in the curriculum area—too high, one felt. She set them a complicated workbook task and insisted they rely on reading the directions themselves and working out how to do it. In spite of several requests for help, she remained firm—they must read the directions and figure it out themselves. Here, then, is a combination of restricted independence in relation to classroom routines and verbal initiation in subject matter and too great an expectation, if anything, for independence in solving personal dilemmas and difficult tasks, especially, one would feel, for a second grade.

Another second-grade teacher (classroom IV–2) also stressed strict rules and routines. "I allow no promiscuous walking around," she said, and "They are never allowed to borrow a crayon because I have found out in years gone by that borrowing crayons can create terrible chaos during your drawing lesson. . . ." She did not allow pencil sharpening in the classroom "as a method of good discipline."

> . . . They must bring two sharpened pencils from home. They are not allowed to even bring their sharpener to school because that creates poor discipline . . . they sharpen them at the desk and spill all over the floor and borrow each other's . . .

As observed, this teacher structured the learning situation as completely teacher-to-child, allowing no discussion or co-operation among the children. Little monitorial carrying out of duties was seen, and the teacher directed dismissal herself, counting to set a time limit for the children. However, she did allocate job responsibilities, saying in the interview, "Having a good monitorial staff and carrying it out well leads to good discipline." She saw monitorial positions as conducive to "good habit formation" for the children—"we make them realize that they're in an orderly room and they're to do things in a nice quiet way"—and she described removing several children from their jobs for not performing them properly. The "dusting monitor" was relieved because she dusted too many things, the "plant monitor" because he put too much water on the plants, the "board monitor" because he did too much talking. "So actually," the teacher commented, "there's a little lesson to be learned in everything they are taught to do." She said she did not have class officers because "the children generally pick the child who fails miserably. They never pick the right child." Her classroom directives stressed posture ("sit nice and tall," "sit up in perfect self-control"), cleanliness (she looks at necks and ears up and down the rows), quiet ("I'm going to look for good reading habits, let us lock our lips," "I'm afraid little people who are talking will not finish first"), and not moving around ("please sit down and draw your own bridge").

Defined areas for initiative in this classroom were two—planning one's time for allotted tasks, and bringing in materials for discussion, if they conformed to the teacher's viewpoint. The first was minimal. The teacher put three tasks on the board for one reading group while she worked with the other. She expected them to move at their own pace from one to the next and to go up and get paper when they were ready for the third (a drawing), and she allowed time at a later period for completion. She saw this as allowing considerable initiative, pointing out to the observers that it was virtually an "individualized program" since the children were working at different things. In her interview, she added that she always provided "fifty per cent more work for them to do when they are able to do it, and as a result of that they are never able to be sitting doing nothing. . . . I find that with the program I initiated, several children in this class have improved a great deal because they never had a chance to waste time." The leeway that exists through encouraging the children to bring in materials for discussion is more real than this supposed training for "planning." Various clippings, projects, and books were reported on in front of the class and, where appropriate, pinned on a bulletin board. The restriction here was that they be in line with the teacher's thinking. If they were, she might interrupt or delay a lesson to follow through and give a child time to "report"; if not, she would cut the child off.

While these two classrooms (III–2 and IV–2) were rated alike on the basis of the teacher interview, the observation revealed that the children were allowed greater leeway for taking initiative in the second classroom. Incidents where children initiated an action or question were all but nonexistent in classroom III–2, where the teacher required virtually complete control. Even when the bell rang, and movement developed in the room, she said, "I did not tell anyone to leave." (One might argue that specially good behavior was being demanded of the children for the benefit of the observers. However, this was doubtless true of all the classrooms, and the only other classroom in which a similar standard was set was the fifth grade in the same school.)

In classroom IV–2 there was some speaking up, even questioning of the teacher. A boy corrected an error she made in sending a monitor on an errand and, after questioning him, the teacher accepted the correction. In another instance, a girl pointed out to her that she was going beyond their assigned work. Two boys helped a girl open the closet

door to get her glasses. When the teacher was introducing the arithmetic lesson, Lucy, who had already reported, went up to her with a picture postcard of a flag. The teacher interrupted herself to say, "Isn't that
lovely, it's our new flag." She asked about the number of stars, called on
various children for answers, and finally sent Lucy to put the card on
the bulletin board. On the other hand, this was the teacher who had
overruled the discussion of Primary Day material which a child had
brought in.

The atmosphere in the remaining two second-grade classrooms was
quite different in the sense that the independence granted the children
in connection with classroom regulations had a more autonomous quality. The teacher in classroom II–2 mentioned some twelve monitorial
positions that involved varying degrees of responsibility. The "paint
monitors" kept the easels clean. The "clothing monitor" called the children to get their coats at dismissal time, while the "class leader" took
charge while the teacher was out of the room. The children volunteered
for the jobs, and the teacher picked them according to what she felt to
be their needs, changing them from time to time. She kept the same
"plant monitor," however, as she was the only child who brought a
plant to school! The "pledge monitor" was changed quite often since
the teacher felt it gave a child—particularly a withdrawn child—a
chance to "stand up in front of the room and lead."

As observed, the children moved around freely to get books from the
library shelves, to distribute and collect books and papers, and to clean
the boards, sometimes simply for the sake of moving. The "pledge monitor" was observed to lead the pledge of allegiance and a song (albeit
somewhat dispiritedly); the "coat monitor" called children to go to the
closet; the "cookie monitor" called turns to come up for cookies. The
teacher ceded responsibility in the latter cases, tending to problems that
individual children brought to her desk. In one instance she allowed
considerable confusion to develop before she intervened to straighten
things out. The learning situation was still structured almost wholly
teacher-to-child, but children could speak up without being specifically
called on, and sometimes they stood and walked toward the teacher in
their eagerness to talk. They spoke up to correct each other, and the
teacher attempted to credit both the correction and the original answer
insofar as possible. She accepted ideas proffered by the children, with
the exception of a boy who spoke out too often and had to be slightly

discouraged. However, when discussion in which the children responded to each other's presentations developed, the teacher would limit it.

The easel was used continuously, with children taking turns in alphabetical order to spend long periods painting. The children kept track of whose turn it was and reminded the teacher if she slipped up. A girl spent a long time wrestling to open a stuck jar top—trying it under hot water, tapping it, etc. She appealed to the teacher, who casually gave suggestions and finally told her to substitute another color. It was not clear to the observers why the teacher did not finally open it for her, but the important point, in contrast to the child with the spilt milk in the first classroom, is that the child felt no reluctance in moving around freely, trying various solutions, and appealing to the teacher.

In the fourth second grade in the study (I–2), the children were seen to move about, consulting each other about work, borrowing things, sharpening pencils, throwing away scraps from cutting, or just talking. A child called the rows to get their coats; others helped a child shut the closet door. During reading, help and interchange were allowed among the children who were not being worked with (if kept within bounds), and the group working with the teacher clustered around her at the board, rather than staying in their seats. The teacher often questioned the group as a whole, allowing unsolicited comments and questions. In the interview, she spoke of involving the children in planning for the day. Each day a different child would write the day's plan on the blackboard. "I have very little to do with it. They know the work we must cover." After writing the regular schedule, the children would add what they want, the teacher said, giving examples like "playing with bells," "drawing and coloring," or "singing happy birthday to the teacher." She said the children led the morning exercises and counted attendance, and there was a wardrobe monitor, an eraser monitor, a milk monitor, a door monitor to close and lock the door at the end of the day, and so forth. When a child could not see the blackboard, he could get up or move to another seat.

As observed, this teacher's reminders for quiet and good behavior were mild: "James, that is better. James has something to say to Joyce and he is now saying it in a quiet voice." "Catherine, are you helping Rhynie? I'm very happy, but I can hear you." "If you throw away scraps, tip-toe to the front of the room." "Oh, Arthur, you must be quiet and not disturb others." "Remember, I don't want to only keep the floor under our desks clean, but the whole floor. We live in the whole room. . . ." She explained in the interview that classroom responsibilities are "to bring in social living really. It's teaching that if you want this responsibility then you must work up to it. It's set up as a sort of honor and you've got the responsibility and must work diligently to get it."

Even in this relatively free classroom, however, there was certainly no questioning of established rules. "In the beginning, I impressed the children with the need for doing a thing a certain way because we are many, and it has to be one way, the right way, or we will get in each other's way," the teacher said. "By doing it this way, they will learn better and be happier. There is always stress on this in our room and our class, and we want things to go well for all of us."

In the last analysis, although movement was freer, there was less independence in the curriculum area than in the more restrictive classrooms. Like the other classrooms, no discussion of curriculum was allowed to develop among the children, except privately. Further, this teacher's technique of questioning was generally the statement of an open-ended sentence which encouraged a predetermined one-word response, one that was often moral laden. This was the teacher who in all sincerity characterized as "discussion" the making of "experience charts" in which she asked "leading questions" to get the answers she wanted.

When one contrasts the two "freer" classrooms with those which are more controlled, the limitations on attempts to describe classrooms through quantitative measures alone stand out sharply. Table 4–3 gives the total number of remarks concerning behavior made in three hours of observation and the proportion of these which were positive or negative sanctions for the eight classrooms, listed in order of high-to-low ratings on the enabling of independent action.

As can be seen, there is no direct relationship between the extent to which independent action is allowed and the number of a teacher's directing or sanctioning remarks concerning behavior. A moment's reflection will show that this is to be expected. A highly controlling teacher can establish so effective a system of discipline that few sanctions are needed, while a much freer teacher might continually set limits on talking and moving about with directives and reminders. Also, a teacher may develop a signal system which is hard to record. One

TABLE 4-3

Relationship of Teachers' Enabling of Independence to Classroom Statements Concerning Behavior

School and Grade	Enabling of Independence*	Total No. Remarks Regarding Behavior	Average No. per Child	Directives and Other Neutral Remarks		Positive Sanctions		Negative Sanctions	
				No.	%†	No.	%†	No.	%†
II-5	8	115	3.4	38	33	0	0	77	67
II-2	8	87	3.1	36	41	11	13	40	46
I-2	8	125	4.2	57	45	26	21	42	34
I-5	7	90	3.0	53	59	0	0	37	41
IV-5	6	103	2.7	31	30	10	10	62	60
III-5	5	81	2.0	40	49	4	5	37	46
IV-2	4	122	3.8	71	58	18	15	33	27
III-2	3	126	3.5	68	54	18	14	40	32

* This rating is a composite of interview and observation ratings.
† These are percentages of the total number of the teacher's remarks regarding behavior.

teacher with a low number of directives said that at the beginning of the year she would establish classroom order by stopping and looking hard at an unruly child until he quieted.

Nor is there any direct relationship between strictness of behavior standards and negative versus positive sanctioning of behavior (that is, criticizing, scolding, punishing, or calling attention to undesirable behavior, as compared with praising, rewarding, or in other ways calling attention to desirable behavior). For the second-grade material, it seemed that a higher proportion of remarks addressed to individual children relative to those directed at the class as a whole might indicate a greater permissiveness, but this did not follow through in the fifth grades. In fact, the only consistencies which emerge from the table have to do with differences between second and fifth grades. As might be expected, there is the trend toward more directives about behavior per child for the second grade (from 3.1 to 4.2 for the second grade and from 2.0 to 3.4 for the fifth), and a higher proportion of these are positive sanctions (from 13 to 21 per cent for the second grade and from 0 to 10 per cent for the fifth).

Leeway for Interaction Among Children

TWO CONTRASTING SECOND GRADES

The relation between "supportiveness," as we have been discussing it, and the enabling of independent action is indirect. On the other hand, the relationship between enabling independence and allowing children to interact is obviously direct, with some overlapping between the two. The teacher in classroom IV–2 who disallowed borrowing of crayons or sharpening of pencils also spoke of allowing the children to talk only before class, in play periods, or in short "whispering periods"; whereas, in the last classroom discussed (I–2), where considerable freedom of movement was observed, the teacher spoke of how important friendships were to the children and how happy she was when they were getting along well. When the more restrictive teacher in classroom IV–2 talked of children's interaction in relation to learning, she commented on those who wanted to talk too much and referred to a child who "buried himself in a book" as getting much more out of the day. When asked about the children's social participation, she kept shifting to her own reactions to the children. As observed, she issued directives for a high degree of quiet and attentiveness, although by default she did tolerate quiet talking. As to crayon borrowing, she said in class, "Boys and girls . . . Jonathan . . . I'm sorry to have to announce this, you are not allowed to borrow crayons. I'm sorry. If you don't have the color you wish, go without." The children were drawing bridges, and she said, "I really don't think people should discuss their bridge, because each one is making a different bridge. Please sit down and make your own bridge." Monitorial duties were structured to minimize interaction rather than to enable it.

By comparison, the teacher in classroom I–2 allowed many opportunities for talking and moving around, she said in her interview, encouraging the children to ask their neighbors for help. "They talk and exchange ideas and help each other," she said. "I will always say, 'If you're having trouble, ask your neighbor to help you.' When I am working with another group, they are to ask someone in their group if they have any questions." She spoke of the importance of friendships to the children and how she liked to see them friendly and getting along. She related how she separated two girls for not paying attention but only moved them one seat apart so that the friendship could remain. "Sarah needs a friend," she explained. "She isn't a popular child."

As observed in the classroom, this teacher allowed considerable talking and moving around by one reading group when she was working with the other. She would limit it from time to time when she felt it was getting beyond bounds with remarks like: "Lucy, are you helping Robert? I'm very happy, but I can hear you"; "Oh, Laura, oh excuse me. Laura, when we have a reading lesson, what is important? How must we speak? In a little voice . . ."; "Oh, Mrs. __ is very upset . . . Donald, that is better. Donald has something to say to Rosalind, and he is now saying it in a quiet voice. . . ." No permission was needed to sharpen pencils or go to the wastepaper basket, and children would stop to chat quietly with each other on the way. There was also casual interplay among the children when monitors distributed books or called rows to get their coats at dismissal time.

The teacher in this less restrictive classroom apparently had sufficient assurance to allow greater freedom among the children without fearing it would get out of hand, while the more restrictive teacher seemed anxious and fearful lest she would lose control. The less restrictive teacher was concerned with structuring co-operative work relations among the children, while the more restrictive teacher felt engendering competition to be useful as a motivational technique. On the whole, the less restrictive teacher (leaving aside a saccharine quality to some of her remarks, perhaps exaggerated for the observers) would appear to more successfully structure relations among the children supportive to a goal of learning. However, there is a drawback to this assumption. *The more relaxed and sociable structuring of relations, it so happened, was combined with lower expectations for the children than those held by the more restrictive teacher.* Again, the complex reality of classroom life contradicted an assumption that supposedly "good" practices would co-exist and reinforce each other. A comparison between the fifth-grade classroom (I–5), discussed a number of times, with its very low value placed on curriculum but a rather pleasant structuring of social relations, and a highly achievement-oriented but restricting classroom (III–5) further illustrates this point.

TWO CONTRASTING FIFTH GRADES
Classroom I–5 was characterized by considerable permissiveness, a casual attitude toward quiet talk and movement, and a high proportion of "neutral" teacher-child interchanges, that is, conversation which is neither didactic, directive, nor evaluative. The teacher was straightforward in her management techniques and did not moralize nor hold one child or group up to the others as an example of good or bad behavior. She was, perhaps, somewhat seductive in her treatment of a favored group of lively boys, although she did not fail to discipline them. She could be firm and, at times, sharp when she felt it necessary, but she generally ignored mock sparring, humorous arguing, tattling, and reasonably quiet talking and moving around—even, in the last instance, of tables and chairs which the children freely shoved into various arrangements for committee work. The teacher asked for quiet and order when calling the children up front for dismissal, but accepted a rather uneven, whispery, and jostling "line." She called the children in groups to pick out books for individualized reading (an optional program in the school for teachers who preferred it), and allowed them time to pore over the books or confer with others about their choice.

The work relations among the children, as observed, were more informally or spontaneously co-operative in this classroom than any other. During the committee work session, the children took on, allocated, and carried through responsibilities among themselves with ease and humor, though the teacher did appoint a chairman. The committee artists or illustrators even felt free to search for supplies in the closet where they were stored. However, these admirable work relations, as we have indicated, occurred in conjunction with a low standard for learning and, indeed, with an over-all minimal definition of goals. This is the classroom where the children's accomplishments were so undermined. The only classroom directives defining work relations during the observation periods concerned reading silently so as not to disturb others and having "just plain ordinary manners" when others were called on. We have already commented on the pathetic level of the work itself in the social studies session—"research" on hopelessly limited questions being conducted within the limits of but one source available to the children, their textbook.[15]

The contrast with classroom III–5 was sharp. Standards for discipline in this class were high, and the teacher lectured the class before dismissal:

> I've noticed by looking out of the window that some of our class are slow in getting on the line. . . . Now you've had many compliments, but I think we need to stop once more and ask is this the *best* we can do . . . ?

In this highly controlled classroom there was little that was not teacher-directed, and any attempt at autonomous behavior seemed thwarted virtually before it had begun. The teacher told the children not to start a task until she had finished giving directions and said, "I'm still waiting for someone who is anticipating what I'm going to say." Control was so well established that it was achieved by fewer, not more, directives than the other fifth grades discussed. There were 81 directives in a three-hour period, as compared with a range of 103 to 115 (see Table 4–3). However, the teacher's high demands for order and self-control were tempered by the fact that she was impartial and consistent.

Brief periods of quiet talking occurred during the short transitions but were quickly and effectively stopped when a new lesson was introduced. Children waited to be called on and were not allowed to speak out, even when a discussion became lively. Monitors took advantage of distributing materials to move around slightly—more than absolutely necessary but only slightly. Nor did more than minimal interaction take place at dismissal time. By the third observation, it seemed that over-all control had been slightly relaxed. When the teacher talked to the ob-servers during a transition period, considerable whispering began, but it was accompanied by much shushing and waving of hands as children told each other to be quiet.

In spite of the stringent control observed, the teacher spoke, in her interview, of how important it was for children to learn independence. She stressed that she wanted to see them "stand on their own two feet," "be self-governing sooner," and "make their own strides quicker." She spoke of giving them responsibilities, such as handling monies for the Red Cross, passing out books and materials, checking rows for health inspection and attendance, and serving as monitors for the lunchroom and the school office. She would like to let the children take over a little more, she said, and she felt "acutely" frustrated that she was not able to reach more of them. However, the class was too large. In her interview, as previously mentioned, this teacher said, "I feel that I domineer the room more than I like, for I feel that the children learn a great deal from each other." She said she had tried more pupil participation but found that it did not work and that she had to get back and take over. The room was, indeed, very crowded, with full and closely placed rows and little space for free movement. Furthermore, since the door was often kept open for ventilation, the highly restricting standards which obtained in the school as a whole would impose their own demands for quiet, even if an individual teacher were not already so disposed.

Co-operation and interchange in relation to work was stated as a value in this classroom despite the strict discipline, and some helping and sharing was assumed. "Come on, you two, wake up, if you're shar-ing a book, share it," the teacher said, and, "Those who are sharing books, put the book on one desk or the other"; "Those of you who are helping each other, that's fine. . . . All right, you've helped your neighbor, let's move on. . . ." Respect for the work of others, and the possibility of learning from them were often stressed. In relation to the curriculum, the teacher would say, "Excuse me, we will add to Natalie's point. . . . She has a very good point . . ."; "I see one girl counting her spaces on each side. That is a good way to get to the half-way mark . . ."; "If you have a question, please raise it; it may help some-one else too . . ."; "Those of you at the board, I wish you'd say what you're doing so that we can follow it." The teacher employed requests for not speaking out while someone else was talking really to define the

learning situation, and not simply as a gimmick for rationalizing discipline. "I'm sorry that hands were up while Harold talked . . . ," she
would say; or, "Give her a chance. What is the question we want to
know? . . . Can you hear her? I don't think so, and she has a very
good point."

The teacher also structured some co-operative work. She seated
children together for some projects, she said, and elaborated:

> Some things are done by groups of children, checking of current
> events material, rating what goes on the bulletin board. . . . Usually
> they choose who they want to work with because they know their own
> strengths pretty well too.

She did not use committee work, but did appoint class leaders to call on
the children for answers to a workbook test. We observed such an instance, however, and as soon as a problem arose, she would take over,
leaving the leader uncertain as to his role.

More than any other teacher, this teacher consciously and deliberately structured intellectual interchange in the learning situation. She
felt children could and should learn from one another and was explicit
about the way she incorporated this principle into her teaching technique. She gave as an example the fact that some children had visited
grandparents in the country, so that she did not have to build a concept
of difference between city and country living from scratch. The others
do it "for those who are uninitiated . . . because they've had experiences." "They can relate an experience with, 'Oh, yes, when I did so-
and-so,' and this is quite fine," she said, and elaborated:

> Whenever some of the things we are doing is within the possibility of
> their understanding, I'll try it to see and you'll find that maybe one or
> two will, and that they in turn will expand on it, and bring it to the
> level of some of those who don't. If you can get it with 25 per cent,
> this may set the tone for the rest.

As observed, the teacher involved the children skillfully and successfully in contributing their ideas to a discussion, using their contributions
and referring to the points of other children already made. *However, it
was always mediated almost entirely through herself.* She was invariably the strict arbitrator, selecting only those aspects of a child's discussion which fitted her own clear, but rigid, concept of what she wanted.
The discussion was never opened up for new possibilities. In one in-

stance she said, "Aha, now you have a disagreement," but she so tightly structured the resolution that the children, initially excited and involved, lost interest.

In sum, this and the previously discussed fifth grade offer alternative "models" to the theoretically ideal climate for learning, where social relations are established that enable children to view each other as partners to be learned both with and from. In the one case, the enabling of considerable interchange and the structuring for cooperative work relations are combined with such low standards and expectations for the children as to defeat their purpose. In the other, the restriction of social interaction is combined with high standards for learning and a structuring for at least one type of cooperative enterprise, that of arriving at the resolution of a problem through class discussion, although so tightly controlled that it is the teacher's judgment, not the actual ideas of the other children, that is the focus.

One of the other fifth-grade classrooms (II–5, see pp. 96–97) fell somewhat closer than either of the above to an ideal model. The last (IV–5), however, presented another alternative. The patterning of group work in this classroom was familiar and unmistakable—that of the "organization man." So central did this seem to the classroom atmosphere that it lent a new significance to the classroom differences we were observing. *What we were looking at was not so much a difference in the quality of education in its more specific sense as variations in how children were being taught to talk and act with their superiors and with their peers. These were variations in patterns of socialization.* The conclusion was making itself inescapable. One could not evaluate—or even understand—the learning process by analyzing classroom life in terms of an ideal model of a climate conducive to learning without also understanding the significance of variations in classroom structures and their relation to differential patterns of socialization in our society.[16]

NOTES

1. M. A. Bany and L. V. Johnson, *Classroom Group Behavior, Group Dynamics in Education* (New York: Macmillan, 1964), p. 3.
2. *Ibid.*, pp. 4–5; M. T. Eaton, G. Weathers, and B. N. Phillips, "Some Reactions of Classroom Teachers to Problem Behavior in School," *Edu-

cational Administration and Supervision, XLIII (March 1957), 129–139; W. R. Flesher, "The Beginning Teacher," *Educational Research Bulletin*, XXIV (January 1954), 12–18.

3. Bany and Johnson, *op. cit.* pp. v–vi, 3, 15.

4. *Ibid.*, p. 14.

5. J. S. Kounin, P. V. Gump, and J. J. Ryan, III, "Explorations in Classroom Management," in W. W. Charters, Jr., and N. L. Gage, eds., *Readings in the Social Psychology of Education* (Boston: Allyn and Bacon, 1963).

6. W. J. Gnagney, "Effects on Classmates of a Deviant Student's Power and Response to a Teacher-Exerted Control Technique," *Journal of Educational Psychology*, LI (1960), 109.

7. R. C. Anderson, "Learning in Discussions: A Resume of the Authoritarian-Democratic Studies," *Harvard Educational Review*, XXIX, No. 3 (Summer 1959), 212 (italics added).

8. See Chapter 1, note 14.

9. Such as those described by Jonathan Kozol in *Death at an Early Age* (Boston: Houghton Mifflin, 1967).

10. Whereas in theory these qualifications in the actual content of a teacher's statement could be taken into account in a sufficiently elaborated coding system, the attempt to do this in practice would necessitate the analyst's having to make an extremely complicated judgment each time, which would simply reintroduce all the potentially "subjective" elements the practice of coding is designed to eliminate.

11. In reporting on a study of some 300 teachers, Philip E. Kraus stated informally that the attempt to describe teachers according to a standardized checklist of some sort was finally abandoned in favor of an individually written thumbnail sketch (see Chapter 3, note 5).

12. That these two should be taken together was indicated by a classroom not included in this particular study, where a high value placed on curriculum and a high proportion of interchange with the children was combined with relatively frequent "negative" responses, although these were direct and straightforward comments on incorrect answers. (Classroom Profile Study, supported by National Institute of Mental Health Grant No. 3M–9135; working papers on file, Bank Street College of Education.)

13. The material from the child interviews is presented and discussed in full in Chapter 7.

14. Part of the excess over other classrooms clustered at the end of the second observation, when the class had been disrupted several times by monitors bringing in stacks of books.

15. For average achievement scores in reading for these and the other classrooms studied, see Chapter 6, Table 6–1.

16. We suggest that this is the reason for the inconclusiveness of so much educational research. After reviewing studies on the sociology of learn-

ing and noting the unevenness of the research, Sarane Boocock comments, "The classroom, the core of the school learning system, presents the most confusing picture. We cannot yet say just what it is that the effective teacher is or does. . . . Satisfying group relations, often perceived as the panacea for all education problems, are not related to learning in any direct or consistent way . . ." ["Toward a Sociology of Learning: A Selective Review of Existing Research," *Sociology of Education,* XXXIX (Winter 1966), pp. 1–45].

C H A P T E R

5

CLASSROOM EXPERIENCE
AS SOCIALIZATION

Teachers define goals for children directly when they teach and set up rules for classroom behavior. Further, they establish goals for behavior indirectly when they praise, punish, or ignore different acts. The influence they exert on children is particularly strong, not only because the amount of time children spend with them is considerable, but also because their sanctions receive powerful reinforcement from a child's point of view due to the fact that they are applied before the watchful eyes of age-mates. This is not to suggest that children necessarily accept the attitudes and goals being presented. Some children internalize them deeply, some accept them casually, others actively rebel against them or casually ignore them. Whatever the response, however, "socialization" is taking place. In whatever part accepted or rejected, the normative expectations for behavior and attitudes presented in the classroom are being learned by children as crucial aspects of the world with which they must cope.

Children also learn to handle the fact that normative attitudes and goals are conveyed in different ways and to differing degrees by different adults. They further find out that some precepts are to be honored in deed as well as word, while others can quietly be ignored as long as they are not openly questioned. Some of the culturally defined ideals they learn are overtly stated and defended. Others, however, just as important, are implied but seldom stated. It is these largely unstated assumptions about how people should act that are so taken for granted as to be considered simply a part of "human nature." It is not generally recognized that they are relative and vary from society to society. They are conveyed to children largely through the way children are treated and through the expectations for their response that are subtly but unmistakably conveyed to them as well as through the way they see others being treated and responding.

In sum, the way the teacher structures both her relations with the children and their relations with each other sets up a behavioral model for them, the implications of which extend far beyond the classroom. To some extent the goals she states for the children and those she implies through her management techniques relate to her individual style, but for the most part they must conform to school patterns which, in turn, relate to general social expectations. It is the failure fully to take this into account which has led to the inconclusiveness of much research on teacher style and its results in the classroom. For example, a series of studies have been made, focusing on "student-centered" versus "instructor-centered" techniques, the assumption being that the former were the more conducive to learning. The concepts of student and teacher centeredness, however, were ill-defined. The psychologist, Mc-Keachie, had this to say:

> With "student-centered" we associate the halo terms of democratic, permissive, insight, affective and student growth. "Instructor-centered" brings to mind the terms authoritarian, Fascistic, knowledge for its own sake, and content-centered. In our psychological subculture the mere labels in our title stack the deck against anyone who attempts to defend the instructor-centered point of view.[1]

McKeachie went on to discuss the contradictory findings of research on the two styles, with a "student-centered" class scoring higher in achievement in one case, and a "teacher-centered" in another. Bany and Johnson comment on such studies as follows:

> Those who analyze the controversy concerning group-centered versus teacher-centered methods generally conclude that those favoring the teacher-centered methods are more interested in course-related material and achievement scores while group-centered proponents are primarily concerned with individual development and emotional needs, hence the discrepancies in the findings.[2]

We are suggesting the further problem that variations in teaching style must be understood within the wider context of the *total model for work-related behavior and corollary goals and attitudes which is being presented to children.* Elementary teaching in public schools is generally "teacher-centered" by comparison with the greater "student-centering" of independent progressive schools, pre-school and kindergarten groups, after-school programs, and so on. However, there are broad, albeit often subtle, variations among public schools. Our argument is that these variations follow from the different patterns of socialization that are taken for granted as applying to different groups of children, and that the effects of contrasting styles can only be fully assessed when this is understood.

In order to explore varying patterns of socialization in the eight study classrooms, teacher-interview and classroom-observation materials were analyzed under the following rubrics:

1. The teacher's formal structuring of relations between herself and the children and among the children through the allocation of responsibilities, class officers, committee work, and the like.
2. The informal structuring of relationships through the way the teacher actually managed the class and what was in fact allowed and disallowed.
3. The goals for behavior imparted to the children through the teacher's differential behavior toward different children and the types of children generally favored, disfavored, or ignored in a given classroom.

Classroom Structuring and Teacher Goals: Interview

In the study schools, the contrasts in classroom structuring and concomitant expectations and goals held by the teacher for the children with whom she was working accorded well with the children's social position. On the face of it, this is perfectly obvious. Any teacher takes it for granted that she changes her approach to fit different groups of children. What analysis revealed was that the differentiation of method is not so much geared to teaching more effectively as to a whole series of often unstated assumptions about desirable patterns of socialization for children of different backgrounds. A description of the fifth-grade classroom in the middle-income white study school, as compared with that in the lower-income Negro school, illustrates this point. Both teachers were capable, experienced, and well-meaning. They had, however, markedly different goals for the children, in relation to both academic achievement and behavior. The following excerpts, collated from the interviews with the two teachers, reveal their different attitudes toward the importance of taking responsibility and showing initiative in carrying out classroom activities.

1. Teacher's goals for the children:

(Interview question: *What kinds of things do you think these children should be getting out of school?*)

CLASSROOM IV–5

As I say to the children, the most important thing is to be able to get along with one another and to have acceptable standards of behavior. In other words to develop into a good human being. That comes first. I think that is the main reason why they come to school, because they can learn how to spell at home with anybody. But the fact that they're working in a group and that they are learning acceptable standards of behavior is very important. I count that number one. And secondly, the intellectual development of the child. That they progress intellectually is

CLASSROOM I–5

First of all, discipline. They should know that when an older person talks to them or gives a command that they should respond, they should listen. That there are times when we do things—there's a time for fun, there's a time for play, then there's a time when we should get down to work. I feel they should learn values, moral values, social values. . . . That a teacher is not here as a policeman but as someone to help. That maybe they might not remember everything they have learned in school, but I think that they should remember a broad concept. They

CLASSROOM IV–5

very important, but that they become decent and intelligent human beings, that's most important as far as I'm concerned.

(Elsewhere in interview) How to be a good human being. . . . Living with a group is not living with your father and mother who give you everything. Living in a group means respect for the rights of others. Living in a group means being careful about bookbags on the floor and not hurting each other. That is mainly the social adjustment that I feel is very important in a classroom.

CLASSROOM I–5

should remember the nice things that happened to them in school.

(Elsewhere in interview) I try to drive into them to be somebody, to try to make something of themselves, that they will not be children all of their lives, that what they do now and how much they learn will shape their adult life.

2. Class officers and monitors:

There is a President and Vice President, one a boy and one a girl, with new elections every month. The President monitors the staircase, reports those who do not cooperate, and represents the class when necessary.

Monitors for the library, the encyclopedia, the window sills, wiping the board, collecting wastebaskets, calling rows for clothing and getting milk are volunteered for, and rotated at election time. Monitors to collect the newspapers, milk money, lunch money, and the bank are permanent. There are two for each job except bank envelopes. Permanent monitors also help in the school library.

Every child has a job to do something. Each child in the class has some kind of job.

There is a President to bring up the line in the morning, Vice President, Secretary to keep track of committees, and Treasurer to collect and record money for GO, trips, or bank envelopes. They are re-elected every three months.

There are no monitors.

3. Teacher attitudes toward leadership and responsibility:

Everyone has a chance to be a leader. This is our classroom. Every

Yes, they [class officers] are elected. I tried once a month for two years—

CLASSROOM IV–5

child has a chance to be a president and wash the board. This is a chore that they love to do, and to be a leader simply means that they sit in the chair and listen to the correct answers, and, of course, I'm always ready with my book of correct answers.

Leaders are for many things. It's a feeling they have that they are conducting the lesson, but actually I am in the background constantly and many times, if there is a wrong answer given, I will interrupt, which is my prerogative, and find out why and explain.

It has great dignity and honor to be voted by your classmates to represent them. We try to give each child a chance by shortening the period. . . . Instead of having an election every four weeks, we have it every three weeks. There is still excitement, even without much selection. . . . I always feel sorry for the child who feels that she is the last one, but I don't know of any other way to do it. Somebody has to be left out. . . . We have to learn not to take that too hard. It happens all the time. Look what happened to Stevenson. He didn't get it. So he had to learn to accept the fact that the [public] body didn't vote for him. We have to accept disappointments too, so I emphasize the fact that everybody cannot be President—it's better to be right. . . .

(Q: *Then you don't have any set helpers?*) Not usually. Sometimes I will say different children, because one child will feel as though he's

CLASSROOM I–5

three years—but I feel that before the child has really gotten into the office, they're out again, so we've done it for about every three months. Then I feel the child has had a good stay, or a good chance in the job to know what he is doing—to know what it is all about.

No [I do not have monitors]. I try to keep the monitorial down as much as I can because of the out-of-the-room business. On Wednesdays we are obliged to serve the office. I will look around for a boy who is neat and clean.

Arthur, lately, has been shining shoes for the assistant principal. When I learned that, I sort of blew my top. . . . I told him, "We learn how to read and write and then wherever you want to go, then you can go." I asked him, "Don't you want to be an assistant principal or do you want to be a shoeshine boy when you grow up?" Of course he said he wants to be an assistant principal. I said, "Well, you get there and learn to read and write and do your arithmetic, and then you can go out and do the other things that you want to do."

CLASSROOM IV–5   CLASSROOM I–5

. . . featured too much . . . I want
them to feel that it's not just the one
child who's able to do it, but everyone else. . . . I have faith in their
ability, so I don't have too much of
one leader. I must add that I have
given them a great deal of experience
in leadership, in that many times
when we check our work, I ask someone to sit in the chair in the front of
the room to conduct it. Every child
has a chance to be a leader. Then we
go around a second time. It isn't a
question of the one who's most bril-
liant. It's a question that everyone's
sitting there and having the feeling
that now he is the leader. (Q: *How
often?*) Every day for practically
every lesson. Of course I oversee
everything. Nothing slips by me but
the child sits there with the feeling
that she or he is the leader. This is
usually when we check our work—
for example, in reading, if we have
to check comprehension questions,
or if we have questions in our social
studies assignment. That gives them
a feeling that they have to be a
leader. (Q: *Oh, I see. They check
from their work?*) Yes, but with my
book open and constantly checking.
But I give them the feeling that they
are the knowledgeable ones.

4. Work committees:

(Q: *Anything else of this sort—leaders—that you do in class?*) Oh yes,
I have beautiful committee work.
. . . It was a hard job getting them
started but they love it. They love it,
and they love the responsibility, and
they can't wait till they get a committee assignment.

(Q: *How do you find committee
work works out?*) It's doing rather
nicely. There are some children that
don't know what to do and I will
have to go and direct them. There's
always one or two that feel, "Oh, I
don't want to work in that group.
They're not doing anything. They're

CLASSROOM IV–5

(Q: *What are these committees for?*) Social Studies, mostly. There are three children assigned to a topic. . . . One of the members is the chairman, another one is the speaker, and another one shows the pictures. . . . It rotates . . . the speaker will become the chairman and so forth. . . . However, each child does the research and . . . they pool their knowledge on what they have researched and give the speaker the information. The speaker makes an outline [which] is just for them to look down at, and they speak without reading. . . . After the speaker is through, then the child who has pictures relative to the subject will show the pictures and explain what the speaker was saying. And after that . . . the chairman says, "Are there any questions," and the children in the seats ask questions. . . . After the questions have all been asked about the topic, the children give contributions . . . so information is shared. It's a very democratic procedure. (The chairman then calls for comments and criticisms.)

They [the children] are challenged. They are listening. They are thinking of ways of adding to a problem—a report—or maybe critically analyzing the committee that's working in the front of the room. . . . The children are always at attention when there's a committee report. I have never seen any group of children that I have had all through the years who didn't listen when fellow pupils are giving them information.

CLASSROOM I–5

just wasting time." I will have to go over and give that group direction, but in the main they are all trying to get their reports out. They want to see their reports up. They want to read their reports to the group, and I think whatever little learning value —how to use the encyclopedias, how to use the index, to learn to look up things, how to use their table of contents, and each time that we have committee work, we're using one of these methods to gather up information. I think it's valuable.

Yes, Jerry is Vice President, the Secretary is Lucy, and the Treasurer is [pause] I think it's Alan.

CLASSROOM IV–5

Then six people are picked [by the chairman] to give him a mark. Nobody is left out because otherwise he'll pick his favorite. This must be an impartial mark. They'll be very good about it. They will give a mark which I usually find correspondent with my mark. Many times five will say B+ and one will say A. We'll pick the B+ because that's the majority. . . . Sometimes . . . they have been unfair in marking . . . and then I go to the rest of the group and I say, "How many of you think this is a fair mark?" and some will say no and some will say yes. I always pick the majority, but, of course . . . the teacher is the final authority. . . . Nevertheless, they should have the experience of evaluating but naturally the teacher who is more experienced should be the final authority in evaluating. . . . On occasion . . . I'll ask why didn't you think that this child was worth A. They might have a good reason. They might say that he didn't stand up straight. . . . He might wiggle and . . . I have trained them to think that poise is very important in front of the room. . . . So I have to remind them that they mustn't be too strict. . . .

I have a committee every day, [which] takes about 40 minutes, sometimes more, because if the children are full of their subject you continue with it.

CLASSROOM I–5

5. Goals for classroom behavior:

They have the privilege of moving about the room to look at the pic-

I feel that a certain amount of movement and talking can go on but I

CLASSROOM IV–5

ture, to get material. They have the privilege of speaking if it is relative to the subject that they're working on. Of course if it becomes loud talk, they can't go on. . . . Of course, when I speak there mustn't be any talking because that's rude. I have a set of rules on the side of the room. I can't remember all of them but one of them is plan your work and No. 4 is be polite. . . . A certain amount of noise you have to expect because there are so many, and children will be children. Unless there's some plain rudeness and disorder, I accept a little talk as part of the day's work.

CLASSROOM I–5

will not allow this . . . when I am up in the front teaching. . . . At committee work, you have to go to the shelf for reference books, or go and see how another is doing, or go to the closet to get a crayon. I don't feel that this is bad. . . . I can't sit at my desk from 9 to 12 or from 12 to 3 without moving, and how much more . . . they have vim and vitality. So I allow a minimum amount. I allow it, but not when I'm teaching. . . . I feel that this is when everything should be still and this is when they have to learn something. This is not a time for talking and moving.

In between a lesson, I don't mind too much if they whisper or they talk to their neighbor, but, as I said, not when I'm talking—not when I'm in front trying to teach a lesson.

6. Techniques for achieving desired behavior:

(Q: *What kinds of things do you do when the children aren't doing what they're supposed to do?*)

If somebody talks and I don't want to say, now you're rude for talking while I'm talking, I just hold my hand up and I say "No. 4," or just four fingers, and they'll know that somebody's being rude. It works. . . .

You would like to know, I'm sure, how I handle a great deal of disorder. I find somebody that is sitting quietly, and I say, "I like the way whosit's sitting. I like the way Evelyn is working." They get the message. Immediately they want to be praised. They want me to like them for something so that it usually works magic. Sometimes I will have

Oh, I call their names. It depends on what the offense is. Under no circumstances will I allow talking on a fire drill. If there is talking, they'll have to come back and maybe write something. One of my pet things has been getting the dictionary and beginning to write. . . . Even the thought of it, the dictionary and writing—you have to look back and forth—it's tedious. It's not the "I must behave myself on the fire drill" type of thing. . . . What else? I might write a note in their notebooks to their mothers. I might change their seat. . . . I might have them stand for a certain length of time.

CLASSROOM IV–5

to say, "I like the way many people are working, but there are a few I don't like," and then they know I'm watching them and that they're not really being cooperative. . . . Sometimes I have to scold, the way I did with Anthony this morning when he was teasing the girls.

(Elsewhere in interview) I really don't like that [tattling], and it's very difficult to get that message across. . . . Let's say Henry will come and talk about Rosemary, and I'll always say to Henry, "You talk to me about Henry, and I'll find out about Rosemary." They usually get that, but it's a difficult thing. Most children want to justify themselves one way or another, and when they talk about somebody else it's usually because they want to inflate themselves or feel that they're helping the teacher, which is not a good way of getting discipline. . . . Many times I have gotten this message across pretty well, because they will come to me and say, "I was disorderly on the stairs," and I usually compliment them for saying that. "I'm glad you told me, it is a fine trait for you to tell me that you were disorderly. Will you try not to do it again?" I tell them that I like it and they do it many times. Sometimes the children are afraid and they won't.

CLASSROOM I–5

Sometimes they sit back in these chairs, and they'll fall, breaking the chairs or loosening the screws or something like that. If this happens more than two or three times, it's not an accident. Then I will have that person stand for a little while [pause]. Go on to the next question. I'll think of something [else]. . . .

(Elsewhere in interview) I feel that a lot of them need the old—maybe mothers do not beat their children nowadays. I do not say this is the answer, but let them know that there is a rod now and then. I know that it did not hurt me any. It gives them respect. I think some of the children have lots of respect and some of the little niceties that little children have.

. . . Ruth talks a little but I don't expect them to be all angels all the time. Really. But you have to yell at them now and then.

(Other forms of sanctioning, elsewhere in interview)

When I say good morning, I usually accent what good things they did. . . . A greeting is about 10–15 minutes, to discuss improvements and manners and so on.

(When pleased with behavior) I will tell them in some form, or I will put my arm around them and give them a little hug or smile at them. Through my manner of talk to them, they will

CLASSROOM IV–5

(On moving from one activity to another) I usually say that we've done a good job with a particular thing, and we need more improvement, but next time we hope that we can get that improvement, and now we'll go on to our next lesson.

CLASSROOM I–5

know that I am pleased. They're fifth grade, and I don't give stars and things like that for good behavior. I think that by you yourself, your smile, the way you talk to them, a gentle pat on the shoulder or a little hug now and then, they will know that you are pleased with their behavior.

(Incidents recounted of sanctioning individual children)

(In relation to a particularly difficult child) I try to tell him all the time that we like Ronald, and we want him to stay. I said, "You want to stay, Ronald . . . because you know if you're going to be disorderly, I'm going to put you in the hanging closet." He said, "I'll stay. I'll stay."

(In relation to another) He's inclined to be angry. I told him that it's hard for me to criticize him. I would rather say nice things about him, and I hate to give marks that are not good. It hurts me more than it hurts him because I, as a teacher, want to know that my children are doing well. I explained my role to him. . . .

I had to speak with him and he is afraid to get criticism for fear that it will be told at home and that there would be a conflict with his parents. . . . So I spoke to him [about teasing the girls out of school] . . . and I asked him to cooperate and not do that again, and if he does, I'd have to send for his parents, because, after all, this is outside of school. . . .

Every now and then, when he starts misbehaving, I say, "Come on now, baby."

She's a little fighter, but then you have to praise her and say, "I think you're a little lady. You're not going to fight."

I've scolded him [about his poor work and not doing homework] and I've written in his report card to his mother that if there is no improvement, although he has the ability, I'm going to leave him back.

He gets mad all the time. . . . If things do not go the way he would like he will not do any work. This went on until I felt that mother ought to know what's happening. I sent for the mother and she asked that I keep a little book for him . . . so I could write his conduct and his work into it each day. He's doing much better, because all I have to do is remind him that the mother will know, and she will really take care of him.

(Q: *What ways do you have to show the children you are pleased with their work?*)

CLASSROOM IV–5

Oh, I compliment them. That is the best way to get children to work. Always commendations, always. Never . . . well, I can't say that I *never* say I'm not pleased. Sometimes I get angry, and say I am not pleased with this kind of paper and I want it rewritten, but, say it's penmanship, I'll always find one word and I say, "This is beautifully written, how about the rest?" . . . This is my best way. It's no use getting myself worn out by saying I don't like this, I don't like that. That would be destructive, not only for the children, but for me. I would never feel as though I were doing a good job if I immediately said, "I don't like anything about you." I always try to stress the positive, accent the positive.

CLASSROOM I–5

I would take their work and I'll hang it out in the hall, or I will hang it up in the room, or I'll put "100-excellent" on it. They like to see that. Most of them love to have their work checked. They love to see the word "excellent" or "very good"—that sort of thing. . . . They love to have their work hung outside the door, so that maybe their friends coming past might see it. If they have done a particularly nice job, I will place it outside the room, or I will display it somewhere in the room. They know by that that I am pleased with their work.

In many respects these two teachers are similar in approach, and both concur with current educational practices. Both saw their role as transmitting values as well as skills and knowledge; both felt they should be positive insofar as possible with the children; both were sympathetic to the needs of children to move around and talk from time to time, though both asked for quiet and order during the formal part of a lesson. However, the contrast is marked between the accent on leadership, on the one hand, and on learning to take orders, on the other. One teacher (classroom IV–5)) spoke at great length about leadership when talking about classroom officers, monitors, and committees, and even compared the children's feelings to those of a defeated presidential candidate. The other teacher (classroom I–5) could not even remember the name of the class treasurer. The first teacher's definition of "leadership" may seem a mockery, so limited is the initiative it ultimately involves. However, it accords with the adult model of the "organization man," where initiative is strictly bounded by one's role in the "organization." Considerable latitude for initiative was actually found in the second classroom due to the relative lack of structure. However, this does not contradict the fact that in the formal work situation, acceptance of authority, not initiative, was critical.

Classroom Structuring and Teacher Goals: Observations

The classroom observations tallied with what the teachers told us in their interviews. In the first classroom (IV–5), the committee reports were handled by the children with great competence and proceeded like clockwork. Three children put material on the board, and one of them, the chairman, announced with a formal manner that the committee's presentation was on the Oregon Territory. A boy gave a well-organized report, presenting information on the history of the territory, its settlement, its products, and so on, referring to notes now and then, but not reading from them. When the report was finished, the chairman announced that pictures would be shown, and the third committee member found and explained pictures in a book showing them as he walked up and down the aisles. During the committee report and picture showing, the children took notes. They maintained a quiet and interested concentration during the first part of the picture showing, but as the "picture shower" moved slowly down the aisles, saying little, they became bored, and there was some quiet yawning and squirming. The teacher walked about, watching, but saying nothing.

The committee chairman then called for "questions," most of which were referred to the reporter, who answered with assurance, referring to his notes now and then. Some of them were: "What kind of fur did they have?" "I didn't hear what happened in 1859." "Would you repeat the nickname of the territory?" "Could you repeat some of the famous cities?" "How many people settled in Oregon?" "What was the first settlement?" "Where was the first settlement?"

Following this, the chairman asked for "contributions," and a boy explained why Oregon was called the "beaver state." Others had pictures to show. The chairman finally announced "comments and criticisms," and many hands went up. Some comments were favorable, like, "Good." "Well organized." Others were critical: "You rocked." "You shouldn't have looked at the board when you were saying the names." "You should have known your information better because you had to look at your paper to answer one of the questions." "They should have a smile on their faces. They look like some kind of prisoners." To this last the teacher explained that sometimes children are nervous when giving reports at the front of the room, although there is no need for them to feel this way.

Finally, markers were appointed. All gave an "A." In another observation, there had been a division of opinion. The marking committee had stood in turn and called out "A," "A," "B." The last marker had hesitated, and then with a shrug, said "A." The teacher then said, quite emphatically, "I think B would be a better grade because they could have spoken up more clearly."

As implied by her interview, this teacher asserted her final authority when it came to the evaluation, but she did not intervene during the reporting itself. However, a review session of mathematics homework presented another aspect of classroom structure. Here the teacher's continual (albeit at times essential) intervention posed for the student leader the problem of how to handle nominal authority while in fact deferring to real authority. The leader during the session, a girl named Maureen, started to call down the rows in order, asking for answers until, for no reason clear to the observers, the teacher took over and started calling on the children. Maureen attempted to continue leading the session, but the teacher kept intervening partly in order to discuss some examples more fully. However, she caused confusion and dissent in the class by forgetting a child who was working out an example on the board and by calling children out of turn. For example, the record reads, in part:

> T moves to the next example, "27 square feet equals how many square yards, Lucille?" Lucille answers correctly. T: "Good, prove it." Yvonne answers correctly again . . .

> Maureen calls Roger, in turn, for the next example. He answers, and Maureen says, "How many agree?" T says, "I'm sorry, I didn't hear. I was talking to George." Roger repeats the answer. Maureen says, "How many agree?" T calls Sarah to explain why. . . .

> (After several more examples) T checks with Maureen as to what example they are up to. Maureen tells her. T calls Harry, then John. Harry and John go up to the front. Janet is talking. Maureen says, "Do you agree?" T says, "Sorry, Maureen, dear, I'm listening to Janet. Sorry, dear, I'm listening to Janet. Janet, would you repeat, dear?" Janet does. . . .

One might well question the value of having a student "leader" for a session which necessarily involves considerable teacher questioning and exposition. However, the lesson in socialization for pupils, many of whom would be moving into the ranks of the "organization men," should be considered. The organizational goal is to move into successive positions of increasing independence and responsibility, and the taking of each step necessitates being able to appraise and handle competently the problems that arise from sharing responsibilities with a superior. The subordinate must make constant judgments of when and how far to show initiative, when to press a point, and when to abdicate, according to the precise structure of the organization and the individual personalities involved. This is co-ordinate with the classroom structure we have described. Furthermore, failure to encourage *true* inquiry on the part of the children in this classroom, emphasis on learning to ask the "right" questions, and stress on superficialities and going through the proper motions are all characteristic of the wariness in our society about the too creative or radical inquiry.

Nonetheless, the classroom we have been describing was patterned for an exchange of information and a pooling of factual material—if not of ideas. Problems were worked out conjointly with one's peers. The children learned from each other and evaluated each other's work.

In the second classroom (I–5), as the interview material suggests, such interaction was at a minimum. Contrast the above episodes with a session wherein children were reporting from their reading on a character they would *not* like to be. The teacher opened by asking Arlene if there was such a character in her book, and Arlene did not answer. "No one you would not like to be in your reading so far?" the teacher said, and turned to Ronnie, "All right, you go to the front of the room and tell us about yours." Ronnie started to talk, and the teacher interrupted, "First tell us the title of the book and the author." He replied, "Little Leaguers," and went on to tell about the boy who had to stay in the house while the others played ball. When he finished, there was no calling for questions or comments from the floor. "All right," the teacher said, and called on Stuart, who leaned against the board and shyly started to speak. He was told to stand tall. Warming up, he gave a rather rambling account of a boy he would not want to be and another who had the mumps whom he wanted to be. . . . The teacher interrupted in surprise, "*Want* to be?" Stuart explained, talking fully, that all the good things happened to the sick boy for in the end he tied the baseball score and won a medal, whereas nothing happened to the other boy. The teacher questioned Stuart further about the details of various incidents, then said, "All right," reaffirmed his choice, and called on Marie. Marie elaborated on a boy hunted by the thieves who had killed his father. The teacher said, "All right, very well told." The session continued in this manner, with the teacher giving directives on posture, on giving the title and author, corrections of grammar, reminders to stick to the point, or questions about the actual content of the story. After remaining quiet for most of the session, the children began to speak out or talk quietly to one another when a story they happened to have read was being reported. At one point someone said indignantly, "He didn't even give the author." The teacher ignored these comments and never opened the floor for formal student participation.

There was some committee work in this classroom, however, and considerable latitude for independence and initiative, although it was primarily in relation to handling materials and supplies and *not the content of the work itself.* The planting session described in Chapter 2 is an example. At the teacher's request, two boys pushed a table near the closet, put a chair on it, and one climbed to the top for a pitcher. Donald gratuitously pointed out its location. The other children were copying homework examples from the board, and paid little attention to this scene, which in some classrooms would have caused quite a stir. Then the teacher directed the children to gather at tables in the front, which they did, with noisy and humorous talk. She doled out dirt and seeds, asking Donald to get tongue depressors for labeling the boxes. He rummaged in her desk drawers, and a girl went over to help him find the markers. Meanwhile the children divided up the work, with lively talk and laughter, although they knew enough to keep their voices from getting too loud. They watered the boxes, labeled them, and carried them back to the table already filled with plants. A girl gave out towels for the wiping of hands, and Donald climbed to the top of the cupboard to return the pitcher. He sat there, his legs dangling, the table and chair having been pushed away, until the teacher ordered him to jump down and take his seat.

The relaxed atmosphere of the session, the easy cooperation and enjoyment of the children, the casual acceptance of considerable noise and movement by the teacher, all were pleasant to observe. What was dismaying, however, was the absence of any academic content or stated expectations of what the children should be learning. There was no exposition by the teacher or structuring for a discussion about what they were doing. It was, perhaps, with a belated recognition of this, particularly in view of the observers' presence, that the teacher told one group to put their plant box in the closet "as an experiment." The directive was carried out reluctantly, and with distress—the children knew well that the "experiment" meant their plants would not grow.

A camaraderie among the students and an ability to share responsibilities were also shown during social studies committee work. Unfortunately, however, so was the failure on the teacher's part to build any real content or learning goals into the classroom experience. The children grouped themselves around different tables, as directed by the teacher, and some set to work quietly and seriously. Others, as befitted their temperaments, wandered around, "getting in on" what was happening at other tables but in some cases asking questions or offering suggestions about subject matter. Several shifted tables around to make a better seating arrangement. Those working on illustrations went freely to get supplies from the closets or the teacher's desk. Yet the topics on which the children were working were pitifully inadequate for a fifth grade. The subject was slavery, and some questions were, "What did the slaves wear?" and "Where were the slaves from?" "Research" was being done in one book only, the text. Further, although the reports were due the following day, some of the children had still to be assigned at the beginning of the session. Also, the teacher overlooked one of her committee chairmen when she checked on the progress of the groups.

Nonetheless, this was a "good" classroom, as classrooms in low-income all-Negro schools go, and the teacher seemed sincere in her desire to help the children. "I feel that if you will be a friend to these children, that they will respond to you, and they do for the most part," she said. She liked them, she said, and found them "a lovely group, quite talkative." "They come through. On the whole, if they are asked to do something, they will respond. . . . I came to class thinking, what can I bring to this child that will help him," she said. "Many teachers are antagonistic to the children here. I feel I would like to help them in any way I can."

However, the limitation in her definition of what she was helping the children achieve negated her good intentions. This limitation was by no means her own. As *socially defined,* the optimal goal for most of these children is the achievement of steady employment and minimal economic and social security. Speaking of her general aims for their schooling, the teacher said, "If they remember something, that will make me feel good." She stated her two main subjects to be reading and arithmetic.

> I feel that the others will fall into place. If they cannot do reading they cannot do so many of the other areas. If they cannot count, what is going to happen when they get out into the street? They will be short-changed so many times and this is what I place my greatest stock on. I feel that you will not lose any greatness by not knowing science, although that today is being stressed, but you will be able to make a living. So when I keep saying reading and math, I want you to understand why.

This view is characteristic of teachers in ghetto schools. When talking about the social studies syllabus, the teacher interrupted herself to say, "A slow class does not have to cover this." Yet hers was a *middle* class on the grade. Is only the very top class of such a school expected to master what should be standard material for all?

Even where this teacher was imaginative in developing activities for the children, she did not follow through and take advantage of what she had opened up. For example, she would have children write to the author of a book they liked, and she spoke of the pleasure it gave a child when he received a response. At the close of the session described above, she said, "Arlene has a letter she received in the mail this morning, and some pictures." She sat down near Arlene's desk, saying, "Come on, Arlene, and read your letter." Arlene went to the front, reading somewhat indistinctly, with a deferential shyness. She stumbled and was prompted by the teacher, who then said, "Show them the pictures. Show them the author. We can't see." Arlene held up the pictures quickly, and started to leave. Jerry said he could not see. The teacher said sharply, but with humor, "Oh, Arlene, stand there. Show them the other picture. All right." Ben complained loudly, "I want to see too," and the teacher responded, "If you can't, you need glasses." The class laughed at the joke, which closed the incident. "Put your books away," the teacher said, "You may put your books away . . . ," with no time for further comment or discussion. The potential offered by the letter was thereby negated rather than developed.

In her interview, the teacher said she tried to "drive into" the children "to be somebody" and "make something of themselves," and she was angry with Arthur for shining the assistant principal's shoes. However, in apparent contradiction with her stated position, this teacher allowed Arthur to take out her high-heeled shoes at dismissal one rainy day and put them in her overshoes for her to change into from her work-a-day oxfords. She took the shoes and put them on without comment, apparently taking a routine action for granted. This incident caused the research team to reconsider the freedom of the children to rummage in her desk and to question whether it bore overtones of the "license" allowed a servant rather than a liberty accorded a respected equal.

The teacher's discussion of the children's home life revealed a contradiction between her actual knowledge of them and her use of common stereotypes about the "culturally deprived." When asked about family sizes she said, "I would say that they are average. Perhaps one or two of the children might be of large families, and the others have just one or two. But, on the average, I would say there are about three or four in a family." However, in the context of discussing motivation, the teacher said, "Mother has so many children that they are lost in the shuffle in most cases. . . ." Similarly, she specifically mentioned seven parents who helped their children and kept track of their work and thirteen others with whom she was in contact; yet, when speaking generally, she referred to the difficulty of reaching the parents. Nor did the fact that she herself was a Negro rescue her from the temptation to fall back on such clichés.

In contrast with other teachers, who in their interviews spoke of wanting the children to "progress intellectually," to "know their strengths and weaknesses," "to develop to the utmost of their ability," and to "like to learn," this teacher saw them as gaining no direct satisfaction from work itself. Instead, she set up a clear dichotomy between learning and enjoyment. Second to learning "discipline" as the result of their schooling, she felt the children should learn there is a time for fun and play and "then there's a time when we should get down to work." She was the only teacher to use what could be a form of learning—copying words from a dictionary—as a form of punishment. She was also the only teacher not to post in some form the names of duties, monitors, or class officers. Instead, this was the classroom wherein one noted a folder containing the names of children receiving free lunch.

Differential Teacher Attitudes Toward the Children

Further contrasts between the middle-income white school and the lower-income Negro school were revealed by material on how the fifth-grade teachers varied in their attitudes and behavior toward the different children in their classrooms. These data were drawn from both interviews and observations. As the basis for assessing the teacher's attitudes, her remarks about each child in the interview were separately collated and rated on a five-point scale for their positive, neutral, or negative feeling-tone.[3] In the classroom observations, each child was identified by name, with the help of a seating plan, and brief profiles of each child's role in the classroom were drawn up for comparison with the teacher's attitudes toward the child, as expressed in the interview, and with the child's status with his classmates, as evidenced by the child-questionnaire. The collation of interview and observation materials on each child was carried out in order to avoid an oversimplified view of the teacher's influence on the group, and to get closer to the several levels at which socialization operates. As has been stated, socialization involves a far more complex pattern of interaction than that between the teacher as a personality and the children as a whole. Interplay of personalities takes place in the context of defined goals and behavioral norms, and each child works out his individual behavior pattern, as he adapts to, identifies with, or rejects the various values that are either stated or implied in the course of ongoing classroom life.

The assumption that ability, achievement, and popularity among both teachers and peers will more clearly reinforce one another in middle-income than in lower-income classrooms was borne out in the two fifth grades under discussion. In the middle-income white school, the children toward whom the teacher felt most positive had an average IQ score some eleven points higher than those toward whom she felt negative. Those toward whom she felt neutral fell in between, although closer to the high than the low scorers. This was not the case in the low-income Negro school. Here *the children about whom the teacher felt positive or neutral had an average IQ score almost ten points lower than those about whom she felt negative* (see Chapter 7, p. 193).

As to "ability" and achievement, the average reading-achievement scores in the middle-income classroom followed the IQ scores, while they did not in the low-income Negro school. In the latter, average reading achievement was the same for the different IQ groups. Although far from being completely culture-free, IQ tests are at least more so than reading-achievement tests, and they indicate the untapped abilities of those more creative and hence often more problematical children who are rebelling against the constrictions of school and society. That they often express the frustration felt by the group as a whole is suggested by a further finding. In the middle-income school the popularity of the better readers and unpopularity of the poorer readers was clear. In the low-income school, however, *it was the slightly better readers with the average IQ who were, as a group, more unpopular than the poorer readers with the higher IQ* (see Table 5-1).

TABLE 5-1

Child Popularity in Relation to
*Reading Achievement and IQ**

School	Sociometric Choice	Number of Children	Average Reading Achievement	Average IQ
Lower-income Negro	3 or more positive choices	7	4.0	93.0
	Not chosen	2	4.3	86.0
	2 or more negative choices	5	4.4	86.0
Middle-income white	3 or more positive choices	12	8.7	120.6
	Not chosen	5	7.9	120.2
	2 or more negative choices	5	7.1	116.6

* It should go without saying that since these are group averages, they show general trends but do not apply to each child. That is, this should not be interpreted to mean that all *better readers are popular in one school and unpopular in another,* but that it is a dominant enough trend to show a contrast in the pattern of social interaction operating in the two environments. (Achievement and IQ scores were supplied by the schools.)

In talking about the Negro children in her classroom, the teacher in the low-income classroom revealed the tendency (common enough, unfortunately) to rely heavily on compliant "co-operative" children and to tangle with those of greater ability whose frustration is presumably leading to rebellion.[4] Murray scored very low on the IQ test, but she said of him with positive affect, "Murray is a well-behaved child, not too good in reading. He gets along with the other children. He's no trouble whatsoever. He's a good boy." On the other hand, her attitude toward Lucille, who scored almost thirty points higher, was negative, and one can see why:

> Now here's a little girl that is very disturbed. She does not want to conform some of the time. I have to treat her with kid gloves, boosting her ego up all the time or she will not do work. She'll just sit there and pout. She's a little fighter. . . . If you don't strike Lucille the right way, she won't work. Sort of on the order of Andrew (also a high scorer on his IQ test, but mediocre in achievement). You have to hit them the right way. . . . If Lucille comes in and you talk to her rough in any manner, she will just say, "Well, I'm not going to. I'm not going to do any work. I don't care."

The teacher's problems with Lucille carried over into her answer about those children in the class who were the least liked. Several of the children she mentioned as disliked were indeed disfavored in the child interview, that is, chosen as children others would not want to sit next to. However, the teacher spoke of disagreements and scrapping with Lucille, and stated that she was one of the least liked children, although the children made no negative choices of her in the interviews.

We should perhaps again emphasize that we do not mean to pinpoint teachers as villains or to hold them responsible as individuals for the poor performance of lower-income children. Nonetheless, they are primary *mediators* of the socialization process. Their behavior must be described to demonstrate how society impinges on growing children, although, as the products of their own training, they are as much the victims of society's problems and limitations as the children. For instance, Corwin writes of the educational system as being "an institution whose function it is to conserve the social order" and goes on to say:

> . . . Persons who expect the schools to eliminate the problems of racial prejudice or religious intolerance ignore the important fact that schools traditionally have been places where such attitudes were reinforced. . . . The schools are a part of society, not apart from it; and as a result, the beliefs of those in control of society find their way into the classroom. . . .[5]

Wrenn writes, "counselors and teachers in general are frequently accused of encouraging conformity, of seeing that students do only what is required." He states this is necessary, but only as a part of the educational process, and continues:

> It is essential to be socialized, to learn systematically what is now known, to build a solid foundation of understanding the present. Such a goal, however, is not an end but the *means to the end* of creating the new and of being oneself. To understand the present and be dissatisfied with it enough to change it, to live as a member of society and yet to develop one's own pattern of being, *is to complete the process* of which present knowledge and socialization are but introductory steps.[6]

This is the ideal and a fine one. In practice, however, it is the unusual individual who has the conviction, understanding, and ability to move beyond the confines of a given institution. We all know well how common it is to start out young and vigorous, with high ideals. Yet it is the extraordinary person who maintains these ideals in the face of resistances and failures that meet the social innovator. It is only to be expected, therefore, that the two teachers we have been discussing would reflect in their attitudes toward their pupils the status system of the society—though, unfortunately, by so doing, they reinforce this system. The teacher in the low-income all-Negro school both reflects and creates the expectation of defeat for the children in her class. She is the teacher whose response to the children's work was negative twice as often as it was positive, and her evaluative remarks addressed to the class as a whole during a three-hour period contrasted sharply with those of the teacher in the middle-income white classroom: "You're not listening," she said, when they did not understand her inadequate explanation. "You need to read desperately," she stated, when reminding them to take their reading home. "It's always the same two or three people that raise their hands," she accused (accurately) when presenting a lifeless and boring lesson. In her interview she saw the children's home life as responsible for poor motivation to work.

In the other classroom, the teacher was working with children most of whom were supposed to be prepared for college entrance. Her lessons were often equally boring and inadequate, but she took herself to task. When asked, "What if they're not paying attention?" she answered,

> If too many children aren't paying attention, that's a message for me. They're either tired or bored or I have exhausted myself. . . . If they're not paying attention because they're not interested, I have to

make myself more interesting. The children are . . . a sort of barom-
eter for me. I have to watch them to see whether I am being interesting enough, or not. If it is complete negligence on their part, then I
will probably call on them to give them more of an interest. . . .

In an attempt to settle down the children who were being noisy, the
teacher addressed the class, "I love the way you're working this morning. I just love it. Your application was perfect. . . . Your oral reading
is good. I want to improve your comprehension." She asked the children to look up comprehension in the dictionary, and said, " 'Understanding,' that's right. That's what we need help with. You all read
beautifully." Later she said, "Good, I'm glad to see your comprehension
reading is improving," and, finally, "It was very nice, children. . . .
Very nice. A commendation for very nice children. I don't want it to
go to your head though. We need to do more work." To performances
not up to par, she said, "Considering the cake sale [held just before the
observation], your reading is good," and, "Well, this was review but
I'm glad we reviewed because many of you children didn't know it."

Teacher Personality and the Socialization Process

One might well argue that the more "positive" teacher style in the
middle-income classroom may simply be a matter of individual personality and unrelated to the children's class position. After all, as one goes
from classroom to classroom in the same school, one observes a wide
variety in the way teachers relate to children. However, the expression
of individual style or personality is always in part defined by the social
context. A woman who expresses one aspect of her personality on Sunday at the beach reveals another aspect when she enters a classroom
Monday morning and assumes the decorum suited to her occupational
role as a teacher. As we have noted several times, teachers will expect
to modify their manners with children, according to whether the school
is in a "good" or "bad" neighborhood and whether the class is "fast" or
"slow." They may see the differences in their behavior as necessitated
by the children's backgrounds, or they may be aware of the role played
by the school and its resources in perpetuating some differences and
creating others. Teachers are seldom aware, however, of the active role
they themselves come to play among the children in reinforcing feelings
of assurance, and expectations of at least moderate success, tying in
with a reasonably positive attitude toward schooling, or, instead, lack
of assurance, suspicion, cynicism, and bitterness.[7]

The manner in which the fifth-grade teacher of the middle-income white classroom expressed her negative attitudes is instructive, since it tallies so well with accepted "middle-class" patterns of behavior. The overt emphasis was always on being "nice." When Ronald dallied at the board, she said, "Ronald, don't you want to do that later?" And again, "Do it later. I want to hear you read. Ronald, *darling*, I want to hear you read. You read so well." And to others, who have not yet come to order, "Richard, I miss you. Where's Arthur, I miss you." This is the classroom in which an observer commented that the teacher tended to compensate for irritation by saying more "nice things."

During the observation periods, the teacher accepted considerable noise as children took advantage of transitions from one subject to another to talk and move around. The impression from reading the record, however, is that this was not real acceptance but resulted from the teacher's fearfulness about really tangling with the children, especially with observers in the room. She was concerned about appearing as accepting as possible and more in control than she was. Behind the scenes, however, a compelling force helped the children set their own limits and not overstep the mark—the threat of nonpromotion. In their questionnaires, as noted in another connection, the children referred to being "put on a list" of those who would not be promoted. Furthermore, in her own account of handling two difficult children, the teacher referred to threatening them—a boy she described as sensitive was threatened with being "put in the hanging closet," and another was threatened with writing his parents about whom she said he was particularly insecure. That these were no more than threats, which in all likelihood would not be carried out, was immaterial in view of the ultimate sanction which pervades the "middle-class" occupational world at all levels—fear of nonpromotion and the blocking of steps toward greater achievement, security, and comfort.

In the second grades in the same schools, we observed similar messages being conveyed to the children, although in different ways by teachers with varying personal styles. The second-grade teacher in the all-Negro lower-income school was warm, motherly, and supportive, a person who showed understanding and sympathy for children who had behavior problems that arose from home difficulties. She spoke of her class as "nice children to work with" and of their maturity, resulting from the home responsibilities which were carried by many of them.

Evaluative remarks in the second grades were generally more positive than in the fifth, and this classroom was no exception. In fact, this teacher's negative remarks related almost entirely to behavior. Nonetheless, her opinion of the children's home experiences and her goals for them were both very low, in keeping with those of the school generally. They pervaded the curriculum in subtle ways. When asked about her program and what she was trying to get across to the children in different areas, the teacher replied that first she wanted to get the children to learn to read. However, asking, "You want me to talk of each area?" she went on to say:

> Well, help, of course, to teach the children to take care of themselves, especially cleanliness. This is a very big problem here. I'm very lucky. The children are pretty clean in this class. Sometimes we discuss, you know, the necessity for changing underwear and not wearing it to bed, and coming in clean and neat. And then good health, the proper foods to eat. . . . And safety, of course . . .

She felt the children were willing, she said, and wanted to do what was right. She hoped they would not end up in the streets, although many teachers felt this was where the children might end after all their efforts. She felt the discrepancy between the material in the readers and the children's own experience was good, since the children's backgrounds were so limited there was little that a reader could be based upon.[8] She saw no contradiction between this statement and her description of the maturing responsibilities the children took on.

In relation to "father figures," she said, "There very seldom is one." Yet a separate survey revealed four of every five children in the classroom were living with their mother and father (or, at least, if one insists on questioning their responses, a "father figure"). Over a half knew both a grandmother and grandfather. In fact several even had a grandparent living with them.[9]

In Chapter 3 we referred to the way this teacher undermined the long and full account of a child's trip to the airport with the inappropriate question, "Who took you?" In the same session, she became caught in a brief but fruitless and embarrassing tangle with a girl who was trying to tell about a trip to the train station to see her father off. She corrected the girl, saying it was her uncle, and when the girl repeated it was her father, the content of the lesson was again sacrificed to inappropriate personal inquiries. The teacher's low opinion of the children's abilities was revealed by her own illustrative example of a lesson in which the discussion moved from airplanes to parachutes to a person being hurt by a 50-cent piece dropped off the Empire State Building. It was the children themselves who were introducing new topics, the teacher indicated, and she told how she pulled the discussion together with a question, "Do you know what this is all about—what we are talking about? One child said, and I was very amazed, gravity. . . ." In this day of TV science fiction to be amazed at a child speaking of gravity is perhaps itself amazing. In any case, this classroom was the prelude to a fifth grade in which the "science" lesson consisted of planting seeds, minus any discussion.

By contrast the teacher in the middle-income white second grade responded affirmatively to the children's accounts of their experiences. Admittedly her response was often excessively "sweet" (her style was startlingly similar to that of the fifth-grade teacher in many respects), with a "how nice," or "how lovely," rather than a serious, meaningful comment. However, she welcomed the children's contributions and included them in her discussion, except in those cases where they did not conform to her own opinions. The response of the children was to become extremely involved in second-guessing the teacher, as the following incident illustrates:

During the spelling lesson the word "fish" was given. "How many don't like fish?" the teacher asked, and scattered hands went up. "Those who like fish stand," she pressed, and most of the class stood up. A few remained seated, however, and she continued, "I'm sorry you are not all standing. I am sorry, since fish is good for you." One of those still sitting slowly slid upward; another sat with her eyes snapping angrily. Somewhat later, the teacher asked the children to list various kinds of fish for their homework. "I hope you will list the fish I like," she said, and the children started to whisper, "Tuna." The whispering rose and the teacher said, "I will tell you tomorrow."

The comparison between the eagerness shown by the children to know even the teacher's tastes, a feature often evidenced in this classroom, and the lack of such interest shown by children in the lower-income all-Negro second grade is informative. Such lack of response from children of poor neighborhoods, familiar and frustrating to many teachers, is all too readily ascribed to lack of interest in learning derived from home backgrounds. In fact, however, this lack of interest and response can be seen as children returning to their teachers exactly what they have been receiving from them.

NOTES

1. W. J. McKeachie, "Student-Centered Versus Instructor-Centered Instruction," *Journal of Educational Psychology*, XLV (1954), 143–150.
2. M. A. Bany and L. V. Johnson, *Classroom Group Behavior, Group Dynamics in Education* (New York: Macmillan, 1964), p. 234. Sexton reports on a summary by John C. Glidewell of research on classrooms as social systems. In Sexton's words, Glidewell and his co-workers on a Social Science Research Council report found that "teachers who are more accepting and democratic tend to affect the social relations of children but not their academic performance." Patricia Cayo Sexton, *The American School, A Sociological Analysis* (Englewood Cliffs, N.J.: Prentice-Hall, 1967), p. 98.
3. Feeling-tone here is distinguished from the content of a remark. A person can talk about some generally positive trait in a disparaging way or a problematical trait with empathy and concern. In order to establish reliability for the ratings, a sample of teacher remarks about twenty-two second-grade children, distributed by school and number of remarks, was rerated. The agreement between the two raters was good: $r = .83$.
4. The assumption that more creative children often rebel against the confines of traditional schooling and become problems to their teachers has been commonly stated. In "The Counselor in a Changing World," Gilbert C. Wrenn summarizes some studies that have yielded positive evidence for the assumption [The Commission on Guidance in American Schools (Washington, D.C.: 1962)].
5. R. G. Corwin, *A Sociology of Education, Emerging Patterns of Class, Status and Power in the Public Schools* (New York: Appleton-Century-Crofts, 1965), pp. 83–84.
6. Wrenn, *op. cit.*, p. 79.
7. For a most insightful discussion of how teachers interpret their classroom problems see Estelle Fuchs, *Teachers Talk: A View from Within Inner City Schools* (New York: Doubleday Anchor, 1969).
8. For an elaboration of this point by the teacher, see Chapter 3, p. 80.
9. Sydelle Sipress, untitled manuscript.

CHAPTER

6

SOCIALIZATION AND EDUCATION IN A "DOUBLE-TRACK" SYSTEM

At the outset, we stated that formal learning was but one aspect of the total socialization process that unfolds during a child's schooling. Indeed, it was perhaps after the broad meaning of "to educate" as listed in Webster—"to bring up a child" or "develop and cultivate mentally or morally"—was becoming replaced by the narrower meaning also listed —"to fit for a calling by systematic instruction"—that a concern with teaching "the whole child" was introduced to restore the full perspective. All too often, however, educational research which aimed to understand the process of "teaching the whole child" focused on the

145

teacher-student relationship in many of its interpersonal aspects, neglecting the full cultural context within which interaction was taking place.

Prior to the emergence of modern Western society, formal education was available only to an elite. It was the development of industrialization, with its need for large numbers of skilled and literate workers, that led to mass education. For example, Napoleon was scarcely a great democrat, yet he recognized it to be in the interest of a strong France for education to be extended beyond the aristocracy and intelligentsia. Schooling remained, however, largely a separate affair for upper and lower classes. Mass education was intended to educate more effective workmen, not to be a channel for upward mobility. If, in the process, it enabled a few of the most gifted to move upward in the social ranks, this was gratuitous, a side benefit.[1]

The democratic ideal has increasingly assumed that an educational system should afford the means for realizing equal opportunity for all. Nonetheless, the structuring of different educational "tracks" persists. In the United States, there is a separate "track" for upper-status groups, whose children attend private schools, while the public schools are a "double-track" system, accommodating most of the burgeoning middle class as well as the "blue-collar" groups. The dream is for public education to enable each individual to realize his potential and prepare himself to find his most useful and congenial niche in society. The reality is the double-track system, blatantly obvious where related to the color line in the South and the focus of increased attention in the North, particularly in the urban centers.

The inequality of education that has recently become a matter of widespread public debate has long been taken for granted by parents anxious to see their children receive the best schooling possible. Children from middle-income areas go to "better" schools or "fast" classes, which feed into special programs in the later elementary or junior high years and into specialized college preparatory high schools. In contrast, urban children in lower-income areas go into poorer schools (or, in heterogeneous neighborhoods, into the "slower" classes in regular schools) which lead into "regular" classes in junior high or separate poorer junior high schools, and they end up in catch-all commercial and vocational high schools where standards are low and drop-out rates high. In rural and smaller urban areas, the physical separation is less clear-cut, but the differentiation of experience for upper- and lower-status children is nonetheless present. There has apparently been little change since Hollingshead documented the class bias running through almost all school activities—not only the academic program, but also in the extracurricular area and the allocation of rewards and punishments.[2]

The most complete documentation of the double-track system in a northern urban center is to be found in Patricia Cayo Sexton's *Education and Income*.[3] Sexton reports both the lower performance of lower-income children and the inequality in their total school experience, housed as they are in older and less adequate buildings (pp. 124–134) and taught more often by uncertified teachers on an "emergency" basis (pp. 117–120). Rather than being overrepresented, they are underrepresented in special remedial reading programs (pp. 33–35) and even more grossly underrepresented in programs for "gifted" children ("gifted" on the basis of IQ tests and the like, pp. 59–60).

This is the reality—a far cry from the dream of equal opportunity through public education. In between the two lies the arena where the personal and political dramas of our society unfold as the dedication of the reformer, the anger of the cheated, and the casual self-interest of the careerist interlock in confused battles. Public protest and debate have led to widespread and varied experimental programs but only to minor reforms. Despite notable successes in a number of situations, budgetary outlays have not been sufficient to bring about significant changes. As each experiment ends, the temporarily lifted morale and heightened interest of both teachers and students wane, and the situation reverts to "normal." Real-estate pressures and status considerations continue to increase the segregation of neighborhoods—by income as well as race—and such plans as there may be for integration in intermediate areas may be rendered obsolete by changing population compositions. Boards of education continue to respond to people of influence, and people in suburban areas continue to resist the expenditure of tax monies on slum-area education in the inner city, while educational budgets continue to be threatened with cuts, not increases.

Parents continue to move out of "deteriorating" areas, when they can afford to do so, in search of greater comfort and better schools, and harassed teachers continue to find it is all they can manage to get through each day. Thus harassed, they either aim for a position in an "easy" middle-class neighborhood or "adjust" to a slum school, adopting tough disciplinary techniques and lowering their expectations for what they try to achieve with the children, a process described in a now-classic study by Becker.[4] It is inevitable that the rationales they adopt to soften their frustration, for the most part, turn against the children; it is difficult for people to take a clear-cut critical or antagonistic stand toward the institution upon which they depend for their livelihood. Instead, they become attuned to the status quo and view with trepidation moves toward greater community responsibility for school affairs in poor neighborhoods.[5]

Institutional structures are buttressed by congeries of habitual acts and acceptable attitudes, through the process whereby people are in part trained and in part self-selected to fit established roles. It is important to restate that although the teacher is focal as the transmitter of her culture in the classroom, *she is not as an individual responsible for its content* but has been carefully fitted for her role. As Spindler writes, teachers "are not selected at random as official culture transmitters; they are trained and accredited to that status and role [since they must] attend teacher-training institutions and graduate with the stamp of approval from the established professional cadre." He continues:

> But professional educational instruction and training consist not only of courses and training in techniques. Every institution with a history and internal organization and a specialized personnel has a culture or, more properly, a subculture. Certain values, symbols, beliefs, and certain basic premises are patterned into the structure and process of the institution. The institutions of professional education—the teacher-training schools and the literature of education—are no exception.[6]

Thus the socialization of teachers starts in their elementary schooling, is carried through to their adult training, and completed as they adapt to their occupational role and to the "culture" of the particular school in which they work. In studying the differential socialization of children, then, we were studying the results of a blend of institutionalized structures and individual adjustments to them.

It was with these considerations in mind that the study schools were selected to represent major social groupings in the public school population. The two major variables, income and race, yielded four different school populations: white children from lower-income homes, Negro children from lower-income homes, white children from middle-income homes, and Negro children from middle-income homes. Schools serving these populations were selected at random since prior knowledge or ready access could have meant a favorable bias on the part of the school administration toward the viewpoint of the Bank Street College of Education.

The sample was selected on the basis of the following data: ethnic composition of New York City schools; the neighborhood income level; the percentage of pupils eligible for free lunch; the degree of school utilization; and average IQ and reading achievement scores. As the basis for selecting sample schools, all those with over 95 per cent white or Negro children were spotted on a map on which income distribution had been plotted as low, middle, or high.[7] Had we been able to increase our sample size, we would have included a school with a majority of Puerto Rican children, representing, as they do, a large and growing proportion of New Yorkers. However, since we could only study four schools with any depth, we dropped from the potential sample all schools with over 15 per cent Puerto Rican children. As further definition to the demographic background for categorization of schools, information on the proportion of Negroes in each census tract from the Special Census of 1957 for New York City and the slum areas indicated in the City Planning Commission Master Plan as "sections containing areas suitable for development and redevelopment" were also indicated on the maps.

An attempt was made to match the Negro and white schools for income level as closely as possible. For this purpose, school lunch data proved helpful, since the number of free lunches served in school relative to the school population has proved a good index of average school income.[8] Eligibility for free lunch, evaluated for each child, is automatic if a family is receiving welfare payments and is otherwise available if income per number of persons in a family does not exceed a certain amount.

Table 6–1 shows the major demographic characteristics of the four study schools. The white school which was first selected turned out to practice "heterogeneous grouping," as compared with the general practice of making up the different classes on a grade to represent different ranges of presumed ability. Classes so selected are widely referred to as either "fast," "middle," or "slow." Since we were studying "middle" classes on the second- and fifth-grade levels, we used this heterogene-

TABLE 6-1
Demographic Characteristics of the Sample Schools

School	Population							Income Level			School Utilization		Average Reading Achievement Scores†	
	Negro		Puerto Rican		"All Other"		Total	Neighborhood	Free Lunch Eligibility				3rd Grade	6th Grade
	No.	%	No.	%	No.	%			No.	%	No.	Degree*		
Lower-income Negro	1,856	87.2	166	7.8	107	5.0	2,129	Low	400	18.8	+745	3-O	2.8	4.6
Lower-income white	210	9.5	165	7.5	1,836	83.0	2,211	Low and some middle	472	21.3	+832	3-O	3.5	—
Middle-income Negro	725	91.2	7	0.9	63	7.9	795	Middle	39	4.9	+114	1-O	3.4	5.5
Middle-income white	8	0.8	0	0	967	99.2	975	High	7	0.7	−187	1-U	4.5	7.7

* U = Underutilized, to first, second, third degree.
  O = Overutilized, to first, second, third degree.

	Utilization Rates
Third (highest) degree of overutilization	Over 150% of capacity
Second degree of overutilization	131 to 150%
First degree of overutilization	111 to 130%
Neutral	91 to 110%
First degree of underutilization	71 to 90%
Second degree of underutilization	51 to 70%
Third degree of underutilization	50% or under

† Third- and fifth-grade scores were used because these were available on a city-wide basis.

ously grouped school for a pilot study to work out and refine our techniques for data collection and preliminary analysis. A second school in the all-white lower-income category was chosen for the core study.

The Middle- and Lower-Income Negro Schools

We have already described contrasting teacher attitudes and practices in the middle-income all-white school and the lower-income all-Negro school with regard to organization of the classroom for leadership and responsibility, and we related this to different patterns of socialization in our society. When the all-Negro lower-income school is compared with its middle-income counterpart, the point is sharpened, for the contrasts are strong and, from the viewpoint of social function, predictable.

The lower-income Negro school was in a run-down neighborhood, one classified for redevelopment, although it did not give an overly congested appearance. With its one-, two-, and three-story attached houses and some trees and parks, its atmosphere was pleasant. The area was mostly residential but contained some small lumber and scrap yards. Forty per cent of the school population—those with the better incomes —lived in two low-cost housing projects. The parents were largely civil servants in the postal service, police force, sanitation department, and transportation. Many of the other families were on relief. The principal of the school stated that he did not feel the neighborhood to be demoralized, citing as evidence the very low breakage of school windows! Since it was chosen to match the all-white school, it was, in fact, at the upper end of the economic range for ghetto schools in the city. The facts of demographic inequality by race being what they are in urban centers, there were no all-white schools at an economic level as low as that of most Negro schools.

The school was built in the 1890's and was scheduled for demolition. It was run down, but the atmosphere in the administrative offices and halls was relaxed and friendly, and the discipline did not appear harsh. The school was extremely overcrowded, although hundreds of children had been transferred to another school at the beginning of the year. The total school population was over 2,000, more than 750 students above capacity. The first grades were on double session, and there were from six to nine classes in each grade, in addition to three CRMD (Children with Retarded Mental Development) classes. The staff was mostly white, and there was a high turnover of both staff and student body, in addition to which children were often shifted from class to class within a grade in accordance with the principle of homogeneous grouping. The principal had three assistants, whose special responsibility was to work closely with the many new teachers. There was an active PTA, consisting mostly of parents from the "fast" classes.

As might be expected, the unequal opportunity that characterizes our society makes middle-income all-Negro schools a rarity. Furthermore, the same social pressures that cause them to be rare just as surely lead to the development of unmistakably middle-class Negro neighborhoods as the only areas into which Negroes who have escaped from the ghetto can move. The middle-income study school was located in such an area, with one- and two-family homes set in small lawns. The neighborhood had been all white in the previous decade, and the first Negroes to enter the community were in professional and other relatively high-status occupational categories. Some of these early newcomers were beginning to move to yet more outlying parts of the city, and, at the time of the study, many of the residents were civil service employees.

The principal of the school had made a strong and highly successful effort to avoid the staff turnover as well as the demoralization and lowering of standards which are commonly allowed to follow a population change from white to Negro in a working-class slum area. What turnover of teachers there had been was normal, and some Negro teachers had replaced white teachers who had retired or taken maternity leave. The school itself, built in the thirties, was cheerful and well kept, with decoratively arranged examples of the children's handiwork greeting the visitor. The building was small, however, and no longer adequate for the student body. The first grade was on two sessions. There was an active PTA chapter, and community organizations used the school as a place to meet.

The atmosphere of the school almost parodied the demands and restrictions placed upon middle-class Negroes—as, indeed, would be necessary in order to prepare Negro children for successful competition in a highly restricted arena. While a teacher in the middle-income white school placed her behavioral demands before the children in the following manner: "I will choose two lovely children to show their book reports to our visitors. I will only choose two of the nicest people, the two with the best self-control," her counterpart in the middle-income Negro school, in lecturing about self-control in the yard, said, "Now you've had many compliments, but I think we need to stop once more and ask, is this the *best* we can do?" To be good, in other words, is never a dependable goal; one must always be *better*!

Situated in a middle-class semi-suburban neighborhood, the school fed into good junior high and high schools. When the rising Negro population caused it to be categorized as deserving of "special services," the principal objected, on the grounds that this would stigmatize the children when competing for entrance into advanced junior high classes. She had instituted a highly organized reading program, and reading levels, which had begun to drop with the turnover, were again on the rise. The cheerful wall decorations, arranged according to the same pattern in all classrooms in the school, the quick and alert chorus of "good morning" to the principal as we were led around to visit, and the almost military precision with which activities were carried on betokened the stringent attempt to keep morale up and prevent any backsliding. The second- and fifth-grade study classrooms reflected the entire school atmosphere, with highly ordered, disciplined, and attentive children, and relatively strict but skillful teachers, whose expectations for academic performance as well as behavior were high. That one teacher was white and one Negro made no difference in this respect.

The marked contrast between this school and that in the lower-income Negro neighborhood (the fifth grade of which was described at some length in the previous chapter) paralleled the different positions in society for which the two groups of children were being socialized. On the one hand, there is the professional or semi-professional Negro, who is constrained constantly to "watch his p's and q's" if he is to be "accepted." On the other hand, there is the unskilled or semi-skilled worker, at best employed in a low-paying but steady job, but for the most part on the fringe of the industrial world, limited to service jobs, semi-employed, or chronically unemployed. The least successful of the former and most successful of the latter obtain the moderately secure position of the civil service worker, with some additional leeway for women in clerical work as well as nursing and teaching.

Different life styles for the two groups have been discussed ever since classics like Davis and Dollard's *Children of Bondage: Negro Personality in the Urban South*[9] and Zorbaugh's *Gold Coast and Slum*[10] were published. Noteworthy among recent contributions have been Franklin Frazier's *Black Bourgeoisie*,[11] for the middle class, and Kenneth Clark's

Dark Ghetto,[12] for the lower class. Both these works, however, stress negative features in great part—the adverse effects of opportunistic self-seeking, on the one hand, and the demoralization of extreme poverty and discrimination, on the other.

The burgeoning literature on working-class Negro life is, on the whole, negative to the point of distortion, conjoined as it is with the theme of "cultural deprivation" as viewed through the sociocentric eyes of middle-class social scientists.[13] Hopelessness, resignation, sullen withdrawal, or angry outbursts, and hungry seizing upon any chance for pleasure or escape: characteristics such as these are expected, observed, and recorded. There is all too little interest in or feeling for quieter (and disquieting) and less dramatic but positive and profoundly human sentiments and coping strengths that come from a common facing of enormous social adversities. In other words, the fullness and variety of lifeways in the ghetto are lost in a stereotype. Hyman Rodman writes, "Characteristics are frequently viewed in a gross manner as, simply, *problems* of the lower class . . . [rather than as] *solutions* of the lower class to problems they face in the social, economic, and perhaps legal and political spheres of life." He gives as an example the one-sided characterization of the Black Muslim movement in terms of segregationist, violent, and primarily anti-white attitudes. "It would be just as easy," he points out, "to refer to their interests in the dignity of the black man, his economic stability, and his moral behavior—including the important stress that they place upon a stable and responsible family." [14]

To return to the lower-income Negro school, it was not what one might think a precursor to a "blackboard jungle" high school should be. Just as at the high school level the overwhelming reality is not a drama of continual rebellion but consists instead of overworked, ineffective, and frustrated teachers and bored, uninterested, and withdrawn children, so in this school the children indicated sheer boredom and a rather admirable patience and tolerance, rather than outbursts of hurt and anger. However, from the teacher's viewpoint, two or three openly rebellious children are all that is needed to command her constant attention and dissipate her energies. Such children dominate the scene, particularly in the "slower" classes in which they are generally placed.

In the study classrooms the children were, on the whole, trying to do what was asked of them. However, as the observers moved from the second to the fifth grade, they were struck by the disappearance of the lively, eager interest and the growing lack of response to the teacher. Part of the reason was the fact that there was little to respond to, as evidenced by the low number of interactions with regard to the curriculum and greater proportion of negative comments about the children's contributions. Table 6–2 gives contrasting figures on teachers' total number of remarks concerning the curriculum addressed to individual children, the interest shown in the curriculum, and the proportion of positive to negative evaluative comments with regard to it, as discussed in Chapters 2 and 3. Contrasts between the lower-income fifth grade in the Negro school and both white and Negro middle-income fifth grades can be seen.

The teachers of the fifth and second grades in the lower-income Negro school, at first impression, did not seem unsupportive of the children. The second-grade teacher was warm and motherly, and the fifth-grade teacher, although somewhat cool and detached, was friendly. The first woman was white, the second was Negro. Both, however, shared a derogatory attitude toward the children and their potentialities as groups. The second-grade teacher denied much of what the children offered from their own experience (as discussed in Chapter 3), although she was sincere and hard-working in her attempts to introduce them to "something better." The fifth-grade teacher, as we have seen, continually derogated and undermined the children's academic contributions. In both classrooms, the children were constantly receiving the message, "You are not going to do very much." They were, in a sense, being taught by hard-working and well-meaning teachers not to learn. In the second grade, the children responded to the learning situation with interest. By the fifth grade, however, the low expectations for their achievement, combined with the lack of challenge in the classroom, had taken their toll. The children fidgeted listlessly, looked distractedly and aimlessly here and there, and waited until something captured their interest.

The researchers were struck by the fact that standards in the low-income Negro classrooms were low for both achievement and behavior. They had assumed that the middle-income schools would stress achievement, and that the lower-income schools would emphasize behavior. Yet it was in the middle-income schools, both Negro and white, that the strictest demands were made. Standards were high for posture,

TABLE 6–2

*Comparisons Among Three Fifth Grades Regarding Curriculum**

	Lower-Income All-Negro School	Middle-Income All-Negro School	Middle-Income All-White School
TEACHER'S STATEMENTS TO INDI-VIDUAL CHILDREN REGARDING CUR-RICULUM			
Total number	82	174 †	174
Average number per child	2.7	4.3 †	4.6
% of remarks on curriculum in relation to total teacher remarks to individual children	44	65	60
TEACHER INTEREST IN CHILDREN'S WORK			
Observation rating	Low	High	Low-medium
Interview rating	Very low	Very high	Medium
Quality	Laconic, even sarcastic	Seemed sincere, though interest expressed in terms of performance ability rather than individual intellectual development	Personal rather than intellectual
EVALUATIVE STATEMENTS TO INDIVIDUAL CHILDREN REGARDING CURRICULUM			
Positive	5	34	28
Negative	15	11	21
Ratio positive to negative	1:3	3:1	4:3
EVALUATIVE STATEMENTS TO GROUP REGARDING CURRICULUM			
Positive	0	1	5
Negative	3	0	1

* *The fifth grade in what was chosen as a low-income all-white school has been omitted from this comparison because its economic class status became ambiguous due to the rezoning and more middle-class composition during the second year of the study when the fifth grades were observed. The figures are based on three hours of classroom observation.*
† *The actual number was 155, observed during periods amounting to 160 minutes. Since one observation was interrupted by a fire drill, the number has been corrected to compensate for the lost twenty minutes, and the average of 3.9 per child corrected to 4.3.*

"self-control," and being "nice," with a variety of favored directives according to the preferences of the individual teacher such as, "Sit tall," "Are our thumbs in the right place?" etc. Behavior is reported as being a primary focus of classroom life in many lower-class schools where there is severe disciplining and punishing of children;[15] however, this is a different matter from setting high behavioral standards for the class-room.

In other words, the goals for conduct and the type of behavior emphasized as either good or bad are quite different in middle- and low-income schools. We have spoken of the stated goal for low-income Negro children as "learning to take orders" or straight discipline—submission as an independent child might see it. This often takes the form of recurrent conflict between the teacher and the several children by whom she is continually plagued, while standards for the other children are relaxed. Such relaxation is not encountered again until one moves up the scale to the private school (or public school in a solidly wealthy area) where the future occupational status and social standing of the children are by and large assured. To make the point most sharply, consider the paradoxical contrast between neatly dressed and scrubbed little boys and little girls in starched dresses, filing out of the "fast class" in the ghetto school, while children of both sexes romp out of the progressive private school in dirty blue jeans. Compared to the exaggerated stress on behavior and control in the more consciously (and necessarily) striving middle-class groups—most strong in the case of the "black bourgeoisie"—the relaxation at *both* ends of the social scale seems pleasant. The drawback is that in one instance it is tied in with acceptance of the children's need for physical freedom, coupled with respect for their potentialities and serious attention to their intellectual development, while, in the other, the relaxed standards are related to lack of respect for the children, and absence of any urgency about preparing them for more than obedience. Although there was a greater acceptance of the children's more idiosyncratic behavior in the lower-income Negro school, it was not in the context of the curriculum that they were allowed leeway for expression of their individuality.

In the middle-income Negro school, although the demands for self-control were exaggerated, and although there was little free play for individual expression, the children were being *taught*. Contrasts between this school and the low-income Negro school were noted by a graduate student teacher after independent review of the study records for the fifth grade. She wrote of the "lack of interest" shown by the teacher in the low-income Negro school and of the fact that it was "not clear whether it is lack of motivation or lack of competence that is responsible for the passivity and dullness of her presentation." She continued, "Though she is allowing the children to 'be' she is also neglecting them and refusing to cultivate and recognize the selves beneath all the activity and busy externalized behavior. She is refusing to relate responsibly to the children as individual people with potentialities and an inner striving for growth and competence." [16]

A systematic comparison of a mathematics lesson in the two Negro fifth grades suggests many ways in which teaching abilities and techniques can be intricately related to goals for and attitudes toward the children's abilities. The following section is quoted from the same study.[17]

> In the way the teacher of [classroom III–5] . . . conducts the arithmetic lessons she communicates much more than methods and principles of arithmetic. She communicates a philosophy about mathematics that puts a primary value on independent thought as the means by which to achieve solutions to problems. This is accomplished in a number of ways: She makes frequent comments that place a value on children's thinking and ideas. She draws the children out in an exploration of multiple methods to solve a problem and only at the end points out the standard and most acceptable way. She carefully emphasizes the adequacy of the alternative methods of solution, thereby rewarding and encouraging the children to think for themselves. In addition to this she is teaching them a principle of . . . thought that relies on "function" or "workability" as the basic criterion to judge the adequacy of any specific method of solving a problem . . . As long as the method of solution which they invent "works" it will be well received. *The teacher, by communicating her attitude that their thinking is of value, also communicates her attitude that they are of value.*
>
> The limiting way the teacher of [classroom I–5] . . . conducts the arithmetic discussions is in marked contrast. "Function" and "workability" are regarded as of little importance. The teacher of [classroom I–5] . . . fastens on particular steps in a solution which become the focus of tortuous attention. Because a certain step is absent the total solution is renounced even though it is perfectly adequate. Moreover, the teacher does not make plain to the children that she expects them to do a problem in the particular way she requires. Therefore they are left with a confused and, we would assume, defeated feeling.[18]
>
> These two teachers differ markedly in other respects in the way they conduct an arithmetic discussion:

The teacher of [classroom III–5] . . . makes frequent accepting remarks. The teacher of [classroom I–5] . . . is very meager in her encouraging remarks.

The teacher of [classroom III–5] . . . conducts the class like a forum, involving the class in a wide participation and minimizing her particular personal relationship to the children. The focus of attention is the work at hand. The teacher of [classroom I–5] . . . does not involve the class as a participating critical body. The children are "called on" to do a problem and the class passively sits by. Her personal reactions get mixed up in the conduct of the lesson. She responds to children's recitations with sarcasm, sternness for minor errors, and she bogs the discussion down on particular niggly points that seem an expression of her own need to emphasize the children's inadequacy.

The teacher of [classroom III–5] . . . consistently and carefully helps children who have difficulty, trying to get them to understand and arrive at an adequate solution themselves. The teacher of [classroom I–5] . . . quickly "gives up" on a particular child who is in difficulty, calling on another to do the problem. She makes no effort to see to it that the first child, who had difficulty, understands.

The teacher of [classroom III–5] . . . protects a child in difficulty from the eager enthusiasm of the class to take over, giving him time and help, communicating to the particular child and to the class in general a standard of fairness and adequate opportunity for each child to work things out for himself. In this way she is communicating a social value and standard of behavior to them, in terms of what she expects of *them*—to give their peers a chance to express themselves. . . .[19] The teacher of [classroom I–5] . . . quickly turns a problem over to a second child when a first is unable to work it out immediately, but in one case she grossly undercuts a child who merely pauses in process of solution and who has expressed her own confidence in her ability to do the problem by the fact that she volunteered. We can only assume that the effect of teacher [classroom I–5] . . . handling of children's hesitancy and difficulty is to undermine their confidence in their own ability to think. Its cumulative effect must surely be to render children insecure and passive. The way the teacher of [classroom III–5] . . . handles similar situations should create in children confidence and security to take a calculated chance.

The teacher of [classroom III–5] . . . uses a thorough technique in presenting material. She reinforces the discussion at each step. For instance, when one child reads the problem to be worked on, she asks another child to explain it. When she senses confusion in the children she stops the discussion to backtrack and go over the steps in solution. The teacher of [classroom I–5] . . . presents problems in confusing and vague language which indicates a lack of thought and analysis. She does not implement, into appropriate action, her insight that the children are confused. She tells them that she knows they are puzzled but she does not follow her statement with a demonstration or explanation.

We have seen then that the teacher of [classroom III–5] . . . is supporting the children in their need to learn and achieve and is carrying on the arithmetic lesson in a way which expresses respect for their individual thinking and effort, and which expresses confidence in their ability to perform and to learn.

The teacher of [classroom I–5] . . . is failing to communicate arithmetic principles and methods in an adequate way. She is letting the children down by not giving them a foundation in arithmetic skills. At each step of the way her teaching is diluted by an intrusion of her own personality. She is not focused clearly on the work at hand. Moreover, in her specific responses to children, and in the way she handles them in situations of difficulty, she is expressing not only a lack of interest in their development but a lack of respect for their efforts, and a lack of confidence in their capacities.

There is, however, another side to the picture, as the report of the study indicates:

When we look at general classroom atmosphere in the two classes, we see that [classroom III–5] . . . is conducted in an atmosphere of almost total control which is the framework set by teacher [classroom III–5] . . . for the accomplishment of serious and concentrated work. Children are not allowed to wiggle in their seats. They are directed in a continual series of work sessions and discussions, moving from one subject to another, with no more break than standing up. The teacher achieves this control by (1) inhibiting the slightest expressions of individuality; (2) being direct, decisive, consistent, and clear in her disciplinary expectations; (3) being generous of her approval and energy in the way she conducts their academic life.

In spite of the fact that the children seem *adapted* to the particular framework of control that this teacher projects, their school life and the total learning situation are limited in important dimensions. The children have no real opportunity to relate to their peers. There is almost no interaction between children in [classroom III–5]. . . . There is a total of only 31 child-child interactions recorded in [three hours of] observations, and of these 22 *are teacher structured,* that is, set up and controlled by the teacher. (An example of such an interaction is the contact that ensues when one child is appointed teacher surrogate and calls on another child.) There are a total of *only nine child interactions* in the classroom records which are not structured by the teacher. Furthermore, these nine interactions are limited. Most of them consist of a quick remark, or a glance across the room. If children talk to one another it is about work. Thus children emerge in [classroom III–5] . . . almost entirely through participation in academic discussion. Contact between them is limited and rare and the children are not seen in significant expressive activity.[19]

The implications of these facts are that the children in [classroom III–5] . . . are valued for their capacity, energy, and integrity in a work situation but they are not accepted as social and emotional beings. The goal-directed, work-oriented environment of this classroom rejects the variations of specific individuals. There is no room for acceptance by any other means than academic work. The environment pares individuals down to a conformity of behavior and purpose which presumably only some children find natural and compatible. We wonder what adjustments those children are making who have no avenue of expression, no means of getting attention and approval, of making themselves known and felt. They have no way of evoking a response from their school world and they apparently have not even the comfort of a relationship with their peers.

In contrast to [classroom III–5] . . . we see in [classroom I–5] . . . that while the children are being "let down" in their intellectual development and are being seriously and consistently undermined when they contact the teacher in a relationship, that because of the casual, disinterested way the teacher carries on the classroom life, children are allowed to "be," to move about the room, jitterbug, chatter to friends, and laugh. Contrasting with the meager *nine* child-child interactions reported for [classroom III–5] . . . , there are 49 child-child interactions reported for [classroom I–5]. . . . (While there are 22 teacher-structured child interactions in [classroom III–5] . . . , there are only three teacher-structured child interactions in [classroom I–5]. . . .) These interactions are not structured by the teacher and many of these contacts are prolonged and involved. Thus, though the children in [classroom I–5] . . . are not learning very much in school and have a problematical adult to deal with in relationships, they are not being impressed into a system which puts clamps and inhibitions into their personal lives. Though the teacher is not helping them to learn, she is not reaching down and stopping the sources of life in the children that make it possible for them to respond, to experiment, to have confident intimate reactions to experience and to each other. Though she is not deliberate in allowing children this freedom, there is some way in which she is allied to them as "free-selves." There is a connection between the indulgence and freedom of expression that she allows herself and the freedom of expression that she allows the children. . . .

Another graduate student, working independently with the study data, contrasted the classrooms in almost the same terms, although she dealt with different aspects of the curriculum.[20]

> In [classroom I–5] . . . there is a much wider range of response [than in classroom III–5] to the classroom situation, although the differences pertain more to personality shadings on a passive-aggressive spectrum than to intellectual functioning.
>
> A low degree of verbalization is common to all the responses, and provides the sharpest contrast to the performance in [classroom III–5]. . . . Most answers are a few words (whereas in [classroom III–5] . . . they were lengthy explanations), and often ungrammatical. The fact that the children are more expansive in their answers to the child questionnaire is a partial clue . . . to the fact that the abbreviated verbalization is not natural to them. The remaining clue is that the teacher does not provide for any other kind of response. Her questions are intended to elicit key words or phrases, not extended sentences. Furthermore, she does not explore anything but the surface of the content. For example, in her presentation of graphs she demonstrates a typically inadequate explanation:
>
> T: "Today in arithmetic we're going to work with graphs. Who can tell me what a graph is? Have any of you seen a graph?"
>
> There is hardly any reaction from the class. The teacher then says, "Today I can't hear you. Some days it's the opposite way around."
>
> ALFRED: "It has lines."
>
> T: "Yes, it's used for attendance."
>
> FRANKLIN: "It's like a puzzle."
>
> T: "It's like a puzzle, he says."
>
> T sends a child to get a newspaper, saying, "We don't know what a graph is." She opens to a page with a graph, so small that the class can hardly see—she has not brought in a good one. "Now do you see what a graph is like? What is it like? What does it do?" She calls on Alfred.
>
> Alfred mumbles something which can't be heard.
>
> T: "It gives you a picture of something you're interested in. Suppose you wanted to know the temperature . . . ," and she proceeds to demonstrate which parts of the graph are used for degrees, days of the week. . . .
>
> The absence of intellectual differentiation and articulation is balanced by the high degree of personality difference that comes through in [classroom I–5]. . . . This is in sharpest contrast to the static picture that emerges from [classroom III–5]. . . . It comes through most clearly in physical movement, child interaction, and distinct relationships with the teacher. In [classroom III–5] . . . , the teacher

relates more or less uniformly to the children. Her classroom structure reinforces this. She instructs the class as one group rather than separate smaller groups. She generally keeps the children poised in a rapid question-and-answer routine. The focus is always on the content. In the lower-income classroom, the structure is much looser. The teacher has many silent work periods following a lesson. The children are given more freedom to wander about, converse with other children, and come up to the teacher individually. . . .

[Classroom I–5] . . . is more relaxed than [classroom III–5] . . . but there is less continuity . . . [classroom III–5] . . . is very directed but there is no time for spontaneous flow and interaction, or a kind of speculation that leads to integration and insight. In her remarks about each child [collated from the interviews], the teacher of [classroom I–5] . . . talks almost solely about the child's social adjustment (his relation to other children, herself, and classroom discipline) and almost not at all about his intellectual functioning. In her remarks on Daniel, the child who has the highest teacher rating, she mentions his likableness and his appearance—nothing about his academic performance.

Again, in her stated goals and ideas of education, the lower-income class teacher gives much less importance to content and sophisticated psychological insights than does the middle-income teacher. The middle-income class teacher talks about the parents' role in building self-control in a child; the lower-income teacher says she thinks the rod is the solution. . . . The middle-income teacher talks about levels of comprehension, analysis, and verbalization . . . ; the lower-income teacher speaks in much simpler terms: "These (reading and arithmetic) are my two main subjects. I feel that the others will fall into place."

Further Comparisons Among the Schools

From the viewpoint of socialization, the two white study schools also revealed a match between expectations and goals held for the children and the style of interaction being encouraged, on the one hand, and general patterns of middle- and lower-class life, on the other. An effort was made to match the Negro and white middle-income schools, which meant choosing a modest white school at the lower end of the middle-income range. The middle-income school selected (IV) was in a rather old but well-kept residential community, with one- and two-family houses and some apartment buildings, old and new. The neighborhood had the reputation of being the "nearest nice neighborhood to Manhattan," and there was apparently considerable population turnover since people moved into the apartment houses as "jumping-off" places for homes farther out. Residents were mostly business and professional people, with some white-collar workers and a scattering lower on the occupational scale. It was not unusual for mothers to be working. The population included many ethnic groups, the largest of which was Jewish, and many children attended afternoon Yeshiva.

The school was built in the middle twenties and was in good condition. It was small, with a little under 1,000 students, and was operating nearly 200 below capacity, with some classrooms standing empty. The staff was well trained and virtually permanent, even including the so-called "substitute" teachers. There was a waiting list of teachers who wished to transfer to the school. Although the turnover among the student body was quite high, the school maintained a high rate of achievement, and half the sixth-graders went on to "special" junior high classes. Parents were actively involved in the PTA, and as individuals concerned with the educational future of their children, many would bring considerable pressure to bear upon the teachers, the principal, and his assistant. Attendance at grade conferences was always close to 100 per cent.

The lower-income white school (II) was in a semiresidential area of some run-down tenements but mostly low attached dwellings, and small factories and machine shops. The area also included a middle-income section with well-kept brick houses on individual plots and some new housing projects, both low- and middle-income. Despite the middle-income projects, the percentage of school families receiving public assistance was still high, and one-fifth of the children were eligible for free lunch. The neighborhood was heterogeneous, the largest ethnic group being Jewish, the next Italian. There were some Negroes and increasing numbers of Puerto Ricans. As it turned out, the school district was "having its face lifted," through a combination of housing developments and rezoning. Therefore the fifth grade, which we studied in the year following our study of the second grade, had a more "middle-class" character than the second. Both were less working class in composition than the school used for the pilot study because of its practice of "heterogeneous" grouping.

The five-story school building was erected in the early twenties. It was nicely painted and kept inside but greatly overcrowded, having doubled its number of classes in five years. All classes except those for mentally deficient children were on double sessions. Turnover was high, with two-fifths of the student body either admitted or discharged within a year. The teaching staff, however, was relatively stable, with few transfers. Changes were due to maternity leaves, retirement, the growth of the school, and the reduction of the 100 per cent regular staff to meet an official requirement.[21] The teachers were expected to take on a great many administrative duties, however, including toileting, dismissal, lunch, etc. Such administrative details were necessarily an important concern of the principal and his four assistants in a school of about 2,200 students which was built to hold only about 1,400. There was an active PTA, consisting mostly of middle-income parents.

We have already referred to the style of interchange in the middle-income all-white fifth grade as being similar to that of the "organization man," initially described by William Whyte and elaborated upon in subsequent social science literature. The neighborhood Whyte described was in a suburban area with a more assured middle-class status than the urban area in which the study school was located. In his chapter on the "organization children" and their school, he mentioned the generally "permissive" attitude of the teachers, by comparison with the somewhat greater controls which we observed. Yet there are marked similarities between the two middle-income schools which set both off against the Negro lower-income study school. For instance, Whyte stated that the "student group is encouraged to take a strong hand in the planning of what they are to be taught," although they "are not exactly put in charge," [22] a statement which suggests the stress placed by the teacher on *partial* responsibility. One study teacher felt it most important that the child should "sit there with the feeling that he is the leader," although she had her book open and allowed nothing to "slip by" her. We have already noted the contrast between this concern with training the children for a certain responsibility and the concern with teaching the children to respond to adult commands expressed by the teacher in the lower-income Negro school, although she herself was not particularly authoritarian and, in fact, allowed considerable independent and random activity to take place in her classroom.

The character of the initiative called for in the middle-income white school (as discussed in detail in the previous chapter) is clarified by points of similarity between it and the "organization society" analyzed by Robert Presthus.[23] Presthus discussed the "weblike pattern of culture, family, and individual," each acting upon and reinforcing the other, so that

> . . . successive authority relationships that begin in childhood . . . continue throughout one's life [and] culminate in a "self-system" that normally includes a *generalized* deference toward authority.[24]

Along with authority and status, Presthus sees small groups as central to bureaucratic structure. The "organization" is, in fact, composed of many small groups, and

> . . . for the individual, this subunit becomes *the organization,* since his work and his life chances are bound up with it. He may develop considerable loyalty to it, regarding other groups as competitors. He will probably form close personal ties with some of his fellow workers. . . .[25]

The grade in the school, the classroom on the grade, the committee in the classroom—these are prototypes of the divisions, departments, and work groups in the organization. In their relations with the teacher, and more remotely with the principal and other school personnel, the students are learning modes of interaction which lay the foundation for work relations in later life. It is in this context that the contrast between the structuring of the work situation in the middle-income white school and in the lower-income Negro school takes on its full significance. The committee structure of the fifth grade in the middle-income white school, with its emphasis on a partial leadership, involving responsibility coupled with a fine sense of when it is appropriate to defer to authority, parallels the pattern of relations on professional or administrative levels of organization; whereas the basically authoritarian (albeit, in this case, benignly so) structure of the fifth grade in the lower-income Negro school parallels the organization of work relations in the factory. It is in the latter classroom that the smooth cooperation and initiative shown by the children are not taken advantage of in the work situation. Only teacher-student interchange and evaluation, but no student interchange, followed committee reports.

Presthus makes an interesting comparison between small group functioning among factory workers and skilled technicians. He describes several studies in which severe criticism was heaped on operators who either exceeded normal production rates ("rate-busters" and "speed-kings") or fell too far below ("chiselers"). "Compliance in organizations is thus encouraged by small group sanctions," Presthus states, but they "vary considerably according to the situation." Ridicule, censure, "even blows," would be resorted to in the factory situation, whereas "in organizations engaged in highly technical work requiring considerable education and training . . . , sanctions are rather more Machiavellian. . . ." [26] It is interesting that the teacher in the middle-income white classroom achieved control at least in part through a technique not mentioned by her but reported by the children—the threat of a "list," presumably of those not to be promoted, on which they might be put.

The middle-income all-Negro school has already been mentioned as socializing the children for a particularly competitive niche in society. Success for a Negro in professional or administrative life not only demands ability and competence in the area concerned, but the constant attention to impeccability of behavior (to which we have referred) and a fine sensitivity about not overstepping unwritten (and unacknowledged, but unmistakable) social requisites for dealing with colleagues and superiors. Negroes know they must be wary of deep-seated and often unexplored attitudes of superiority in their white counterparts, to whom they must show subtle deference if they are not to be considered as "having a chip on their shoulder" and being "overaggressive" or otherwise "difficult to get along with." Furthermore, middle-rank positions may occasionally be accorded to Negroes, but channels to full leadership are generally closed.

With this in mind, the structuring of teacher-student relations in the middle-income Negro school is instructive. Leadership is formally assigned but devoid of real responsibility. It is in the second grade of this school that the teacher says officers head the lines "and get to sit on the stage in the auditorium." In both second and fifth grades, the teacher structures her relations with the children and their relations with each other to a greater degree than in any of the other schools. In the second grade, speaking out is reprimanded, and whispering is seldom tolerated. The teacher said she used to allow talking during snack times but decided it was better to read the children a story. Monitorial duties are restricted and not allowed to become a basis for interaction. Children were even called up row by row to throw out milk containers at snack time. Yet the teacher felt she had not achieved her goal of "complete discipline." The emphasis on control, however, was tied in with high goals for academic achievement, an expectation that the children would learn. The teacher was capable, a good technician, and the children's accomplishments gave her real satisfaction.

In her interview, the fifth-grade teacher stressed independence and teaching the children to "stand on their own two feet" as goals. This was the teacher who said she domineered the classroom too much, but who spoke of the difficulty of doing otherwise since the class was so large. She spoke of allotting various responsibilities. Her classroom, as observed, however, allowed little leeway for children to show responsible initiative. Monitors' duties were so limited that their tasks did not become the basis for interaction. Here, too, monitors took materials from the teacher to be given to one pupil in each row to be passed back. Class leaders functioned in a purely formal way and were constantly superseded by the teacher. Some working together was allowed but not through formal committees. Little was not directed or restricted in the classroom. When the teacher lectured the children on their yard behavior, she said they had received good reports but could they not still do better? The teacher did, however, give the children responsibilities directly related to the curriculum, such as handling money for the Red Cross—this was "real math," she felt. She felt the children could learn from each other and structured for class interchange very skillfully, although always through herself. Her expectations for the children were high, her tasks demanding, and she favored those children who worked very hard or had shown marked improvement.

Style of Teacher-Student Relations and the Curriculum

What is the relation between the socialization patterns we have been discussing and *teaching* in the strict sense? Statistically, schools in lower-income neighborhoods are inferior with regard to the adequacy of the plant and experience of the teachers; standards are lower, and the curriculum is sparser. However, this by no means implies that teachers are uniformly better in middle-income schools. In our study they were not. As it happened, the better teachers, when evaluated along the lines discussed in Chapter 2, were in the middle-income Negro and lower-income white schools, while the poorer teachers were in the middle-income white and lower-income Negro schools. Yet a poorer teacher in a "good" school was more successful in her classroom than one in a "poor" school. The sheer level and richness of curriculum content in the fifth grade in the better school meant the children were being exposed to more, although the teacher's ability to explicate the material was limited. The children were being taught more, in a narrow sense, although they were not necessarily being taught *better*. They were responding to the higher standards and the higher expectations. But how? What does this mean? What we have been trying to reveal is the way a pervasive atmosphere, stemming from the very structure of our society, expressed in the organization of the school system and embodied in the teacher's assumptions about different groups of children, adversely affects the teacher-student relationship and the teaching function. Of the many ways that doubtless exist, we have explored three which have made themselves sharply evident in our material: (1) derogation of children through negative evaluation of their work; (2) negation of the children through failure to respect contributions offered from their own experience; and (3) relating to the children in ways that prepare them for subordinate social roles in which they are not expected to show initiative or take responsibility.

We have described in detail the derogatory style of the teacher in the lower-income Negro fifth grade. While the number of her negative remarks with regard to behavior as well as school work was not particularly high, and while she was not unfriendly with the children, the ratio of negative to positive evaluative comments on their work far exceeded that of other teachers. Following this through, we saw how she expressed attitudes in her interview that threw light on the way she made the children appear responsible for her own failure to be clear in her arithmetic session. In contrast, the teacher in the middle-income fifth-grade classroom, when inadequate in an arithmetic session, was hypocritical, but not derogatory; she bored and confused the children, but she did not *blame* them in the same way.

We have also spoken of the fact that failing to respect children means one does not involve their experiences in the curriculum, and examples were given from discussions on transportation. In the middle-income white classrooms, the teachers dealt with what the children said directly or, if they were not really listening, would at least make supportive, accepting comments. In the lower-income Negro school, when one adds to the cutting-off of or otherwise nullifying a child's proffered experiences, the negation of his very being in texts and materials, and the constant (albeit well-meant) correction of his grammar and syntax, one can only ask how strong a child would it take not to get the message that what he has to say is worthless and to feel an increasing reluctance to say more than the necessary minimum.

People who are familiar with really demoralized schools, where children do not learn because the teacher-student relation has degenerated into a direct pitched battle and children are hit, yelled at, threatened, and shut in closets, might feel that all this is somewhat precious. However, to explore the limitations of relatively benign classrooms reveals some of the reasons why so many concerned and motivated teachers continue to fail, and why introducing social heterogeneity into a school or classroom, without corresponding teacher retraining, falls so far short of what is needed.

So far we have focused on the inequalities in schooling which it is the first responsibility of a school system, which is theoretically committed to equal opportunity, to correct. As to what the children bring, it is perfectly obvious that the sheer time, space, and materials available in working-class homes are not equal to those available to middle-class children. This is quite different from saying, however, that the children are not ready, willing, and eager to learn; it is quite different from assuming lack of parental aspirations, an assumption that any number of studies have contradicted.[27] The findings of a study comparing the kindergarten performances of children from successful Head Start programs with matched groups of children without benefit of such experience give one pause. With good kindergarten teachers, the Head Start children did better; with poor kindergarten teaching they did, not the same, and not just slightly better, but worse.[28] The very success of their prior training unfitted them for the reality of school life. They still showed greater "readiness for learning," however. One can only assume it would not last long.

But what about the children? How do they see school? What are their attitudes toward their work and their teachers? How does school fit in with their expectations, as they phrase them, for their future lives? What is the nature of the interplay between school and community in their lives? These questions will form the focus for the next chapter.

NOTES

1. R. L. Pounds and J. R. Bryner, *The School in American Society* (New York: Macmillan, 1959), Chapter 3.
2. A. B. Hollingshead, *Elmtown's Youth* (Part III, New York: John Wiley, 1949). Hollingshead's findings were systematically tested in six urban and suburban areas in New England, New York, and Pennsylvania; social status was found to correlate with receiving rewards in terms of academic marks and prizes, classroom favors, and student office holding. See S. Abrahamson, "School Rewards and Social Class Status," *Ohio State University Education Research Bulletin*, XXXI (1952), 8–15. Later studies are summarized by Patricia Cayo Sexton, *The American School, A Sociological Approach* (Englewood Cliffs, N.J.: Prentice-Hall, 1967), pp. 54–55.
3. New York: Viking Press, 1961. Various surveys have documented similar patterns in other major cities: Pittsburgh Board of Public Education, *The Quest for Racial Equality in the Pittsburgh Public Schools* (Pittsburgh, Pa.: 1965); Robert J. Havighurst, *The Public Schools of Chicago* (Chicago: Board of Education, 1964); Fels Institute of Local and State Government, *Special Education and Fiscal Requirements of Urban School Districts in Pennsylvania* (Philadelphia: 1965); Massachusetts State Advisory Committee to the U.S. Commission on Civil Rights, *Report on Racial Imbalance in the Boston Public Schools* (Boston: 1965). According to the U.S. Office of Education report, *Equality of Educational Opportunity* (Washington, D.C.: U.S. Government Printing Office, 1966), the so-called "Coleman Report," regional variations in unequal school facilities exceed those for racial or ethnic minorities. However, Harold Howe, II, U.S. Commissioner of Education, writing in *The New York Times Annual Education Review* (January 11, 1967), pointed out that ". . . 'average' is a tricky notion, often concealing more than it conveys. In New York's case, for example, the school district with the highest expenditure per pupil spent almost seven times as much as the district with the lowest. Such inequities . . . characterize every state in the Union. . . . Typically in our schools we spend less on the child who comes to school with a disadvantage and more on the fortunate youngster. . . ."
4. H. S. Becker, "The Career of the Chicago Public Schoolteacher," *American Journal of Sociology*, LVII (1952), 470–477. That the situation remains substantially unchanged is implicit in the myriad programs to broaden teacher attitudes and the failure along these lines reported by the President's National Advisory Council on the Education of Disadvantaged Children.
5. The varying reactions to community control of school affairs were exemplified by the responses to New York City's decentralization plan

developed by the Mayor's Advisory Panel on Decentralization of the
New York City Schools (McGeorge Bundy, Chairman) in the report
Reconnection for Learning (New York: 1967).

6. G. D. Spindler, "The Transmission of American Culture," *Education
and Culture* (New York: Holt, Rinehart and Winston, 1963), p. 156.

7. For materials on the ethnic breakdown of New York City elementary
schools in 1958, we are indebted to the Bureau of Housing, under
Frances A. Turner, and the Office of Budgetary Statistics of the Board
of Education. Unfortunately, racially and economically homogeneous
school populations are easier to find than heterogeneous schools, and
really balanced schools (those within 40:60 proportion of white and Negro children) are extremely rare. The "Allen Report" of 1964 stated: "We
must conclude that nothing undertaken by the New York City Board of
Education since 1954, and nothing proposed since 1963, has contributed
or will contribute in any meaningful degree to desegregating the public
schools of the city. Each past effort, each current plan, and each projected proposal is either not aimed at reducing segregation or is developed in too limited a fashion to stimulate even slight progress toward
desegregation" [*Desegregating the Public Schools of New York City*,
report prepared for the Board of Education of the City of New York by
the State Education Commissioner's Advisory Committee on Human
Relations and Community Tensions (May 12, 1964)]. According to *The
New York Times Annual Education Review* (January 12, 1968), desegregation gains have been so minimal as not to have kept up with the
growth of the school population. Before the 1954 Supreme Court decision, there were 2.2 million Negro children in all-Negro public schools
throughout the country; by 1968 there were 2.5 million.

Income data for neighborhoods were taken from the New York
Market Analysis of Population and Housing for New York City and
Suburbs, compiled by The New York Mirror, News Syndicate Company, Inc., and The New York Times Company, based primarily on
the 1950 Census of Population and Housing. A "low" income was under
$3,000; "middle" was from $3,000 to $5,000; and "upper" was above
$5,000. Some specific zones have changed in New York City since that
time, but the pattern of demographically homogeneous zones, which
is critical to patterns of differential schooling, has changed not at all.

8. For data on the School Lunch Program, we are indebted to the Elementary School Division of the Bureau of School Lunches, Board of
Education, New York City.

9. Washington, D.C.: American Council on Education, 1940.

10. Chicago: University of Chicago Press, 1929.

11. New York: The Free Press of Glencoe, 1957.

12. New York: Harper & Row, 1965.

13. In a review of some of this literature, Charles Valentine refers to the
"well-nigh tyrannical power of the association between poverty and

pathology in the minds of social scientists concerned with understanding their own social system" [Charles A. Valentine, *Culture and Poverty, Critique and Counter-Proposals* (Chicago: University of Chicago Press, 1968), p. 120].

14. "Middle-Class Misconceptions About Lower-Class Families," in A. B. Shostak and W. Gomberg, eds., *Blue-Collar World, Studies of the American Worker* (Englewood Cliffs, N.J.: Prentice-Hall, 1964), pp. 61, 65.

15. As most fully documented in J. Kozol's *Death at an Early Age: The Destruction of the Hearts and Minds of Negro Children in the Boston Public Schools* (Boston: Houghton Mifflin, 1967). See also Kenneth Clark, *Dark Ghetto, Dilemmas of Social Power* (New York: Harper & Row, 1965), pp. 134–136.

16. J. Sloman, "Teacher Values, Teaching Techniques and Style of Classroom Management in Two Fifth Grades," Master's essay (New York: Bank Street College of Education, 1962), p. 85.

17. *Ibid.*, pp. 75–82.

18. Italics added.

19. Italics in the original.

20. M. Newfield, "A Comparative Study of Fifth Grade Children Selected from a Lower and Middle Income Negro School," Master's essay (New York: Bank Street College of Education, 1965), pp. 62–65. It might be stressed that Miss Sloman and Miss Newfield worked entirely independently of each other; they did not know each other, and never met in the course of the study.

21. As a move toward equalizing staff teaching experience in higher- and lower-income neighborhoods, no school could have more than 80 per cent regular—that is, nonsubstitute—teaching staff.

22. W. H. Whyte, Jr., *The Organization Man* (New York: Simon and Schuster, 1956), p. 384.

23. R. Presthus, *The Organizational Society, An Analysis and a Theory* (New York: Random House, 1965).

24. *Ibid.*, p. 144 (italics in the original). Presthus also wrote: "Success now requires extended university training, and such training is the prerogative of middle-class families who employ child-rearing practices that give their children the inside track by emphasizing striving, punctuality, and the suppression of unprofitable emotions. These attributes prove functional in big organizations, now the main sources of status and prestige. As a result, those who possess these attributes assume power and replace themselves with men who reflect their own image. In such ways the socialization process is tuned to the organization's demands for consistency, conformity, and the muting of conflict" (pp. 133–134).

25. *Ibid.*, pp. 156–157 (italics in the original). The group leader finds himself in an ambiguous position, according to Presthus: "Here, the

ambiguity of goals in organizations may be seen. To retain his position and preserve the hope of future rewards, each subleader must honor organizational values and at the same time retain the loyalty of his own group by defending their interests against competitors within the system and against neglect by the elite. Although he is torn between such conflicting demands, his own career is in the hands of his superiors, and we can assume that he will give priority to their claims. They will measure him by the loyalty, dispatch, and affirmation with which he carries out their policies. Thus the price that the subleader pays for marginal power and great expectations is loyalty upward" (p. 139).

26. *Ibid.*, pp. 161–162.
27. T. V. Purcell, "The Hopes of Negro Workers for Their Children," in Shostak and Gomberg, eds., *op. cit.*, pp. 144–154.
28. M. Wolff and A. Stein, "Six Months Later, A Comparison of Children Who Had Head Start, Summer, 1965, with their Classmates in Kindergarten, A Case Study of the Kindergartens in Four Public Elementary Schools, New York City," Office of Economic Opportunity Project, 141–61, Study I, sponsored by Ferkauf Graduate School of Education (New York: Yeshiva University, 1966), mimeographed. See also *The New York Times*, Sunday, October 23, 1966, p. 1.

C H A P T E R

7

CLASSROOM GOALS FROM THE CHILDREN'S POINT OF VIEW

In a brief interview, each child was asked a number of short direct questions about his school experience, such as, "Suppose tomorrow someone told you it was up to you as to whether you wanted to go to school any more? What would you do?" "Why?" and, "Do you think you'd miss anything if you didn't go?" They were questioned about the kinds of things children do that made their teacher happy, the kinds of things the teacher did not like, and what she did about both. They were also asked simple questions about their occupational goals, their school work, and their friends and classmates. Examples of the last topic were: "If you could choose all by yourself, which child in the class would you

175

like best to sit next to?" "What children in class don't you particularly like?" "How come?" "What kind of things do children in your class do that annoy you most?" [1] The interviewers were well aware that answers to questions such as these would be influenced by the children's desire to say the right thing to someone who, despite assertions to the contrary, would doubtless be identified with their school. This was no drawback, however, since a major aim of the questionnaire was precisely to find out what the children thought the "right things" to be, that is, how they defined the expectations their teachers and their schools held for them.

Interviews were distributed across classrooms as follows:[2]

	NO. INTERVIEWED	NO. IN CLASS
Second Grade:		
Lower-income Negro	23	30
Lower-income white	22	28
Middle-income Negro	34	36
Middle-income white	29	32
TOTAL	108	126
Fifth Grade:		
Lower-income Negro	26	30
Lower-income white	32	34
Middle-income Negro	38	40
Middle-income white	36	38
TOTAL	132	142

The deliberately vague and open-ended phrasing of many questions afforded the children the opportunity to interpret them freely. This allowed the researchers to ascertain the extent to which children interpreted school-related or teacher-defined goals in terms of behavior rather than academic performance, how they defined standards for behavior, and whether academic performance was seen as a matter of simply meeting more or less arbitrary requirements, or whether some feeling for *true learning or understanding* might be involved. As analysis proceeded, it soon became apparent that responses to the questionnaire related as often to the school differences we have noted as to the children's presumed home and neighborhood experiences.

The set of questions pertaining to peer relations was subjected to further analysis in an effort to explore relations between teacher attitudes and child responses. Patterns of response were compared both with observational material on classroom interactions among the children and with children favored or disfavored by the teacher in her interview or through her distribution of praise or criticism in the classroom. The aim was to explore the relation between teacher attitudes and child responses by comparing the children's perception of the goals for their behavior with those the teacher either stated directly or implied through her treatment of them.

The Children's Views of Their Adult Roles

On the whole, school is a fixed factor for young children to be attended without regard for any present or future satisfaction it may offer. Thus, to the question as to whether they would go to school if they did not have to, most of the study children replied, yes, they would. They replied also that school would help them to become what they wanted to be when they grew up. School-to-school differences occurred, however, both in the adult roles they projected in answer to the question, "What do you think you'd like to be when you grow up?" and in their picture of the way in which school would help in the attainment of these roles.

Social-class differences appeared in the occupations named by the children. Even at the second-grade level, they had some generalized picture of the occupational status hierarchy and of their position within it.[3]

As Table 7–1 indicates, this hierarchy is more clearly differentiated for boys than girls. The majority of girls in all schools chose the culturally defined female roles of teacher or nurse, which would be a step up for low-income groups and, in middle-income groups, would defer to the class-linked occupational role of a husband. The only girl in the four second-grade classes to opt for professional status was in the middle-income white school, while in the fifth grade, several such choices were from the middle-income white and Negro schools. Conversely, none of the sales, service, and factory choices came from the white middle-income school, while nine were made in the lower-income Negro and white schools and three were in the second-grade middle-income Negro school. Of the 117 girls answering the questionnaire, only four chose to interpret what they would like "to be" as wife, mother, or housewife.

Nine out of fifteen second-grade boys and fourteen out of twenty fifth-grade boys answered the question in terms of professional occupations or, in two instances, business, in the middle-income white

TABLE 7-1

Children's Responses to "What Do You Think You'd Like To Be When You Grow Up?"

	Low-Income Negro				Low-Income White				Middle-Income Negro				Middle-Income White			
	2nd Grade		5th Grade		2nd Grade		5th Grade		2nd Grade		5th Grade		2nd Grade		5th Grade	
	Boys	Girls	Boys	Girls	Boys	Girls	Boys	Girls	Boys	Girls	Boys	Girls	Boys	Girls	Boys	Girls
No.:	10	13	11	15	12	10	17	15	18	16	20	18	15	14	20	16
Professional and artist	2	0	2	0	0	0	10	0	3	0	9	5	9	1	14	2
Clerical, teacher, nurse	0	12	0	10	0	6	2	10	0	10	0	9	0	11	2	11
Sales, service, factory	1	1	6	4	4	3	0	1	4	3	4	0	1	0	2	0
Public service, armed forces	6	0	2	0	8	0	4	0	8	0	7	0	2	0	1	0
Wife, mother, housewife	0	0	0	1	0	1	0	1	0	0	0	1	0	0	0	0
Other	1	0	1	0	0	0	1	1	2	2	0	2	3	1	1	3
No answer	0	0	0	0	0	0	0	2	1	1	0	1	0	1	0	0

school. In contrast, there were but two "doctor" choices and two "artist" choices in the lower-income Negro school. By the fifth grade, the seven-year-old boy's "policeman-fireman-soldier" answer gave way to sales, factory, or construction occupations in this latter school, while in the middle-income Negro school considerable professional choices appeared. The rise that can be seen in the table for professional choices by the fifth grade in the lower-income white school did not simply reflect age or greater chances for white children, but instead the changing class composition of the neighborhood. As aforementioned, the building of middle-income projects plus the rezoning of the school district were moving this school into a more middle-class category, and the differences in it between the year we worked in the second grade and the following year when we worked with the fifth grade were noticeable.

Both in their projection of future roles and in their ideas as to how school would help achieve these roles, the children were, of course, still too far from the adult world for their answers to be taken literally. Nonetheless, there were important variations in the relative specificity and appropriateness of the pictures the children held of the connection between their schooling and their later lives. By the fifth grade the majority of the children responded that school would help them toward a given occupation through teaching them various subjects and through preparing them for further education, with college clearly

*References to Learning as Preparation for Future Occupations**

Second Grade:
   Lower-income Negro: Learn, read, write, print, draw, listen
   Lower-income white: Learn, read, write, words, spell, math, show books
   Middle-income Negro: Learn, read, write, words, spell, numbers, count, draw, build, watch, listen
   Middle-income white: Learn, read, write, spell, math, science, "learn about space, earth, sun, humidity," draw

Fifth Grade:
   Lower-income Negro: Learn, read, spell, math, count, sew, draw, build, sing
   Lower-income white: Learn, read, write, math, algebra, add, subtract, divide, figures, figuring problems, shorthand
   Middle-income Negro: Learn, read, write, spell, math, science, anatomy, social studies, art
   Middle-income white: Language, words, math, figures, decimals, fractions, add, anatomy, "understand and know the world," "share ideas," typing

* *Answers on behavior, etc., are omitted.*

stated as a goal by many children. This is in keeping with studies that have shown college to be a stated aim for many working-class as well as middle-class families.[4] However, there were variations by income in the specificity of references to subjects learned as preparation for further training and future occupations. What is significant here is that the answers suggest that this specificity reflects the different school experiences we have been describing as much as it does the different home backgrounds.

As noted earlier, most of the study children replied affirmatively when asked whether they would go to school if they did not have to. In analyzing the reasons they gave in answer to the question "Why?" clear differences appeared in variety and specificity of responses from second to fifth grade and from school to school. Part of the broader range might follow from the slightly larger number of children responding, but this increase would be far from accounting for the whole:

Second Grade (all answers):
   Low-income Negro: Like school, learn, reading, writing, drawing
   Low-income white: Like school, learn, writing, drawing, homework, get a job when grow up
   Middle-income Negro: Like school, learn, reading, writing, miss work, playing, learn to be good, like teacher, want to go to college, want to be doctor or scientist
   Middle-income white: Like school, learn, writing, spelling, arithmetic, science, social studies, painting, drawing, get education, keeps me busy, friends, like work, mother makes me, be dunce without college, without it I'd be stupid, learn things for hard job

Fifth Grade (all answers):
   Low-income Negro: Like school, learn, reading, writing, get education, not be dumb, learn to be right, learn to play with others, mother wants it, be teacher or nurse, "they'd look back in my files and I wouldn't have anything on my school record"
   Low- (and middle-) income white: Like school, learn, reading, writing, mathematics, get an education, not be stupid, be smart, be able to help kids with their work, college, study to be lawyer or doctor, for marines, for business, earn lots of money when a man, make a living, pass tests for jobs, "without education whole world would collapse," manage finances and go to bank, for my future
   Middle-income Negro: Like school, learn, reading, spelling, mathematics, social studies, social conversation, interesting things in school, get an education, won't be dumb, to be doctor, to be school teacher, to be something, get a good job, learn—go to college—get all those nice jobs, go around the world, "don't want to miss what parents missed—be better in certain things," "school is good for children," classmates
   Middle-income white: Like school, learn, better education, not be dumb cluck, college diploma to get job, get into good business, be doctor, biologist, college, have to support family—better jobs, "want to be a scientist—don't want the

Russians to get ahead of us," "put it to use when I get older," "to answer my kids' questions when I grow up and not look stupid," "in school they keep you busy," "it's interesting—if you don't learn to read, you'd have a useless life," "love to read, love science and nature," have nice teacher—play together, "if I didn't, I'd get a hammer over my head, from my father" (and, for the answer as to why would *not* go to school if the choice was there, "two words —I'm lazy!").

In addition to the increasing explicitness of answers with increasing age and income level, there begin to be suggestions that work can be useful, interesting, and self-fulfilling as well as remunerative. Here one is touching on part of what is often implied by the loose ascription, "middle-class values." The assumption has often been that faulty communication between teachers and students from low-income homes follows from the "lower-class values" of these children, who have difficulty with the "middle-class values" of teacher and school. It has been our contention that this is a vast oversimplification of the case, and that the school is, in fact, not presenting "middle-class" values to working-class children unless this is interpreted to refer specifically to the "middle-class " views of the teacher toward "lower-class" children whose role in society is seen as restricted. In other words, the school is conveying *a middle-class image of how working-class children are and how they should be*—an image which emphasizes obedience, respect, and conscientiousness as desirable, rather than ability, responsibility, and initiative, and which expects deviance to be unruliness with regard to behavior and apathy with regard to curriculum. It is our further contention that through projection of this image upon the children, teachers help perpetuate the very behavior they decry.

As an illustration of this differential interpretation of and response to behavior, consider a situation in a fifth-grade middle-income white school not included in the study. On the basis of a disagreement with the teacher, the children "went on strike" and refused to participate in their mathematics lesson. Before any such incident would have taken place in a "slum school," potential leaders ("troublemakers") would have been identified and isolated in one way or another, if necessary with the support of the principal. In this instance, however, given the relatively high status of the children's parents in this particular neighborhood, the last thing the teacher wished was that the principal or parents should hear that her class had been out of control. She begged the children to cooperate, and, having sufficiently asserted themselves, they eventually did. Thus the response of the teacher to unruly behavior implied that it could be accepted and corrected (albeit deplored), whereas in a low-income classroom far less defiant actions are commonly responded to as innate and incomprehensible intransigence on the part of the children.

Children's Attitude to Work in Relation to Their School Experience

In order to see how the children perceived expectations for their behavior, they were asked what their teachers liked and disliked and what the teacher "did about it." In all the classrooms, children saw their teachers as being more concerned about good or bad behavior than academic work and performance. From 12 to 32 per cent of the second-grade children mentioned good work among the things that made their teachers happy, while from 73 to 88 per cent mentioned good behavior. In the fifth grade, more children referred to work (56 to 69 per cent), even though the range of responses dealing with behavior (65 to 88 per cent) was similar to that of the second grade (see Table 7–2).

The emphasis on behavior was even sharper when the children were asked what their teacher disliked. One suspects that questions about what the teacher likes draw the more formal answers—the parallel to the teacher's overtly stated goals in the classroom—while questions about her dislikes draw responses about those actions which, in fact, make the children fearful of drawing her active displeasure. While from 69 to 77 per cent of the second-graders included some mention of behavior in their answers, only from 3 to 35 per cent included references to work. For fifth-graders, the answers on behavior run from 87 to 96 per cent and on work from 4 to 33 per cent. Even these percentages give the teacher the benefit of the doubt. References to what are essentially work-related routines, rather than actual work achievements, are included in the work category, which would decrease even more if they were dropped out.

Educational ideologies hold that the maintenance of discipline should be a means to academic learning and not an end in itself. However, the effort put into enforcing discipline and "proper" behavior in the study classrooms was such that the children saw this area as the more salient for teacher approval and disapproval. Other writers have considered the structure of the school as an institution and have com-

TABLE 7-2

Work Versus Behavior Responses to What Does and Does Not Make the Teacher Happy

	Behavior*		Work*		Number
	No.	%	No.	%	Interviewed
Low-income Negro school					
Second grade					
Teacher likes	19	76	8	32	
Teacher dislikes	16	69	2	9	23
Fifth grade					
Teacher likes	17	65	18	69	
Teacher dislikes	25	96	1	4	26
Low-income white school					
Second grade					
Teacher likes	16	73	5	23	
Teacher dislikes	17	76	3	14	22
Fifth grade					
Teacher likes	25	78	18	56	
Teacher dislikes	28	88	4	12	32
Middle-income Negro school					
Second grade					
Teacher likes	30	87	4	12	
Teacher dislikes	26	77	1	3	34
Fifth grade					
Teacher likes	25	66	25	66	
Teacher dislikes	33	87	11	29	38
Middle-income white school					
Second grade					
Teacher likes	25	88	7	24	
Teacher dislikes	20	70	10	35	29
Fifth grade					
Teacher likes	28	88	24	68	
Teacher dislikes	34	94	12	33	36

* *Totals exceed 100 per cent since a child's answer that mentioned both work and behavior was counted twice. A common practice of using the first response only and not counting the rest was not felt to be appropriate for present purposes.*

mented on the fact that its custodial nature is in constant conflict with its professed educational function.[5]

Children's responses on teacher likes and dislikes reflected the pattern which was found in our observations and which deviated from our original expectations—the strong emphasis on behavior as well as work in the middle-income classrooms when compared with the low-income classrooms. The negative sanction against poor work in the middle-income Negro and white fifth grades was more strongly felt than in the low-income classrooms (29 and 33 per cent mentioned teacher disliking poor work, in comparison with 4 and 12 per cent). It was also more strongly felt in the middle-income white second grade than in the others (35 per cent mentioned teacher disliking poor work, in comparison with 3, 9, and 14 per cent). However, the stronger sanction against poor work did not mean a dropping off in the perception of a strong negative sanction against bad behavior in these classrooms. (Eighty-seven and 94 per cent of middle-income fifth-grade children mentioned the teacher disliking bad behavior, which is the same as the 88 and 96 per cent of low-income fifth-grade children who answered similarly. For second grades, the figures are 70 and 77 per cent in middle-income classrooms, and 69 and 76 per cent in low-income classrooms.)

Thus the children's responses further emphasized the inadequacy of our initial assumption that greater emphasis on work would involve lesser emphasis on behavior and vice versa, and that classrooms could be evaluated in terms of their relative stress on one as compared with the other. Instead of a greater or lesser emphasis on behavior as such, it was the *qualitative definition of behavior* which was significant. The differences in definitions of behavior which emerged from the child questionnaires paralleled those which were observed in the classrooms, and it was easy to match the children's reports with their counterpart in the teacher-interview and observational material. The second-grade children in the more "permissive" low-income classrooms spoke of such things as sitting quietly and being good as pleasing the teacher and "not hollering," "doing what told," "listening," "not making the teacher scream." In the middle-income Negro classroom, where formal and rigid behavior was stressed (behavior required for successful competition in a highly critical white society), there were ten explicit mentions, out of thirty-four answers, of sitting or standing "up tall." In the white middle-income second grade, there were eight mentions, out of twenty-nine answers, to "self-control" which was stressed in the classroom and which is part and parcel of the training for an authoritative social role.

Good peer relations were referred to as pleasing the teacher by several children in the fifth-grade middle-income white classroom. They stated she was happy when "we get along with other children," when "we are good sportsmen—when we lose, some of the kids start to cry," and when "we try to help everybody . . . [and are] courteous to each other." In another fifth grade, "getting along with each other" was mentioned by one child but, apart from an idiosyncratic answer, "when they aren't afraid to dance with a girl," there were no mentions of good peer relations as pleasing the teacher in the other fifth grades or in any of the second grades. There were but one or two mentions of friends in most classrooms, or none at all, in response to the question about what a child would miss if he did not go to school. However, four children in the middle-income Negro fifth-grade classroom and six in the middle-income white fifth grade spoke of missing friends or social life.

Although answers about peer relations are so few as to be suggestive rather than definitive, they afford a good example of the way in which school-defined goals can tie in with neighborhood social patterns and the way they reinforce one another; this contrasts with the view that sees the school as simply responding to independent neighborhood differences. In a middle-income school there is more likelihood for a child to have visiting relations out of school with some of his school "colleagues" than in a low-income school. Parents have more time and facilities for and interest in the children's social life in and out of the classroom. In the middle-income neighborhood, there are parties for school friends and acquaintanceship with other parents through the PTA, in contrast with the low-income neighborhood, where friends are necessarily on the block or at least nearby, and where they are not as likely to be in the same classroom, given the greater number of classrooms in a grade in the larger low-income schools. The structuring of the learning situation to involve closer peer relations in a middle-income classroom can both use and strengthen existing social patterns.

The marked variations in the degree and extent to which children refer to work in their answers about what the teacher likes or dislikes are illustrated graphically in the following compilation. As can be seen, in the fifth-grade middle-income classrooms there is (1) an increasing explicitness in the references to subject matter, (2) more references, not just to completing work, but to its correctness and to doing extra work, and (3) the emergence of references to attitudes toward work. The fact that the children are here reporting what they see their teachers to be asking of them casts new light on the commonly held assumption that a presumably greater motivation for success in school among middle-class children derives solely from their home backgrounds. An examination of their content shows the children's answers to reflect the kinds of practices which were observed in the classroom and discussed in the teacher interviews. On the whole, the children are apparently repeating what their teachers have said or done, rather than expressing

Verbatim References to Work in Responses to What Does and Does Not Make the Teacher Happy

1. *"What kinds of things do children do that make your teacher particularly happy?"*

Second Grade

LOW-INCOME NEGRO	LOW-INCOME WHITE	MIDDLE-INCOME NEGRO	MIDDLE-INCOME WHITE
Do work	Do work in spare time	Take something out to do	Read in class library
Listen, watch	Write story by self	Doing work right	Nice drawing
Reading	Color lightly like T says	Read	Take time on drawing
Good when you write	Do extra work	Know things	Good work habits
Read quiet	Write, read nice		Learn work
Reading, studying			Good work
Finish work, know how to read			Good work, good painting
Jane reads and writes			Work good
			Work quietly

Fifth Grade

LOW-INCOME NEGRO	LOW-INCOME WHITE	MIDDLE-INCOME NEGRO	MIDDLE-INCOME WHITE
Do arithmetic right	Do homework	When finished with work, get book and read, math, reading, social studies, spelling	Do our work quietly
Do their work (2)	Do the work (2)	When T busy try to do things you don't know; pronounce a word	Finish assignments
Work by themselves	Do work the T likes	Do good work, busy when visitor comes in	Study as soon as get into room
Draw something pretty	Answer questions	Do things without her standing over you, keep busy when she talking to someone	Do work fast and quietly, think about problems for while, just don't put any answer down that comes to our head
Draw, hear Sarah talk because she comes from South, write	Turn out work at right time	Reading to yourself	Finish working
Stand up and answer her	Work good, don't talk while doing lessons	Art, drawing, drawing maps	Do our work (2)
Drawing, read, write	When you get 100 on papers, write neatly		Try to do school work when they just don't rush, smile when they work and happy and enjoying it
Draw, write	Do work quietly, homework in		
When somebody knows how to pronounce a big word	Do your work good, catch up		
Draw a calendar, draw Uncle Ben, arithmetic	Learn what she teaches us		
	T comes in and sees us studying		

LOW-INCOME NEGRO	LOW-INCOME WHITE	MIDDLE-INCOME NEGRO	MIDDLE-INCOME WHITE
Know how to read, compositions	math or social studies, good marks	Bringing in extra homework, bringing in current events	When T says something wrong like she has the wrong date and children raise hands or walk up and tell her
Arithmetic, spelling, social studies	Do good on tests	Don't make sounds when work, listen, and read to selves when she writes on board	
Penmanship, writing, good speech at all times	Read silently		Do homework, good writing, good oral reading
Drawings	Do extra homework, write neat, get better, do something for science, book report	When talking to visitor, get out book	Bring in extra work, bring buzzer or bell to show
Write to authors, nice work, bring in homework and current events	Work a lot and do all homework	Good homework, extra work, bring in articles, stamps, countries	Do math good
Ask children to find out something and they do it	Bring in science projects and book reports, make up plays	Bring current events	Work very well
Not talk when supposed to work; good mark in arithmetic	Algebra, read, spelling, songs	Lucia draws nice, brings in things she doesn't ask for, Edward can do math very fast	Learn things
	Math paper right, do math or spelling tests neatly		Have special committees and special reports they weren't required to
	Work like math, reading, social studies	Bring in current events, study social studies well, get prepared for the reading	When reading and stop and talk about something very good, do lessons good, math good
		When finish a story, she asks question and you tell her right meaning and main idea	Study, work hard
		Have all their homework	Work well, good speech, work nicely, write nicely
		When they raise their hands	Do math or something she likes us to get all right
		Do their work and finish	
		When T talking to parent, take out books and read, do arithmetic when she is busy	Answer questions correctly
		When she is out of room and no one talks, gets reported, do our work	Write well, speak well, do math right, do homework
		Drawing and writing nicely	Do math right, spelling and reading, stomach all their work and the committee gets A+
		Know the answers to questions	

1. *"What kinds of things do children do that make your teacher particularly happy?"* (cont'd)

LOW-INCOME NEGRO	LOW-INCOME WHITE	MIDDLE-INCOME NEGRO	MIDDLE-INCOME WHITE
		Fifth Grade (cont'd)	
		Bring in a lot of current events, news from papers, maps and things When they do good work	

2. *"What kinds of things do children do that your teacher doesn't particularly like?"*

Second Grade

LOW-INCOME NEGRO	LOW-INCOME WHITE	MIDDLE-INCOME NEGRO	MIDDLE-INCOME WHITE
When they're happy and stand around doing nothing, put heads on desks When draw When write on blackboard when not supposed to	Run to get library book Let book fall and mess them up Not wait for T to finish at board before beginning work	Bad, don't do homework	Not learning and listening, not doing spelling right Talk too much, poor drawings Not good, poor work, run around asking questions they should know Boy broke someone's glasses, finish in a hurry Talk to children working Get half finished, not do work expected, then ask for more Talk too much, tell others answers Talk or sit when should be doing something Do reading, drawing at wrong times Say what's on the board is wrong when it's right

LOW-INCOME NEGRO	LOW-INCOME WHITE	MIDDLE-INCOME NEGRO	MIDDLE-INCOME WHITE
			Hurry, work not good, do nothing
			Talk, laugh, rush to T, hurry through work
			Coming to T, annoying, not good work, hurrying, half finish
			Not mind, don't do work, fool around

Fifth Grade

LOW-INCOME NEGRO	LOW-INCOME WHITE	MIDDLE-INCOME NEGRO	MIDDLE-INCOME WHITE
Get up and walk around, talk and not do work	Don't get an example right	Don't do work	Not doing work (2)
	Not do any work	Don't bring in homework (2)	Not doing homework, not completing work (2)
	Don't do their work	Don't finish their work	Do our lessons very bad
	Don't turn in work at right time	Talk when work to do	Try to get away with the homework
		Don't get book	Do work sloppily, talk in between work
		Disturb other people	Don't finish our work, don't put headings on paper, don't dot our "i's" and cross our "t's" or put a period at the end of a sentence
		Bother other people, yell out loud when she asks somebody else a question	Copy, annoy other children while they're working
		Having to ask other children what the work is, not bringing in neat work	Not get good marks on math test
		When we do math and she calls someone for the answer and they yell out	Don't do work properly, don't do it on time, and on tests get all examples wrong
			Don't understand work T explained 3 or 4 times

their own attitudes. For example, the middle-income white fifth-grade references to speaking up and engaging in good discussion, correcting the teacher, and pausing to think about a problem before answering are recognizable as characteristic of that classroom. The few references to work that occurred in response to the question, "What does school teach you about how you should act?" also reflect classroom differences. In the low-income fifth grades these took the form of not interrupting or talking when someone else had the floor. A child in the middle-income Negro fifth grade said, "Not to talk and how to be quiet—when you first start school, you can't sit still for a long time and work by yourself." An equally explicit remark from a white middle-income fifth-grader was, "If somebody talks to you, don't answer back unless it's to get what assignment they missed or something," and a classmate's answer, unique for this question, was, "Always know your facts."

Contrasts among the classrooms with regard to the emphasis on work were even sharper in answer to what the teacher did *not* like. Here the second-grade middle-income white classroom and both fifth-grade middle-income classrooms stood out, with considerably more references to poor work. As a corollary, in the question about how the teacher acted when she did not like something, there were no mentions of bad marks in either of the low-income Negro classrooms, while in the other classrooms from 19 to 41 per cent of the children made some reference to grades, conduct marks, or report cards. The weight of threatened negative sanction was little felt for poor work in the former classrooms but strongly felt in the middle-income fifth grades and the white middle-income second grade. Again, one could argue that this was differential perception on the part of the children, according to their previously held value scheme if the interview material did not tally so well with the classrooms as observed. As a humorous example, one child in the middle-income white second grade sagely answered that when his teacher was displeased by a child, she "pretended to put 'U' on the report card."

In short, the children's accounts of how the teacher rewarded and punished closely paralleled and in some cases filled out the picture of the teachers' classroom management techniques (discussed in Chapter 4). To be sure, the picture given by the children is more lively than that observed, with teachers "hollering" and "screaming" and getting red in the face. One would expect a teacher not to lose her temper with observers present and would assume that she did at other times. However, there were only two specific practices mentioned by the children which were not recorded in the classroom observation or teacher interview or which might not have readily been inferred from these materials, and these fitted the comparative picture of differential controls and expectations we have been presenting. They were the threatening "list" for nonpromotion, supposedly kept by the middle-income white fifth-grade teacher, and hitting as a form of punishment in the low-income Negro fifth grade.

In response to the question, "What would you like to do in school that you don't do now?" the children's stated desires for more and harder work increased with income level:

| | Second Grades | | Fifth Grades | |
	NO. OF CHILDREN MENTIONING WORK	% OF RESPONDENTS	NO. OF CHILDREN MENTIONING WORK	% OF RESPONDENTS
Low-income Negro	5	22	7	27
Low-income white	3	14	6	19
Middle-income Negro	8	26	17	45
Middle-income white	8	28	18	53

In all classrooms, however, and in the fifth grades as much as the second, the responses of the children reflected their reaction to the restrictions of the school day. Some 50 per cent or more of the children in every class expressed the desirability of more time for pleasant activities such as gym and various kinds of games, art, music and craft activities, and school trips. References to the desirability of academic activities were as follows, with most answers implying a child would like more of a subject already given:

Second Grade:
  Low-income Negro: Read, write, number work, "read books that James reads"
  Low-income white: Real writing, number work, learn mathematics, homework
  Middle-income Negro: Read, write, write like third-graders, write stories (3 responses), arithmetic
  Middle-income white: "Read for fun," more math, homework, spelling harder words (3 responses), "arithmetic where don't have to write," geography, history, science, "study big reptiles like dinosaurs"

Fifth Grade:
  Low-income Negro: "Individualized reading" (actually the system in this class), write, "easy arithmetic," more science, do arithmetic and spelling better, do work better, "work all the time—write to authors"

Low-income white: Lot of math, science (2), social studies (2), French, algebra, "get ahead in my work"

Middle-income Negro: Reading, math, spelling, French, Spanish, science, social studies, "a book with paper that I could write stories in," "be good in math," "catch up in math," "take general course," "get a higher reader and learn higher math and do what sixth grade do," "study geology and astronomy," "engineering, electric shop and woodwork shop," nursing

Middle-income white: Math, algebra, social studies, language (5 responses, including some French, some Spanish, some simply language), spelling, chemistry, "harder work," "find out about dinosaurs," "spelling bees—learn more from them," "sixth-grade math or higher subjects," "more nature working with animals"

Relations Among Teacher Attitudes, Sociometric Preferences, and Achievement

Other questions showed the same "fit" between the children's answers and observed differences in teaching, classroom management practices, and teachers' expressions of goals and expectations. Questions about the children's attitudes toward their peers indicated the way the children accepted teacher goals and attitudes as they tried to please her. They were asked what their classmates did that annoyed them, whom they would like to sit next to in class, and whom they did not like and why. As might be expected, 50 per cent or more answers to the question as to what annoyed a child concerned noise, talking, fighting, and teasing of one kind or another. The number of answers that referred explicitly to disturbing work varied from classroom to classroom as follows:

	Second Grade		Fifth Grade	
	NO.	%	NO.	%
Low-income Negro	5	22	3	11
Low-income white	9	40	8	25
Middle-income Negro	4	12	7	18
Middle-income white	9	31	12	33

These figures have to be considered in relation to how much confusion and disruption of work was in fact allowed in a classroom. In the second grades, the frequency of responses varied from the relatively low percentage in the highly controlled middle-income Negro classroom, through the somewhat less controlled classes to the highest percentage in the most "permissive" setting. By the fifth grade, however, differentially perceived goals entered in, for while degree of control may have contributed in part to the relatively low percentage in the highly disciplined middle-income Negro classroom, it cannot account for the considerable difference between the low-income Negro and middle-income white classes. Furthermore, answers in the former referred only to talking going on while a child was working; in the latter they also referred to another child looking at one's work and copying, to talking during tests and, in a unique reply, to making "fun of me because I'm not so good at math." The fact that there is a slightly greater variation in the second grade than in the fifth grade in the low-income Negro school is interesting. Mentions of copying and of "noise disturbing the speed of work" occur in the second grade. The number of answers involved are far too small to make the variation significant in any technical sense, but the trend is suggestive of the widening gap between the classrooms with respect to academic goals as the children move up the grades.

Variations from second to fifth grades in the pattern of sociometric choices, that is, preferred and disliked children, conformed to the findings of other studies in that fifth-grade positive choices were directed toward a wider range of children than were second-grade choices. Studies of classroom favorites typically show "stars" in the lower grades, with more stereotyped answers directed toward a few children, in contrast with greater individual selectivity by the fifth grade and a "clique" pattern or two or three definable clusters surrounded by a periphery of less popular children and "isolates." Variations among the study classrooms in the present case, however, were suggestive of other differences across social groups (see Table 7–3).

Children could give several choices to the question which children they "did not particularly like," or they could answer "no one," and in all classrooms they found it easier to make positive than negative choices. This was the more true in the second grades and particularly in the Negro classrooms. In the fifth grades, negative choices increased considerably, but less in the low-income Negro classroom than in the others. They averaged little more than one choice for every two children, while in the other classrooms they were about one per child. Positive choices, in part due to their greater number, were wider ranging than negative. In the second grades they were wider ranging in the low-income schools, with the star pattern most pronounced in the white middle-income classroom.

The sociometric questions put to the children were placed in the classroom context: "What child would you like best to sit next to?" and

TABLE 7–3

Patterns of Sociometric Choice

	Average No. Positive	Choices per Child Negative	% Children Chosen Positive	Negative
Low-income Negro school				
Second grade	1.6	0.5	62	20
Fifth grade	1.7	0.6	87	33
Low-income white school				
Second grade	1.5	0.7	71	43
Fifth grade	2.0	1.0	82	21
Middle-income Negro school				
Second grade	1.9	0.4	53	38
Fifth grade	1.8	1.0	67	42
Middle-income white school				
Second grade	1.5	0.7	44	30
Fifth grade	2.0	1.0	76	45

"Who would you choose next?" Sociometric questions may be phrased in terms of accompanying a friend to a movie, inviting a friend home, and so on, but our purpose was to stay close to the school situation and examine school-related goals and attitudes toward peers. The assumption has been that the clash of "values" leads to a lower-class pattern of peer alliance vis-à-vis the teacher by contrast with the greater identification of middle-class children with the middle-class teacher. We have questioned the simplistic formula of "value clash" and have examined the role played by the teacher in the influencing of children's motivations and identifications. Therefore, the questions raised by the sociometric material were: who were the favored and disfavored children; to what extent did choices seem independent of teacher preference; or to what extent did they mirror her attitudes?

The rating of the affect shown by the teachers in their descriptions of individual children was described in Chapter 5. The distribution of these ratings for the fifth grades was as follows:[6]

	Low-income Negro	Low-income white	Middle-income Negro	Middle-income white
Very positive	1	1	2	2
Mildly positive	7	10	5	10
Neutral	7	12	18	25
Mildly negative	11	9	11	1
Very negative	4	1	3	0

As can be seen, the teachers' evalutions of the children parallel the children's status as groups in the eyes of society, with Negro lower than white, low-income lower than middle-income. Nor can the more negative teacher attitudes expressed toward the Negro children be considered a result of simple race prejudice, for both of the teachers in these classrooms were themselves Negro women.

Not only was there a general downgrading of Negro and low-income children, but it was directed more sharply toward the *more* able children in these groups. As stated in Chapter 5, the teacher-favored children in the middle-income white fifth grade had an average IQ score that was eleven points higher than those toward whom the teacher felt negative, while in the low-income Negro fifth grade those about whom the teacher felt positive or neutral had an average IQ score that was almost ten points lower than those toward whom she felt negative. Given this situation, an alliance of peers might well follow from a defensive attempt on the part of low-income children to preserve their self-respect. In the middle-income white fifth grade, there was a meshing of teacher and peer favor, ability and achievement; the better readers were more popular with the other children than the poorer readers who were more unpopular. In the low-income Negro fifth grade, the better readers with average IQ's, or those children who were presumably the more school achievement oriented, were more unpopular than the mediocre readers with higher IQ's, or the more able but nonconforming children.

The following figures show teacher affect ratings viewed in relation to reading achievement and IQ in the middle-income white and low-income Negro fifth grades:

	Teacher Rating	Number of Children	Average Reading Achievement	Average IQ
Low-income Negro:	Positive	8	4.3	84.4
	Neutral	7	4.0	84.2
	Negative	15	4.1	93.2
Middle-income white:	Positive	12	8.4	122.8
	Neutral	19	8.7	118.3
	Negative	7	7.0	111.7

These figures dramatically indicate the effect of the teacher's negativism toward the presumably more able children in the low-income

Negro classroom. Despite an average IQ almost ten points higher than that of the positively and neutrally viewed children, scores of the negatively viewed children averaged slightly lower on reading achievement. This is in marked contrast with the positive correlation between IQ and reading achievement in the middle-income white classrooms.[7]

A study by Rosenthal and Jacobson, which focused directly on the effects of positive teacher expectations on children's performance, reinforces some of our own conclusions about the significance of teacher attitudes.[8] Rosenthal and Jacobson found that children who were, in fact, randomly chosen but who were believed by their teachers to be potential "spurters" who would show considerable gain during the academic year, did on the whole make greater gains than their classmates. The teachers also described these children more favorably in relation to their disposition, curiosity, and chance for success in life. The gains were particularly marked in the first and second grades, then tapered off, and, interestingly enough, did not affect the fifth grade, where child roles were presumably more firmly established, until the second year of the study.

When Rosenthal and Jacobson inquired more closely into teacher attitudes and children's performance, they found *an unfavorable response to children who progressed when they were not expected to.* They comment, "It would seem that there are hazards in unpredicted intellectual growth." Where this unfavorable response to intellectual growth was most marked, however, was in the "slow-track" classrooms in a school which was attended by some middle-income children but mostly by low-income children, including Mexican-American families and families on welfare. Rosenthal and Jacobson write:

> When these "slow-track" children were in the control group, where little intellectual gain was expected of them, they were rated more unfavorably by their teachers if they did show gains in IQ. The more they gained, the more unfavorably they were rated. Even when the slow-track children were in the experimental group, where greater intellectual gains were expected of them, they were not rated as favorably with respect to their control-group peers as were the children of the high track and the medium track. Evidently it is likely to be difficult for a slow-track child, even if his IQ is rising, to be seen by his teacher as well adjusted and as a potentially successful student.[9]

The authors speak of the need for more research into the nature of teacher-child interaction and the means by which a teacher may unwittingly communicate her expectations to a child and influence his conception of himself and his "anticipation of his own behavior." [10] Our study has thrown light on some of these means, though we would assume there are many more.

NOTES

1. For the full child questionnaire, see Appendix III.
2. Since up to six or seven children were absent on the day interviewing was undertaken in the low-income second grades, children who were absent in the fifth grades were interviewed on a later day. It was decided that if changes in responses of previously absent children occurred due to conversations with other children, they would be very slight and would be offset by the advantage of a more complete interview series. The smaller number of interviews in low-income classes, with the exception of the white fifth grade, should be noted, since in and of itself it might affect the range and variety of answers relative to the middle-income classes. However, as shall be seen, it is not sufficient to account for the kinds of differences we shall be discussing.
3. This is at variance with the unrealistic aspirations of Negro children reported in some earlier studies, but it is in keeping with more recent research. Such studies and various considerations possibly involved, such as changes over time and from the urban North to the rural South, are discussed in A. J. Lott and B. E. Lott, "Negro and White Children's Plans for Their Futures," in J. I. Roberts, ed., *School Children in the Urban Slum* (New York: The Free Press of Glencoe, 1967), especially pp. 354–361.
4. For a summary of such studies, see Theodore V. Purcell, "The Hopes of Negro Workers for Their Children," in A. B. Shostak and W. Gomberg, eds., *Blue-Collar World* (Englewood Cliffs, N.J.: Prentice-Hall, 1964), pp. 151–152.
5. C. E. Silberman writes: ". . . it is overwhelmingly clear that one of the principal reasons children do not learn is that the schools are organized to facilitate administration rather than learning—to make it easier for teachers and principals to maintain order rather than to make it easier for children to learn. Indeed, to a degree that we are just beginning to appreciate as the result of the writings of such critics as Edgar Z. Friedenberg, John Holt, and Bel Kaufman, schools and classrooms are organized so as to *prevent* learning or teaching from taking place" [C. E. Silberman, "Technology in the Schools," in P. C. Sexton, ed., *Readings on the School in Society* (Englewood Cliffs, N.J.: Prentice-Hall, 1967), p. 246].

6. The total of thirty-three and thirty-nine, instead of thirty-four and forty children in the low-income white and middle-income Negro classrooms, respectively, is due to the transfer of children to other schools.
7. The figures for the low-income white classroom show an almost neutral relationship, in contrast with the above two classrooms. The interesting figures for the middle-income Negro classroom cannot be compared with the others because of the complicating factor that the "reading track" system in that school meant the children shifted classrooms for the reading lesson.

	Teacher Rating	Number of Children	Average Reading Achievement	Average IQ
Low-income white	Positive	11	6.2	96.7
	Neutral	12	6.1	95.4
	Negative	10	6.1	98.7
Middle-income Negro	Positive	7	6.9	103.2
	Neutral	18	5.6	92.6
	Negative	14	6.5	93.1

8. R. Rosenthal and L. F. Jacobson, *Pygmalion in the Classroom: Self-Fulfilling Prophecies and Teacher Expectations* (New York: Holt, Rinehart and Winston, 1968).
9. R. Rosenthal and L. F. Jacobson, "Teacher Expectations for the Disadvantaged," *Scientific American*, CCXVIII, No. 4 (1968), 22.
10. *Ibid.*, p. 23.

C H A P T E R

8

CLIMATE FOR LEARNING

In this study of school experience for city children, we have taken the contemporary view of what ideal education in our society today should be. We have assumed learning must be related to a child's own prior experience and understanding, and that it can only be built on a foundation of respect for him as an individual and on the effort to meet him at least to some extent on his own terms. It can be argued, with good reason, that contemporary methods have proved to be no more effective than others, that children learn in all manner of ways that do not seem to follow the rules set down by educational psychologists, and that traditional, formal rote learning has been as successful as more recent methods. However, it is hard to argue against the position that whatever the method, the respect for a child's ability to learn what he is being taught and the expectation that he will learn it are of profound importance for successful teaching.

We have accepted the view that building a *conceptual* basis for thought is essential for true education and have assumed that concepts learned in school are affected in great part by the teacher's structuring of the child's involvement in that learning—to the extent that he is actively engaged by the teacher in the first place. It is important to ask: Is a child in effect second-guessing the teacher, trying to determine what relatively arbitrary way of phrasing an answer the teacher has in mind? Or may he be engaged in attempting to remember a body of set material, factual data, and technical operations? The former involves learning social and nonintellectual—if not directly anti-intellectual—techniques for "getting along"; the latter the acquisition of essential skills and standard knowledge. Instead of either of these, may the child be following the teacher's line of reasoning as a process is presented or actively reinterpreting his own prior experience, knowledge, or feelings in relation to a particular subject? These are conducive to the building of a conceptual basis for true intellectual exploration and mastery.

In analyzing the teaching process in the classroom, we kept in mind the responsibility now taken by the school for socialization of children in a very broad sense and the fact that formal schooling (or lack of it) affords almost the sole path toward the attainment of occupational roles in adult life. We were concerned to understand ways in which the educative function of the school is compounded with its sociological function of perpetuating existing class statuses with children staying on the same rungs of the occupational ladder as their parents. We explored ways in which teachers unwittingly help perpetuate a system of inequalities by reflecting in their behavior and attitudes the stereotypes and shortcomings of a society dominated by "middle-class" materialistic, nonhumanistic, and nonintellectual perspectives. We wished to define how such broad social considerations influence the two factors generally seen to be the primary determinants in the educational process: namely, the concept and methodology of teaching as mastered by teachers during training and their individual personalities and characteristic styles of approach to children.

In order to examine the manner in which the social functions of the school impinge upon classroom life, we focused upon covertly and informally conveyed goals and expectations for children, as well as upon those which are directly stated or enacted. Such inquiry into the interplay between sociological and educational considerations necessitated close interdisciplinary collaboration among social anthropologists, psychologists, and educators, as well as the reliance on a variety of analytic techniques. Our view of the classroom as a social system involved a concept of patterned variations in the choices for behavior available to children and in their consequences for children, according to different subcultural contexts. Therefore our study called for schools which would represent differences in the socially crucial factors of income and race.

As we studied classroom materials and weighed them against the ideal for optimal teaching, we saw how many of the problems that have been raised by critics of the educational system and other researchers were expressed in classroom life. In Chapter 2 we outlined certain effects of inadequate teacher training. We observed some competent drill and training in basic skills, but when it came to building concepts through involving the children in discussion, we saw the parroting of educational dicta with little understanding either of what concepts are or what goals for leading a discussion might be. In Chapter 4 we detailed some effects of poor training in classroom-management techniques, noting the point made by others that psychological generalizations about individual children are generally substituted for confrontation of the real problem, which is how to work with groups. New teachers virtually put aside all they have ostensibly learned when they first face a classroom alone, and they start over on the basis of their own judgment and what they learn from experienced teachers in their school.

In Chapters 3 and 5 we described the consequences for teaching and management styles that follow the lack of well-grounded and realistic pedagogic goals. With reference to the school's role as a major socializing institution, we illustrated the tendency of teachers to fall rather spontaneously into the transmission of standards and goals often adverse to educational ideals. We viewed the school as on the whole geared for a rather rigid adaptation to the status quo, and we described the ways curriculum areas involving social content are approached in a *rationalizing* and *moralizing* spirit, rather than in a *scientific* and *humanistic* one. We saw how, as a result, there was a failure to objectify the world and the actions of people in it, or to deal with social processes as if they were like natural processes, that is to a major degree orderly and understandable. Management techniques, we pointed out, develop in large part in response to the status structure of the society and its unstated implications for how children of various groups should be treated, rather than in accord with some goal for an optimal learning environment.

Throughout the study we have attempted to emphasize the paradoxical role of teachers. Teachers are the central carriers or perpetuators of school practices that socialize children for a future status in accord with the status of their parents—often at the expense of *education* itself—but it does not follow that, as individuals, they are in a position easily to do otherwise. Teachers cannot simply interact with the children in their classrooms, according to their desires and personal style. Instead, their behavior often takes on characteristics beyond their immediate aims or intents. They must adapt their style, not only to the children, but to the institution, to the principal's requirements, to the other teachers' attitudes, and to the standards according to which they will be evaluated. Teachers screen school functions and directives to suit their own convictions to the extent possible, but usually in a context where demands are heavy, the needs of the children great, and the limitations of their training considerable. There is little allowance in teacher schedules for the reading, discussion, and intellectual development as essential for effective performance at lower levels of schooling as at the university level. Furthermore, the teachers' custodial function often outweighs their educative function: constant paper work intrudes on their teaching time; the requirement of control in the classroom is often beyond what is desirable for a good learning situation; and conformism to the institution, rather than creative teaching, is the key to success. Teachers are pressured, in other ways, to take the easiest course, which is to conform to and perpetuate the dominant "culture" of the school, the dominant expectations for the children and styles of dealing with them.

In Chapter 6, we discussed ways the above general limitations are compounded in their adverse effects on low-income Negro children, whose school experience contrasts sharply with that of white middle-income children. The low-income white classrooms and middle-income Negro classrooms fell in between in different ways but each with characteristics recognizably in keeping with the children's family status in society. Other studies have documented the gross differences in school facilities and experience and training of personnel in low-income areas —the lowered standards and the greater punitiveness accorded low-

income and especially Negro low-income children.[1] What our analysis
has added is the way in which individual teachers, with different personalities or habitual styles for relating to others, translate them to "fit"
established attitudes and expectations for different groups of children.
For example, the teacher working with white middle-income fifth-grade
children took responsibility for her own limitations and spoke of
reacting to their lack of attention as a cue to her, indicating the need for
her to arouse their interest. On the other hand, the limitations of the
teacher working with low-income Negro children were ascribed to the
children, and boredom on their part was attributed to their presumably
limited attention span.

We also observed that a generally friendly teaching style did not prevent a basic nonsupportiveness of learning in the low-income Negro
classrooms. The second-grade teacher was warm and motherly and
seemed genuinely to like the children; the fifth-grade teacher was
friendly and trying to do her best. Yet in both cases the children's very
being, their existence, as well as their contributions, were being denied
or undermined. Albeit pleasantly, lower status roles were being structured for the children, in contrast with the middle-income white classrooms; poorer images of themselves were being presented to them.
With regard to the distribution of previously discussed ratings, the
middle-income white and lower-income Negro fifth-grade classrooms
were not that far apart:

		Sum of Ratings on Management Style: Supportiveness, Enabling of Independence and Leeway for Child Interaction	Teacher Interest
Lower-income Negro:	5th	18	Low
	2nd	23	Medium-low
Lower-income white:	5th	25	High
	2nd	24	Medium
Middle-income Negro:	5th	14	High
	2nd	9	High
Middle-income white:	5th	17	Medium
	2nd	12	Medium

However, when considered from the viewpoint of expectations for children, goals being defined for them, and respect for their ability to learn,
the two schools were at opposite poles.

The children's relative lack of involvement in the low-income Negro fifth grade, in comparison with the second grade in the same school, tallied with the widespread experience teachers have had with the falling-off of interest shown in ghetto schools, and with the growing gap in test scores between middle-income and low-income children. On the basis of analyzing classroom differences and their subtleties in our study schools, and viewing these differences against the background of a rapidly growing body of literature on education, cognitive development, and life styles, we have argued that the change seemed sufficiently accounted for by the children's school experience itself.

A prevailing argument is that deficiencies that poor Negro children bring to school due to the impoverishment of their circumstance are so extreme as to make it virtually impossible for them to be taught. The out-of-school difficulties for low-income Negro children are of course undeniable. Social organization comprises an interlocking network of institutions, each reinforcing the other, and the school can no more be entirely responsible for perpetuating inequalities in our society than can any other single institution. However, the importance of the school is equally undeniable, and our data indicate its complicity despite its formal commitment to ameliorating, rather than aggravating, the difficulties of poverty.

We have seen how contributions of low-income Negro children could be cut off and undermined and how interest could be stifled with irrelevant personal remarks; we know, from other studies, the further inequities within the schools. Furthermore, in the low-income Negro fifth grade we observed the classroom to be structured for *less responsibility and initiative than the children were actually taking in the classroom itself, although outside of the immediate learning situation.* Questions about their studies indicate a self-confident feeling on the part of second-graders in this school and a drop by the fifth grade considerably below all other schools.[2] The expectations projected on the children in the school become their own as they move from second to fifth grade. The success of many children from low-income homes, despite all the difficulties in and out of school, attests to a determination to overcome all odds that cannot be explained within a theoretical framework that sees motivation destroyed by age five or six, previous to school entry.

On the basis of our material we have argued, further, that the substance of negative school experiences for Negro children cannot be conveyed by the phrase "value clash" unless the concept is reinterpreted. In order for the phrase "middle-class values" to apply to teacher attitudes, it must include as central the middle-class feeling of superiority over those who are lower on the social scale and the greater readiness on the part of relatively secure middle-class people to accept a Panglossian image of "this best of all possible worlds." What we observed in the classroom was not the attempt to "impose middle-class goals" on the children, but rather a tacit assumption that these goals were not open to at least the vast majority of them. *The "middle-class values" being imposed on the low-income Negro children defined them as inadequate and their proper role as one of deference.* Despite the fact that some teachers in the low-income schools stated their felt responsibility to set "middle-class standards" for the children, their lowered expectations were expressed by a low emphasis on goal-setting statements altogether. In a three-hour period, clear-cut overt goal-setting statements numbered 12 and 13 for the low-income Negro school, 15 and 18 for the low-income white school, and 43 and 46 for the middle-income white school.

This is not to say that there are not wise and dedicated teachers who are imbued so deeply with the belief that all children are capable of learning and discovery that they communicate this to comfortable and deprived alike. For every Jonathan Kozol or Herbert Kohl who have written of their experiences in ghetto schools, there must be hundreds of anonymous teachers who have found ways to reach poor children. More common, however, is the person who starts his teaching career with the assumption that all children can learn as something of a question or a wish, and who is disillusioned when his attempts to teach in a poor neighborhood are beset with so many difficulties. Not fully comprehending the web in which he is caught, he does not turn the responsibility back on himself or (at least in any open way) on the school system. It is easier to place the responsibility where he is told at every turn it lies—with the children. In a middle-income neighborhood he would be held responsible by parents and principal for a large percentage of failures; in a low-income classroom he generally would not be held responsible.

Implications for Innovation

The implications for innovation in the technology of education suggested by this study are various but far from new. The importance of proficiency in the concepts and content of particular disciplines as essential to helping children explore ideas in any depth in the classroom, the need for training in the specifics of involving children actively as participants in learning experiences, the urgency of teacher training which translates techniques for both teaching and management of the classroom from the realm of airy abstraction into the practical realities of school life—these and other desirable improvements have been discussed elsewhere. Our primary aim has been to throw light on the extent to which supposedly strictly educational questions such as these can be intricately related to the congeries of structural relations and concomitant attitudes surrounding educational institutions in our society.

In view of the extent to which inadequate teaching practices are institutionally based in the structure of the school, it is interesting to note the extent to which demands for change made by community leaders, parents, and teachers alike have involved restructuring. Three major institutional changes have been sought: equalization of schools in all demographic respects and/or social heterogeneity of the student body in any one school; formal roles for parents and community leaders in the running of the schools, particularly in low-income and minority areas; and professionalization of the teaching status. There is no need here further to underline the fundamental importance of equalizing educational facilities, expenditures, standards, and, in short, eliminating the whole "double-track system" with its categories of "good" and "bad" schools. Nor can it be too strongly emphasized that teachers in elementary schools, and especially in junior high and high schools, must have time for their own course preparation and greater freedom to make decisions about curriculum content if their performance is to be substantially improved. Categorically, as students of social structure, we would say that the restructuring of the relation between the school and the community it serves directly, with a formal role for parents and community leaders in decisions concerning the children's education—a virtual reality in well-to-do communities—would do more to eliminate the lack of respect generally held by teachers for children of poor backgrounds than all the workshops that could be organized. Indeed, this is doubtless why this innovative step has been viewed with such alarm—upsetting traditional status lines is always threatening.

Other proposals for reform, coming from both within and without the educational system, have involved curriculum content. We have described some of the difficulties teachers have with methods emphasizing a conceptual understanding such as in mathematics, but our major emphasis has been on course content in reading and social science texts. The awareness that school materials should reflect the diversity of American society and a growing disaffection with the blondish suburban Dick and Jane textbook family and their prototypes throughout the grades have resulted in the production of somewhat more diversified materials. By and large, however, teachers must use those texts and materials which are available, and choices of additional books continue to be largely restricted to ones which embody the same pallid Dick and Jane image of "middle-class" life and the implication that it is the best, indeed, the only valid way of life. Of course, some teachers do not actively and enthusiastically endorse the textbook world and try to remain neutral or to introduce, albeit cautiously, the notion of a world encompassing different and equally valid ways of life which cannot be measured solely according to their deviation from the idealized textbook family. The teacher of the white low-income second grade who stated her concern with imposing her own attitudes on the children was able to build her transportation discussion on the experiences of truck driving of their fathers and other relatives. She brought easily into the discussion the use of jeeps on Israeli farms, with a tone implying that the people of that country were part of the total (and acceptable) "we" and not of "other" (by implication strange and somewhat inferior) people.

Related to the concern with ameliorating the stereotyped content of school texts, there have been proposals to liberalize the emphasis on "correct" speech so pervasive in classroom life by teaching "standard English" as "a second language." Accepting a "second-language" approach enables children to speak and learn in their own vernacular and be introduced, formally, to "standard" usages much as they would be introduced to French or Spanish. Unfortunately, this principle may involve an exaggeration of differences between standard English and its colloquial variants. Nonetheless, it can help to resolve the problem of how to deal with the *content* of a child's contribution, rather than the style of delivery (with a long discussion cut short with, "Do not say 'ain't' "), while recognizing the fact that standard English is, willy-nilly, a requisite for occupational success in many areas.

A great many programs have involved the education of teachers as to life styles in low-income and ghetto areas as the basis, presumably, for improving their ability to communicate with poor and minority-group children. Our close look at classroom functioning has indicated the naïveté often found in connection with such programs and makes it clear that a greater sophistication is needed if they are to be more than superficial and patronizing statements of intent.[3] Improvement is called for along three lines:

1. Clarification of ideas involved in the "culture of poverty" concept. Reinterpretation to exclude traditional middle-class stereotypes of lower-class inabilities. Substitution of the understanding that life styles involve coping mechanisms for dealing with objective circumstances, and that demoralization, defeat, and despair indicate the breakdown of these coping mechanisms, resulting from the sheer weight of oppression and deprivation, but do not constitute the content of the "life style," "culture," or "value system" itself.[4]
2. Clearer insight into "middle-class values" and the nature of the cliché the phrase has become. Opening again the question of what, in fact, these values are and adopting a more critical attitude toward the implication that, however defined, the phrase implies it to be something complete and entirely desirable and in its present form not to be questioned.
3. Recognition of the fact that some of the "new" ideas about how to educate low-income children are little more than a rediscovery of Dewey. Following from this is the awareness (helpful in eliminating a "do-gooder" attitude) that insights gained from research into learning problems of low-income children can lead to needed improvements in education for *all* children.

These points have been raised at different times in this book, but it may be worthwhile here to summarize our opinions as they crystallized during the course of the study. That the "culture of poverty" concept has constantly tended to become a new phrasing for old stereotypes

about the poor and about people of color is to be expected; it has occurred, not only among teachers, but among social scientists as well.[5]
Unfortunately, to become a social scientist by no means makes a person
automatically immune to biased attitudes toward those considered by
the relatively secure to have "failed." Thus literature on educating the
poor has been replete with euphemisms. Instead of "lazy," the poor are
now said to be "fatalistic" and "apathetic." Instead of "lacking ambi-
tion," they are considered unable to "delay gratification" or "plan for
the future." Instead of being "stupid," they supposedly have verbal patterns that do not allow for abstract thought. Furthermore, the position
taken in the Moynihan report on the Negro family is that "family instability," leading to poor educational motivation and achievement and
hence limited job opportunities, is basic to the "tangle of pathology"
which is characteristic of ghetto life.[6] The public health psychologist,
William Ryan, has offered a stringent criticism of the Moynihan report
on both empirical and theoretical grounds. For example, he points out
that reported rates of illegitimacy among Negroes, rather than being an
index of a vaguely defined state of "family instability," reveal no more
than the following:

> Negro and white girls probably engage in premarital intercourse in
> about the same proportions, but . . . the white girl more often takes
> Enovid or uses a diaphragm; if she gets pregnant she more often ob-
> tains an abortion; if she has the baby, first she is more often able to
> conceal it and, second, she has an infinitely greater opportunity to
> give it up for adoption.[7]

On the basis of similar examinations of other aspects of the report,
Ryan states:

> . . . it would be far more reasonable to conclude not that "family in-
> stability" leads to a "tangle of pathology," but that poor Negro families
> —that is, half of all Negro families—are bitterly discriminated against
> and exploited, with the result that the individual, the family, and the
> community are all deeply injured.[8]

Thus, Ryan places as the primary issue discrimination and its continuing effects, rather than an historically based "family instability." Faulti-
ness in the line of reasoning that poor educational achievement, caused
by family instability, is mainly responsible for low incomes and unemployment among Negroes is revealed by a series of studies showing that

additional years of education do not automatically lead to substantial improvement in income level and employment.[9]

On the basis of studying poor people in Washington, D.C., the sociologist, Hylan Lewis, is also critical of lumping together things for which "there is no necessary relationship . . . such things as places lived in, one parent in the household, hunger, prospects for cognitive development, unconventional language, neglect, and immorality." [10] Lewis suggests focusing on "syndromes of poverty-related behavior" as a concept which is more discriminating and manageable than such concepts as "culture of poverty," "culturally deprived," or "lower-class culture." Different strategies for dealing with poverty and their variations should be studied, he states, and of particular importance, truly "clinical" cases of family demoralization should be distinguished from the majority. He writes:

> The amount of diversity among low-income families is frequently overlooked and underrated in popular and scientific thinking. Much of a basic strain toward conformity to standard values and practices in this segment of the population is missed or ignored because of these tendencies to underestimate heterogeneity, and changes in family life among the poor . . .
>
> Our view is that it is probably more fruitful to think of different types of poor families reacting in various ways at various times to the facts of their position and to relative isolation rather than to the imperatives of a culture of poverty or of the slum. It is important that we do not confuse life chances and the actual behavior of people . . . with the basic values and preferences of people in poverty.[11]

Somehow as a result of "culture of poverty" discussions, the "middle class" has claimed for itself as exclusive characteristics a cluster of so-called "values," ranging from such things as neatness, cleanliness, and orderliness to drives like motivation for success and ability to plan toward it. Lewis points out two things that sensitive and thoughtful teachers already know: it is a distortion to project what may be true of "clinical" or extreme cases of demoralization onto the poor as a whole; and it is a further distortion to assume that a lack of opportunity for achieving a desire is the same as not having the desire. Most teachers are well aware that most children, albeit from very poor homes, are taught to be neat and clean, and that really slovenly children are the exception. Since these children from demoralized homes are so often placed together in "slow" classes, for teachers of these classes the stereotype is closer to the reality.

As for the confusion between goals and the possibility of achieving them, David Gottlieb, Assistant Director of the Plans and Programs branch of the United States Office of Economic Opportunity Job Corps, writes the following:

> From my own research and the reports of others, I have yet to hear of a youngster who seeks to live in poverty, alienation, or despair. I have not come in touch with a youngster who comes out of poverty who has voiced a desire for a life in the slums, inferior housing, unemployment, or crime. I have yet to meet a youngster who comes from a broken home who holds the same goals for his own adult life. I have yet to hear a poor youngster say, "Man, I dig poverty—I love this social milieu."
>
> If there is, then, a common end or goal that all youth aspire to, it would be something we could call "the good life"—a life free of unemployment, poverty, social alienation, family chaos, and mental and physical illness. . . .

Where the difference lies, states Gottlieb, is that "poor youths aspire to those things that are at the entrance of the good life, while the more affluent deal with the fringe benefits that come with a living knowledge of the good life." [12] The latter, as would be expected, also know more precisely what they want and how to get it since they are already well on the road.

Our impression is similar to Gottlieb's. Differences among groups of children in relation to school seem more a matter of responses to different possibilities for achieving generally similar goals than a matter of widely divergent goals. One would expect the "haves" to hold somewhat different attitudes about their society than the "have nots." One would expect them to be on the whole more optimistic about it, more attuned to it, willing to conform to its demands; conversely, one would expect the "have nots" to be more disaffected, withdrawn, cynical, angry, and less willing to commit themselves to a striving that stands a poor chance of success. (There is bitter irony in the remark of the study teacher in the low-income Negro second grade that the textbook family image was probably good for the children in that it might inspire them to want something better than they had.)

One would also expect to find what is, in fact, the case—enormous variations among children of the poor. Apart from the exigencies of individual life histories, there are many different streams of tradition that enter into lifeways of the poor. Some follow from different national and religious traditions, others from rural or urban backgrounds, and yet others from the influences of different occupational settings. These variations have become blurred by an overriding emphasis on a "culture of poverty." Even more serious, however, has been the failure (indicated by Hylan Lewis) to distinguish between valued aspects of traditional life style and day-to-day responses to enormous objective difficulties. As Alvin Schorr puts it, "the attitudes that are associated with the culture of poverty, viz., orientation to the present, passivity, cynicism, are a realistic response to the *facts* of poverty." [13]

In an article on "Traditional Values and the Shaping of American Education," Merle Borrowman points out that concepts of work, authority, and community do not pass from the descriptive to the normative—into the arena of culturally defined values in the true sense—until "human emotion and preference become strongly attached to them; that is, when people feel a community 'ought' to have certain characteristics, and that 'good' people have one attitude toward work and play while 'bad' people have another." [14]

To confuse immediate behavioral responses with goals or values is to ignore the totality of a cultural heritage. Nowhere is this more than in the case of Negro Americans, the richness of whose culture is attested to by writers who have devoted themselves to the analysis of its content and diverse historical sources. Albert Murray, for example, has elucidated the Negro sense of being a people in an extended definition of the word "soul" and the traditional values, interests, and understandings the term encapsulates. [15] These cover a broad range—from behavioral style and manners, particularly of speech, through such widely recognized features as "soul music" in its various manifestations and "soul food," to a deeply felt sense of common history and cultural expressions.

Some of the connotations Murray gives for the term are the following: "sophistication, as in any Negro stylization in which references and meanings are *signified* (by gesture and innuendo) rather than stated outright in conventional terms familiar to white people, hence also . . . anything which makes Negroes laugh but which puzzles most whites present"; "music which goes with the robust Negro genre of rawhide-beneath-patent-leather elegance"; "any black-oriented behavior . . . in the interest of a black cause"; "any esthetic projection expressive of black American experience"; "authentic, as from deeply felt human passion as expressive of innermost being, as opposed to artificial or phony, as from mechanical technique without emotion"; and "expression which reflects knowledgeability earned through profoundly personal involvement." To reduce truly cultural meanings and traditions such as these to a homogeneous stereotype through the term "culture of poverty" not only becomes an insult to the people involved, but makes a mockery of the culture concept itself.

Yet this is not the whole story. Just as we are far from a full definition of the cultural heritage possessed by the different groups who make up the poor of our society, so are we far from an accurate depiction of middle-class life. On the one hand, in contrast with the "culture of poverty," middle-class children have become pictured as possessing clear goals which they pursue with confidence of attaining satisfaction from their achievement. That this is scarcely the case is attested to by suburban parents wringing their hands over their recalcitrant children and adolescents who unpredictably destroy property, leave school, experiment with drugs, and aggressively adopt slovenly habits. Somehow the image of well-motivated children and able, directed parents moving them along the road to college, success, and satisfaction has been entirely divorced from the continuing humanistic and scientific critique by psychologists, poets, and philosophers of contemporary alienated, automated, "one-dimensional" man. In this case the middle-class image emerges as more negative than the image of the manual laborer: greater concern with external appearances at the expense of inner satisfactions; greater anxiety caused by individual deviants, in contrast with a less critical acceptance of others; and a guilt-ridden drive to validate the self through worldly success, at the expense of self-acceptance and ability to gain satisfaction from what one has. Middle-class people who are quick to state what they feel to be the limitations of this image when they locate themselves and the people they know within it might do well to adopt the same critical stance when they appraise material on the working class.

The third and final point concerns the belated rediscovery of Deweyan educational principles in connection with working with poor children. That all children like "activities," that learning must be based on experience and experiment, that these should be related to prior experiences insofar as possible in the children's own terms—these have been central themes in progressive school curricula for a long time. The importance of learning more about the world of working-class children and of building realities from their world into the curriculum have their counterpart in the more effective education of children generally. Concern is expressed that our "well-educated" children, too, are not that well educated, that they are trained for test-taking—for the performance of set tasks quickly and ably and not for humanistic understanding or for innovative exploration. How can they be when they are so largely taught a myth—a myth for lower-income and middle-income children alike? Not only is the existence of this country's majority virtually denied in the classroom, but any "controversial" issue is avoided. The bland version of the world presented in the classroom contradicts reality, not only for lower-class children, but middle-class children as well; it contradicts the personal reality of their own powerful emotional surges and the external reality of violence and seeming chaos that TV daily brings into their homes.

The psychologist, Jerome Bruner, comments on "the passivity of the process we call education." Rather than emphasizing "the art of approaching the unknown, the art of posing questions," the stress is "upon gaining and storing information . . . in the form in which it is presented." Furthermore, it is a watered-down information, denying feelings, characterized by "the embarrassment of passion." He describes young Christopher Columbus as presented in a popular social studies text:

> Young Chris is walking along the water front in his home town and gets to wondering where all those ships go. Eventually he comes back to his brother's cobbler shop and exclaims, "Gee Bart, I wonder where all those ships go, whether maybe if they just kept going they wouldn't come back because the world is round." Bart replies with pleasant brotherly encouragement. Chris is a well-adjusted kid. Bart is a nice big brother. And where is the passion that drove this obsessed man across uncharted oceans . . . ? Everything is there in the story except the essential truth—the fanatical urge to explore in an age of exploration, the sense of an expanding world. . . .

Bruner goes on to say that "the pablum that makes up such textbooks" is justified as touching more directly on the life of children. And how is this life seen by text writers and publishers?

It is an image created out of an ideal of adjustment. The ideal of adjustment has little place for the driven man, the mythic hero, the idiosyncratic style. Its ideal is mediocentrism, reasonableness, above all, being nice. Such an idea does not touch closely the deeper life of the child. It does not appeal to the dark but energizing forces that lie close beneath the surface. The Old Testament, the Greek myths, the Norse legends—these are the embarrassing chronicles of men of passion. They were devised to catch and preserve the power and tragedy of the human condition—and its ambiguity, too. In their place, we have substituted the noncontroversial and the banal.

When we strive to attain adjustment "by shutting our eyes to the turmoils of human life, we will not get adjustment, but a niggling fear of the unusual and the excellent," Bruner concludes.[16]

The house with the white picket fence is no more than a superficial reality for anyone—well off or not. Yet it becomes reified as the ultimate in living. It is presented as the goal of education—indeed, it is, perhaps, the goal of *schooling* today. Meanwhile, there is the wonder, the mystery, the terror, the beauty, the challenge of a world become one, a world so interdependent that mankind as a whole must arrive at consensus about his future or destroy himself.

Never has the truism been so valid that today's generation must solve the problems of tomorrow in fundamentally new ways. Yet the idea becomes no more than another platitude in the moralistic context of school texts, where the illusion is maintained that the world is not full of questions for children and adults alike, but that it is full of things that are defined and known in terms of either right or wrong. The teacher knows what and which they are, and the children will learn. The history of mankind is taught as if it had developed according to decisions made by important people who were on the whole either very good or very bad. That history has developed through myriad actions by multitudes of people, a great many of whom were poor, is not told to children in their early years but is learned by those who go on to college, the vast majority of whom are *not* poor. The basic myth of the elementary classroom leads, not only to the denial of their existence for many school children, but to a denial of the truth for all.

NOTES

1. The findings of the Coleman report on *Equality of Educational Opportunity* [James S. Coleman *et al.* (Washington, D.C.: U.S. Government Printing Office, 1966)] appeared to discount the importance of these differences for children's performance. Unfortunately, Coleman used entire school districts as units when averaging such things as instructional expenditures per student. Further analysis of his data does reveal school inequities, especially those related to teacher attitudes and abilities, to be significantly related to children's achievement [see Henry S. Dyer, "School Factors," and Samuel S. Bowles, "Towards Equality," *Harvard Educational Review*, XXXVIII, No. 1 (1968)].

2. Responses to the questions, "How are you at reading? at arithmetic? very good, medium good, not so good?" (Answers in per cent.)

	Reading				Arithmetic			
	Very good	Medium good	Not so good	Other DK, NA	Very good	Medium good	Not so good	Other DK, NA
Low-income Negro school								
Second grade	44	30	26	0	44	30	26	0
Fifth grade	19	47	34	0	0	47	53	0
Low-income white school								
Second grade	32	41	18	10	27	55	5	14
Fifth grade	36	55	6	3	23	58	16	3
Middle-income Negro school								
Second grade	32	47	15	6	29	53	9	9
Fifth grade	39	53	8	0	18	42	37	3
Middle-income white school								
Second grade	28	62	7	3	28	62	10	0
Fifth grade	50	45	5	0	31	58	11	0

Similar questions were asked of middle- and lower-income Negro children—60 boys and 60 girls at ages 6–8 and 12–14—in Durham, North Carolina. Increasing assurance of the "upper"-income children with increasing age was reported, and a drop in assurance was reported for low-income boys and no rise for girls in the older group [Regina M. Goff, "Some Educational Implications of the Influence of Rejection on Aspiration Levels of Minority Group Children," in E. T. Keach, Jr., R. Fulton, and W. E. Gardner, eds., *Education and Social Crisis, Perspectives on Teaching Disadvantaged Youth* (New York: John Wiley, 1967), p. 225].

3. Therefore, an extremely important development in this area is that

which stems from teachers themselves, as they attempt to establish rapport with parents and other community people in the effort to increase their own understanding and to build the basis for more effective communication with poor and minority group children. "The Teachers Incorporated" an example of such a development, established a group of teachers to work in decentralized schools in Harlem and the Lower East Side of New York City with the basic goal of improving the quality of education for "inner city" children.

4. For a full discussion of the theoretical shortcomings in the "culture of poverty" concept, see Charles Valentine, *Culture and Poverty, Critique and Counter-Proposals* (Chicago: The University of Chicago Press, 1968).

5. Davidson and her co-workers documented the negative view of workers held by college students of the types who would become teachers, psychologists, and social workers [H. H. Davidson, F. Riessman, and E. Meyers, "Personality Characteristics Attributed to the Worker," *Journal of Social Psychology*, LVII (1962), 155–160]. A dramatic illustration of how this bias can operate in practice is afforded in a study of Rorschach diagnoses in relation to class, in which it was found that essentially identical records were interpreted differently according to the class designation of the patient. Individuals said to be "lower class" were diagnosed as more maladjusted than their middle-class counterparts and more frequently categorized in terms of psychosis and character disorder, while parallel middle-class records were characterized as neurotic and normal [W. Haase, *Rorschach Diagnosis, Socio-economic Class, and Examiner Bias,* unpublished Ph.D. dissertation, New York University, 1956 [quoted in F. Riessman, "New Approaches to Mental Health Treatment for Labor and Low Income Groups, A Survey," National Institute of Labor Education (February 1964), mimeographed, p. 4]. Brill and Storrow likewise report middle-class patients as considered more treatable than lower-class patients [N. Q. Brill and H. Storrow, "Social Class and Psychiatric Treatment," *Archives of General Psychiatry*, III (1963), 340–344].

6. U. S. Department of Labor, *The Negro Family, the Case for National Action* (Washington, D.C.: U. S. Government Printing Office, March 1965).

7. W. Ryan, "Savage Discovery: The Moynihan Report," *The Nation* (November 22, 1965), p. 381.

8. *Ibid.*, p. 382.

9. S. Bowles, "Towards Equality of Educational Opportunity?" *Harvard Educational Review*, XXXVIII, No. 1 (1968), 96–98. Not only does the gap between earnings of Negroes and whites *increase* with educational level, but, Bowles writes: ". . . one competent piece of research using U.S. Census data suggests that for Negroes in the North, the economic gains associated with additional years of education beyond

the eighth grade are comparatively minor, and that at a number of points in the educational career of a Negro youth staying in school for an additional year results in an actual reduction in the present value of expected lifetime earnings."

10. H. Lewis, "Syndrome of Contemporary Urban Poverty," *Psychiatric Research Report No. 21,* American Psychiatric Association (April 1967), p. 7.

11. *Ibid.,* pp. 8, 10.

12. D. Gottlieb, "Some Social Aspects of the Teacher-Student Interaction Process," in Gordon J. Klopf and William A. Hohman, eds., *Perspectives on Learning,* Papers from the 50th Anniversary Invitational Symposium, Bank Street College of Education (New York: Mental Health Materials Center, Inc., 1967).

13. A. L. Schorr, "The Nonculture of Poverty," *American Journal of Orthopsychiatry,* XXXIV, No. 5 (1964), 907.

14. M. L. Borrowman, "Traditional Values and the Shaping of American Education," in Nelson B. Henry, ed., *Social Forces Influencing American Education,* 60th Yearbook of the National Society for the Study of Education (Chicago: The University of Chicago Press, 1961), pp. 144–145.

15. A. Murray, " 'Soul': 32 Meanings Not in Your Dictionary," *Book World,* in *The Washington Post,* June 23, 1968, p. 6.

16. J. S. Bruner, "Learning and Thinking," *Harvard Educational Review,* XXIX, No. 3 (Summer 1959), 186–190.

A P P E N D I X

I

(A) Outline for the Characterization
of a Classroom (Teacher)

(B) Outline for the Characterization
of a Classroom (Children)

APPENDIX I(A)

OUTLINE FOR THE CHARACTERIZATION
OF A CLASSROOM (TEACHER)

Class:_____

I. TEACHER—CURRICULUM
  A. *Curriculum Content*
    1. Schedule:
      (a) Weekly Schedule—T Interview
      (b) Schedule—Observation No. 1
      (c) Schedule—Observation No. 2
      (d) Schedule—Observation No. 3
      (e) Periods Observed

SUMMARY AND COMMENTS

Time Spent on Classroom Activities	Observation No. 1	Observation No. 2
Language Arts	MINUTES	MINUTES
Reading (oral and silent)		
Reading Workbooks		
Phonics		
Spelling		
Penmanship		
Story telling (T or children)		
Creative writing		
Other		
Mathematics		
Social Studies		
Science		
	TOTAL	TOTAL
Health		
Art		
Music		
Play Period		
Show and tell		
News		
Gym or Recess		
Milk and Cookies		
Other		
	TOTAL	TOTAL

Time Spent on Classroom Activities	Observation No. 1	Observation No. 2
Routines	MINUTES	MINUTES
Transitions		
Discipline (Individual)		
(Group)		
	TOTAL	TOTAL
Interruptions		
Other		
	TOTAL	TOTAL

2. Texts and materials: (T Interview)
   (a) Texts—name and level:
   (b) Materials—use and source:

SUMMARY AND COMMENTS:

3. Statements about the curriculum from T Interview:

SUMMARY AND COMMENTS:

4. Analysis of curriculum content: (Obs.)
   (a) Degree of integration and development of content (inter-relatedness of subject matter, clarity of underlying concepts, etc.).
   (b) Relation of content to children's experiences.
   (c) Depth, richness, and variety.
   (d) Style of learning and thought (development of "adventurous" and/or "systematic" thinking, practice in routine skills, nature of involvement in thought process).
   (e) Value content of material from teacher's statements, texts, and displays.
B. *Presentation of Content* (Obs. and T Interview)
   5. Originality of presentation:

Stereotyped presentation			Original presentation	
1	2	3	4	5

(Routine, unimaginative development of ideas and presentation of materials)	(Imaginative, resourceful development of ideas and presentation of materials)

OBSERVATIONS   1 2 3 4 5
INTERVIEWS   1 2 3 4 5

REMARKS: *

* Note any areas which deviate from rating.

6. Flexibility of presentation:

Inflexible presentation			Adaptive presentation	
1	2	3	4	5
(Rigid conforming to routine, impatient with interruptions, remarks, or digressions; closes discussion)			(Adaptable to pupil interests—taking advantage of pupils' remarks to clarify ideas or heighten interests; broad scope; encourages discussion)	

OBSERVATIONS 1 2 3 4 5
INTERVIEWS   1 2 3 4 5

REMARKS:

7. Variability of presentation:

Varies presentation for individuals			Does not vary presentation	
1	2	3	4	5
(Standards and assistance geared to differences in individual ability)			(Sets same standards for all pupils; no differential encouragement or assistance)	

OBSERVATIONS 1 2 3 4 5
INTERVIEWS   1 2 3 4 5

REMARKS:

8. Frequency of assistance:

Assists children often			Assists children seldom	
1	2	3	4	5
(Often suggests aids, provides hints, clarifies, or gives assistance)			(Leaves children alone in the learning process)	

OBSERVATIONS 1 2 3 4 5
INTERVIEWS   1 2 3 4 5

REMARKS:

9. Effectiveness of planning:

Ineffective planning			Effective planning	
1	2	3	4	5
(Poorly planned programming, undecided what to do next; time wasted, especially with children who are not directly working with T)			(Carefully planned programming, directed toward objective; able to anticipate and move along without time wasted)	

OBSERVATIONS 1 2 3 4 5
INTERVIEWS 1 2 3 4 5

REMARKS:

10. Clarity of presentation:

Clear presentation			Unclear presentation	
1	2	3	4	5

(Clear, definite, comprehensible) (Confused, indefinite, incomprehensible)

OBSERVATIONS 1 2 3 4 5
INTERVIEWS 1 2 3 4 5

REMARKS:

11. Breadth of knowledge used in classroom:

Displays limited fund of knowledge			Displays broad fund of knowledge	
1	2	3	4	5

(Seemingly limited background in subject material; unsatisfactory or incomplete answers to pupils' questions; failure to depart from text for illustrations or explanations) (Evidence of broad background in subject or material; complete, accurate, and satisfying answers to questions; ability to draw examples from various sources, fields, or personal knowledge)

OBSERVATIONS 1 2 3 4 5
INTERVIEWS 1 2 3 4 5

REMARKS:

12. Language in classroom:

Child-like language			Mature language	
1	2	3	4	5

(Uses child-like language level, small vocabulary, "simple" sentence structure; talks down) (Mature vocabulary, "complex" sentences; accustoms pupils to hearing "good" mature English, to learning new words and concepts)

OBSERVATIONS 1 2 3 4 5
INTERVIEWS 1 2 3 4 5

REMARKS:

13. Style of participation:

Allows undirected participation	Encourages active, constructive involvement	Exacts passive participation
1 2	3	4 5
(Allows disorganized discussion; random and undirected participation)	(Encourages constructive participation in recitation, discussion, planning, etc.)	(Discourages discussion; expects waiting for turns, listening, etc.)

OBSERVATIONS   1   2   3   4   5
INTERVIEWS   1   2   3   4   5

REMARKS:

14. Use of information:

Supplies information		Information tied in with discussion	
1 2	3	4 5	
(Provides information which must be digested and returned in same form)		(Gives information and encourages pupils to inquire and explore its meaning)	

OBSERVATIONS   1   2   3   4   5
INTERVIEWS   1   2   3   4   5

REMARKS:

15. Opportunity for children's participation in planning daily curriculum: (Obs. and T Interview)
16. T's interest in children's work: (Obs.)
    (a) Degree of interest:

	Low		High
Reading	1	2	3
Arithmetic	1	2	3
Social Studies	1	2	3
_____	1	2	3
_____	1	2	3
_____	1	2	3

    (b) Quality of interest:
17. T's evaluative techniques in relation to curriculum content:
    (a) How and when praise or blame is used. (Is response varied according to the product or is it routinized?)
    (b) How teacher deals with correct answers. (Evaluating, accepting, opening up further lines of reasoning, etc.)

   (c) How teacher deals with incorrect answers. (Evaluating, correcting, seeking out the errors in reasoning, etc.)

   (d) Frequency of techniques:

      _____ (if correct) Neutral acceptance or affirmation

      _____ (if incorrect or partial, closing statements)

         _____ Corrects or completes (neutral)

         _____ Passes on to another child without comment

      _____ Evaluates positively:

         _____ Supportive comment

         _____ Humorous comment (if incorrect)

         _____ Other

      _____ Evaluates negatively:

         _____ Criticism

         _____ Sarcasm or disparagement

         _____ Invidious comparison

         _____ Other

      _____ Opens up or seeks errors

      _____ Other or unclear

II. TEACHER STRUCTURING—FORMAL

A. General Arrangements

18. Arrangement of tables, desks, numbering of rows, etc. (Cf. plan of room) (Obs. and T Interview)

   (a) Space provisions for *possible* free interaction in the classroom. Locate.

   (b) Implications of T's arrangement of children in rows, at tables, etc., for social interaction:

19. Placement of equipment and supplies (Obs. and T Interview)

   (a) Openness and availability of material for children. Locate.

   (b) If not, describe what a child must do to get at the supplies.

20. Activity groups (reading, mathematics, social studies, gym, trips, art, etc.): (T Interview)

   (a) Groups:

   (b) Rationale: (Criteria used to place children in each group.) Permanence of groups. (If groups changed, on what basis and with what regularity?) Overlapping.

21. Use of buddy system (activities, responsibilities, names of children): (T Interview)

B. Rules (T Interviews and *explicit directives* to class)

22. Posture:

23. Neatness of person, neatness of desk:

24. Noise allowed (no talking, quiet talking, noisy talking, other):

   (a) During what activities does T allow talking? How much?

   (b) T's statements of techniques used to regulate talking:

25. Movement allowed: (State kind of movement: no movement, up

from desk for acceptable errands with T's permission, up from desk for acceptable errands without asking, free movement.)

    (a) During what activities does T allow movement: What kind? How much?

    (b) T's statements of techniques used to regulate allowable movement, and movement which is against the regulations:

C. *Routines*

  26. Method of effecting transitions: (Obs.—Repeat for each transition)

    (a) Transition from _____ to _____.
Method or methods used, in sequence: _____

       i. Indirect statement.
      ii. Direct statement.
     iii. Determination by routine.
     iv. Determination by children's choice.
      v. Determination by children's request.
     vi. Determination by perception of interest level of the group.
Time span: from _____ to _____.
If accomplished in seconds, give an approximation.
Give account of transition below:

    (b) T's use of cues in effecting transitions: (Obs.) (For example, cue words such as "all right," behavior such as clearing one's throat, switching lights on and off to gain attention, etc.)

  27. T's statements regarding transitions: (T Interview)

  28. Shifting of groups from one activity to another: (Obs., T Interview) (Give old group arrangements, new group arrangement, activity shifting from and to, and characterize movement.)

  29. Individuals leaving the room: (Obs., T Interview)

    (a) Describe the routine a child follows when he wishes to leave the room.

    (b) During what periods is leaving allowable, what periods not allowable?

    (c) How many children may be gone from the room at the same time?

  30. Getting in line: (Obs., T Interview)

    (a) Describe the routine of getting in line.

    (b) How are children placed in line (for example, tall children to the rear, tall boys with tall girls)?

  31. Milk and cookie distribution: (Obs., T Interview) (Describe how conducted.)

  32. Distribution of texts and materials: (Obs., T Interview)

(Who distributes the texts and materials? Do they differ for each activity? State persons. Describe routine.)

33. Other:

34. Delegation of responsibility: class officers, monitors, etc. (T Interview)
    (a) What are the positions for which children are chosen as class officers and monitors, etc.?
    (b) What criteria used to choose children for these positions? If differ with each position, list positions with criteria.
    (c) Are there elective offices? If so, how are the candidates chosen? By T, then an election? By children, then an election? How are elections conducted?
    (d) What are the duties and privileges appended to each position?
    (e) List children who hold positions and name positions they hold:

III. TEACHER STRUCTURING—INFORMAL
   A. *Informal Structuring of the Teaching Situation* (*Obs.*)
      35. Mathematics:
          (a) Describe the way in which T structures the activity in terms of the major orientation: (T-oriented, oriented to individual child, group-oriented with "radial interaction," etc.):
          (b) Latitude for choice—groups assigned or self-chosen.
          (c) Patterns of response called for by T. (Describe how T calls forth responses in terms of hands up, by rows, by individual, group response, spontaneous response, etc.)
      36–38. Repeat for reading, social studies, other.
   B. *Differential Treatment of Children* (*Obs., T Interview*)
      39. Partiality: (Obs.)

Partial				Fair
1	2	3	4	5

(Special criticism, attention, or approval given to individuals)	(Criticism, praise, attention distributed among pupils as deserved)

      40. Emergence of children: (T Interview)
          (a) T's judgment of children:
              "Bright" children:
              "Slow" children:
              "Problem" children:
              "Good" children:
              "Unusual" children:
              "Quiet" children:
              Other:
          (b) Summary descriptions:

41. Emergence of children: (Obs.)
    (a) T-initiated interaction directly pertaining to subject matter: (Obs. I & II)
    (b) T's evaluative techniques directly pertaining to subject matter: (Item 17)
    (c) T's control mechanisms pertaining to behavior: (Item 52)

    [NOTE: Forms for recording data for items 41–a, 41–b, and 41–c may be found at the end of Appendix I(A).]

C. *T's Enactment of Rules and Routines:*
    42. T's perception of children's interactions: (T Interview) Names of friendships and cliques she observes.
    43. Attitudes she expresses toward such formations: (T Interview)
    44. Time allowed for free interaction: in curriculum period, in play or "free" periods. (Obs., T Interview)
    45. Ways and degrees to which T directs activities during free periods: (Obs.)
    46. Intervening: (Obs.)

Intervening				Non-Intervening
1	2	3	4	5

(Quick to move into children's problems to structure, assist, or in any way handle or settle)

(Children left to work out problems for themselves unless —or even if—they threaten the whole situation)

REMARKS:

47. Imposes severe limitations   Limitations scarce and mild

1	2	3	4	5

REMARKS:

48. T mandatory, "lays down the law," expects compliance

Exchanges ideas, encourages suggestions, requests criticism, allows wide range of choice

1	2	3	4	5

REMARKS:

49. Frequent disciplinary friction   Lack of disciplinary friction

1	2	3	4	5

REMARKS:

50. Consistency with which T disciplines:

Consistent				Erratic
1	2	3	4	5

REMARKS:

51. Effectiveness of enforcement:

Very effective   Not effective

1   2   3   4   5
_____

REMARKS:

52. Control mechanisms:
    (a) Frequency of techniques: To Individuals   To Groups
        Simple directives _____
        Signals _____
        Direct praise _____
        Mildly negative questions, statements, and warnings _____
        Scolding _____
        Explicit use of the word "shame" _____
        Direct threat _____
        Threatens withdrawal of affection _____
        Physical control negative _____
        Physical control positive _____
        Removal from group _____
        Promises _____
        Moralizing _____
        Indirection _____
        Calling on outside authority _____
        Calling for competition among children _____
        Request to please, or statement of T's pleasure _____
        Pointing out child or group as positive model _____
        Pointing out child or group as negative model _____
        Neutral interchange _____
        Other _____
        _____

    (b) Give all examples.
    (c) T's reaction to child-child conflicts: (Obs.)
        List all incidents, and state nature of situations, whether
        T clamps down, lectures, takes sides, disregards, other.
    (d) Situations which T most often controls: (Obs.)
53. Partitive or integrative techniques: (Obs.) (For example, praise
    or blame for individual given indirectly through holding up the
    child's work to the class, praise or blame for the group, how
    given. Summary statement from Items 17 and 52.)
54. T's view of her enactment: (T Interview)

IV. BEHAVIORAL MODES: VALUES AND ATTITUDES
    A. *Behavioral Modes*
        55. Description of T:
            (a) Appearance and dress
            (b) Facial and bodily movements
            (c) Quality and demeanor of voice

(d) Degree of assurance conveyed to observers and interviewer

(e) Level and tone of verbal communication with children

(f) Types of nonverbal communication; physical contacts

56. Maturity of manner:

1	2	3	4	5

(Self-pitying, complaining, demanding, indicating envy or jealousy)   (Well-controlled emotionally, natural in manner, realistic)

OBSERVATIONS   1   2   3   4   5
INTERVIEWS   1   2   3   4   5

REMARKS:

57. Self- or pupil-directed:

1	2	3	4	5

(Talks of self more frequently than pupils; seeks for pupils to satisfy or please her rather than oriented toward satisfying or interesting pupils)   (Talks often of pupils, oriented toward their needs more than her own, or possibly toward fulfilling their needs as the way of satisfying her own)

OBSERVATIONS   1   2   3   4   5
INTERVIEWS   1   2   3   4   5

REMARKS:

58. Cheerfulness:

1	2	3	4	5

(Depressed, frowning, skeptical, appearing to see and call attention to potential bad)   (Cheerful, appearing to see and call attention to potential good, anticipated good in future)

OBSERVATIONS   1   2   3   4   5
INTERVIEWS   1   2   3   4   5

REMARKS:

59. Approachability:

1	2	3	4	5

(Distant, condescending, remote, formal, not in contact with children)   (Close, warm, approachable, keenly reactive to children)

OBSERVATIONS   1   2   3   4   5
INTERVIEWS   1   2   3   4   5

REMARKS:

60. Alertness:

1	2	3	4	5

(Bored, passive, preoccupied,   (Buoyant, enthusiastic, active)
physically inactive)

OBSERVATIONS   1 2 3 4 5
INTERVIEWS   1 2 3 4 5

REMARKS:

61. Confidence of manner:

1	2	3	4	5

(Unsure of self, faltering, hesi-   (Sure of self, self-confident)
tant)

OBSERVATIONS   1 2 3 4 5
INTERVIEWS   1 2 3 4 5

REMARKS:

62. Steadiness:

1	2	3	4	5

(Loses temper, impulsive, in-   (Unruffled, even-tempered,
consistent, temperamental)   calm, stable, consistent)

OBSERVATIONS   1 2 3 4 5
INTERVIEWS   1 2 3 4 5

REMARKS:

63. Response to children's attempts at autonomous behavior: (Obs.)
    (Give all incidents)
    Accepts (allows time for completion, gives opportunity for ini-
    tiation). Channels (redirects). Thwarts (or interrupts). Respects
    (gives latitude for choice and revision).
64. Noninstructional service to pupils: (How much? Document.)
    (Obs., T Interview)
B. *Values and Attitudes*
    65. T's classroom statements of motivation and goals for children:
        (Obs.)
    66. Content of T's rewards and punishments: (Obs., T Interview)
    67. T's view of self and role: (T Interview)
    68. T's view of children, their parents, and social background: (T
        Interview)
    69. Summary statement of T's values and attitudes, stated and im-
        plied: (T Interview)

T-initiated interaction directly pertaining to subject matter: (Obs. I & II)

Name	Hand Up Called	Hand Not Up Called	Hand Gesture Unrecorded	Unrecorded Response	Total	Spontaneous Response	Remarks

TOTAL

Specify:
1. A—Arithmetic
   R—Reading
   S—Social Studies
   O—Other

2. G—Group response
3. C—Correct
   W—Wrong
   o—(unknown, irrelevant, etc.)
   P—Partial answer

FORM 41-b

T's evaluative techniques directly pertaining to subject matter: (Item 17)

Name	Correct				Incorrect					Incomplete or Partially Wrong				
	Accepts	Evaluates Pos.	Neg.	Uncl.	Opens Up	Corrects	Evaluates Pos.	Neg.	Uncl.	Seeks Errors	Com-plete	Evaluates Pos.	Neg.	Uncl.	Opens Up

FORM 41-c

T's control mechanisms pertaining to behavior: (Item 52)

Name	Directive or Signals	Praise or Reward	Mildly Neg. Sanction, Ques., Dir. or Warning	Other Punitive	Moralizing	Calling for Competition	Request to Please T	Using as Pos. Model	Using as Neg. Model	Other

OUTLINE FOR THE CHARACTERIZATION
OF A CLASSROOM (CHILDREN)

Class:_____

I. CURRICULUM
  A. *Ability and Achievement* (Interviews with T, Observations, Child Questionnaire)
    1. Age and IQ scores
    2. Reading level and/or other test scores
    3. T's judgment of ability and achievement
    4. Indirect evidence of ability from observation
        Interaction and verbal level with other children;
        interaction with T; physical competence
    5. Evidence of ability from Child Questionnaire
  B. *Reaction to Task* (Obs.)
    6. Involvement in the task: mathematics (repeat for reading, social studies, other)
        Give account of children's response to opening, carrying on the task, and closing. (See Item 26, Teacher's section, Transitions, and Item 35, Informal Structuring of the Teaching Situation.)
        Scales: When taken _____
              Observation No. _____
      (a) Extent of attentiveness to task:

1	2	3	4	5
Virtually all	c.70%	c.50%	c.30%	Almost none

      (b) Quality of interest of the participants:

1	2	3	4	5
Enthusiastic, "keyed up"			Passive, compliant	

      (c) Relation to work: Ease in getting started:

1	2	3	4	5
Need answers, directives			Get under way readily	

      (d) Relation to work: Carrying on the task:

1	2	3	4	5
Need constant encouragement, worry about details			Proceed on own, requiring only occasional encouragement or assistance	

235

(e) Noise level:

1	2	3	4	5
Very quiet				Loud, hectic

(f) Movement:

1	2	3	4	5
Much movement				Little movement

7. Reaction to ideas of other children versus reaction to ideas of T:
   List incidents showing
   (a) Evidence of reaction to T's ideas
   (b) Evidence of reaction to children's ideas
   (c) Effect on class of T's reaction to a child's idea
   (d) Comments
8. Classroom response to success and failure:
   (a) List incidents showing response to individual success and individual failure
   (b) Comments

C. *Mode of Cognition* (Obs.)
   9. Nature of classroom participation:

1	2	3	4	5
Active (Manipulating things, ideas; active, having direct experience)			Passive (Passive, vicarious intake of facts and information)	

Reading	1	2	3	4	5	Social Studies	1	2	3	4	5
Arithmetic	1	2	3	4	5	Recess	1	2	3	4	5
_____	1	2	3	4	5	_____	1	2	3	4	5

REMARKS:

10. Adequacy of response: (in relation to T's standards)

1	2	3	4	5
Less than required		Adequate		Fuller than required

Reading	1	2	3	4	5	Social Studies	1	2	3	4	5
Arithmetic	1	2	3	4	5	Recess	1	2	3	4	5
_____	1	2	3	4	5	_____	1	2	3	4	5

11. Range of frequency, correctness of response:
    (Summary of Item 41a, Teacher's section)

(a) Total number of responses observed
(b) Range (names of high and low children, and number of children in middle categories):

Names and number of children	Number of responses	Number correct	Number incorrect or partly correct

12. Style of children's responses or statements:
(Analysis of responses where children either elaborated or clearly determined the content or direction. Simple, factual, and yes/no responses not included.)

(a) Categories:

Procedural	_____	(related to curriculum only)
Logical	_____	(describes reasoning process, or puts facts together toward conclusion)
Factual	_____	(gives information)
Definitional	_____	(gives formal type of definition)
Personal	_____	(refers to self or family in relation to subject)
Irrelevant	_____	(statement seemingly unrelated to subject)
Other	_____	
Uncertain	_____	
Total	_____	

(b) Incidents:

13. Style of response:
(a) Comparison of number total responses and child-elaborated or directed responses:
Total number of elaborated or child-directed responses _____
Total number of all responses (Item 11, Children's section) _____
(b) Individuals with high number of elaborated or child-directed responses:
(c) Individuals with high number of total responses:

II. CHILDREN'S SOCIAL RELATIONS

A. *Response to Routines and Controls*

14. Carrying out of formal responsibilities in classroom (monitors, etc.)
Give name of child, formal role title, and behavior observed.

14a. Child-initiated statements regarding classroom management:
Curriculum procedures _____ (Items from procedural category
Rules and routines _____ of style of responses, Item 13)
Behavior of other children: Reporting to T _____
Interceding on behalf
of other children _____

15. Noise level: (Obs.)
    (a) Noise level under varying conditions:

1	2	3	4	5
Very quiet			Loud, hectic	

Noise level generally	1	2	3	4	5
T is working with whole class	1	2	3	4	5
When T is working with part of class, individual child, or at desk	1	2	3	4	5
When T is out of room	1	2	3	4	5
Transitions	1	2	3	4	5
Other	1	2	3	4	5
Other	1	2	3	4	5

REMARKS: (Especially what part of class or particular children contribute to noise level at a given time.)

(b) Posture:

1	2	3	4	5
Sit up straight at desk, hands folded, or in formal reading or writing position		Relaxed but composed	Sprawl or slouch at desk	

17. Movement: (Obs.)
    (a) Movement under varying conditions:

1	2	3	4	5
Much movement			Little movement	

Movement in general	1	2	3	4	5
Movement when T is working with whole class	1	2	3	4	5
Movement when T is working with part of class, individual child, or at desk	1	2	3	4	5
Movement when T is out of room	1	2	3	4	5
Movement during transitions	1	2	3	4	5
Other	1	2	3	4	5
Other	1	2	3	4	5

(b) Purpose of movement:

1	2	3	4	5
Purposeful coming and going			Purposeless, scattered coming and going	

18. Class response to sanctions directed at whole class: (Obs.)
    (a) Speed of response:

1	2	3
Immediate	After long time	

    Is there much individual variation in speed of response?
    Yes _____ No _____
    Which individuals observed to respond quickly?
    Names:
    Which individuals observed to respond slowly?
    Names:
    (b) Quality of response: (Rank frequency used with "1" as high
    and "0" when not applicable. List names of children who
    respond this way.)

    RANK

    Active obedience—does efficiently what T demands. _____
    Names:
    Passive obedience—begrudgingly and inefficiently
    does what T demands.   _____
    Names:
    Objects to T's demands.   _____
    Names:
    Disobeys T's demands, so that further sanctions are
    necessary.   _____
    Names:
    Other.   _____
    Names:
    (c) List incidents:
19. Individual child's response to control: (Obs.)
    (a) Names of individuals sanctioned who respond quickly:
    (b) Quality of response to T's sanctions: (Rank in order of
    frequency, using "1" as most frequent and "0" if not ap-
    plicable; and list names of children responding in these
    ways.)

    RANK

    Active obedience—efficiently does what T demands. _____
    Names:
    Passive obedience—begrudgingly and inefficiently
    does what T demands.   _____
    Names:
    Objects to T's demands.   _____
    Names:
    Disobeys T's demands.   _____
    Names:
    Other.   _____
    Names:

(c) Names of children who incorporate T's sanctioning power by tattling, or by telling other children directly to do something (i.e., stop talking, fighting) when not monitors:
(d) List incidents:
20. Class response to T's sanctioning of individual:
    List incidents and state category into which they fall when applicable:
    (a) Identification with T—does class seem to mirror T's attitude when individual is sanctioned?
    (b) Identification with child, actively hostile to T—does class seem antagonistic to T when she sanctions individual?
    (c) Identification with child, actively fearful of T—does class seem threatened when T sanctions individual and seem to take it as warning to themselves?
    (d) Lack of involvement—does class seem to sit by passively as if sanctioning of individual has no bearing on them?
    (e) Identification with child and T—does class seem to understand rationale and accept sanction as fair?
    (f) Other—specify.
B. *Interactions Among Children*
    21. Descriptions of observed groupings not directly structured by T: (Obs.)
        (a) Degree of observability of child-child interactions

1	2	3	4	5
Low				High

How many interactions were recorded:
(b) Names and pairings and trios evident, and form:
    (T: talking; P: physical; O: other—smile, look, etc.)
(c) Distribution of interactions:
(d) Names of children with high level of interaction
(e) Names of children with low level of interaction
(f) Pattern of interactions:
    Are pairing or trios within sex____cross sex____
    Other characteristics of pattern of observed interactions:
(g) List incidents where context and content of interactions are recorded.
22. Content of observed interactions:
    (a) Talking: RATE
        In general   ____ (Rate little, medium, much)
        Quiet interchange   ____ (Rate rarely, sometimes, often)
        Arguing   ____ (Rate rarely, sometimes, often)
        Unclear   ____ (Rate rarely, sometimes, often)

(b) Physical interchange: RATE
    Casual touching, bumping _____
    Mock fighting   _____
    Serious fighting   _____
    Unclear or other   _____

(c) Are following categories of interaction evidenced?
    RATE
    _____ Children learn from or with each other.
    _____ Children enjoy each other; evidence of straightforward, enjoyable interchange.
    _____ Children gang up against each other; evidence of group-group, group-individual animosity.
    _____ Children test worth against other children; evidence of physical and verbal aggression between individuals.

23. Descriptions of sociometric groupings: (Child Questionnaire) (See teacher's perception—Item 42, Teacher's section.)
    (a) Pairings and trios evident:
    (b) Highly chosen children:
    (c) Underchosen or nonchosen children:
    (d) Rejected children:
    (e) Children mentioned in questionnaire on non-sociometric questions: (Give names, frequency mentioned, and behaviors for which mentioned.)
    (f) Other sociometric patterns:

III. CHILDREN'S BEHAVIORAL MODES, VALUES, AND ATTITUDES

A. *Modes*

24. Apathetic   Alert

1	2	3	4	5

(Inattentive, indifferent, half-hearted participation)   (Respond eagerly, anxious to participate, attentive)

REMARKS: (Including names of atypical children.)

25. Obstructive   Responsible

1	2	3	4	5

(Interrupting one another, quarrelsome, sullen, obstinate, refusing to participate, or demanding attention by waving hands constantly)   (Cooperative with one another and with T but seek help when needed, orderly without specific directions from T)

26. Uncertain   Confident

1	2	3	4	5

(Demonstrate fear of partici- pation, hesitance, embarrass- ment, shyness, confusion)	(Willing to try new problems or activities, participate freely, speak with assurance, not un- duly disturbed by mistakes)

27. Dependent   Initiating (within T limits)

1	2	3	4	5

(Rely on T for explicit direc- tions, unable to proceed with initiative, unable to take lead or responsibility)	(Volunteer ideas and make suggestions, resourceful in pro- ceeding without direction and taking lead)

28. Evidence liking for T   Evidence dislike for T

1	2	3	4	5

29. Signs of satisfaction: (Obs.)
    (a) When pleasure is shown:
    (b) How pleasure is shown:
    (c) Names of children showing satisfaction:
    (d) List incidents:
30. Signs of tension: (Obs.)
    (a) When tension is shown:
    (b) How tension is expressed:
    (c) Names of children observed as showing signs of tension:
    (d) Incidents:
B. *Goals and Attitudes* (Child Questionnaire Data)

APPENDIX

II

Teacher Interviews

FIRST TEACHER INTERVIEW *

LEAD QUESTION	POSSIBLE FOLLOW-UP QUESTIONS	RATIONALE
1. Could you tell me a little about this class?	Range of children's abilities. How the children are doing scholastically. How well the children get along together. How the class compares with other classes.	How T views the children's ability and performance, and her preliminary attitudes to the children as a group.
2. How would you describe the children?	The unusual children and what they are like. The children who are doing top work. The children who are doing poor work.	T's definition of the unusual children; who they are. The ones she sees as the "good" learners and "poor" learners. T's attitude toward children.
3. How much concern do the parents express for their children's learning?		T's attitude toward the parents' concerns, and specifically what they are.
4. What do you think the parents consider as your most important job as a teacher?		What T sees as the meaning of her function to the parents. T's attitude toward parents.
5. In what ways can the parents be most helpful to their child in school?	Areas where help is desired, and not desired. Ways of conveying this to parents.	T's expectations for the parents. How she deals with them and sees her role in relation to the home.
6. How much contact do you have with parents from your class?	Conferences. PTA meetings. Active parents.	T's attitudes toward the adequacy of her contact with the parents and specific data on contact with parents.
7. From your knowledge of the parents, what picture do you get of the children's home life?	Space for homework. Family cohesion.	Specific information on the children's background, and how their home environments are oriented to school.
Also, what is the average size of the families? How many of the mothers work? What do the fathers do?	Uniformity or lack of uniformity of fathers' occupations.	T's attitude toward the children's backgrounds.

---

* Developed by Phyllis Gunther.

LEAD QUESTION	POSSIBLE FOLLOW-UP QUESTIONS	RATIONALE
What backgrounds, ethnic and religious, do most of the children come from?		
8. Let's go back to the classroom. Could you tell me something about how you have worked out the classroom routines?	Seating arrangement. Arrival to classroom. Bathrooming. Milk and cookies. Dismissal. Cleaning up. Belongings from home	Specific information on T's structuring of classroom routines. T's attitudes toward the meaning of classroom functions to the children.
9. What do you do about talking and moving around in the classroom?		Specific information on T's handling of talking and moving around. T's attitude toward children's communication with each other and its place in the classroom.
10. How do you move from one activity to another?	Expectations for children when they have finished their work. Termination of one activity and beginning of a new one.	Specific information on how T structures transitions. T's attitudes toward children's independence.
11. Could we go over the schedule of your program? I would like to write it down so the observers can plan their visits.	T's keeping to her schedule.	Information on T's program and her allocation of time.
12. Could you tell me about the texts that you use?	Adequacy of them for children's abilities and for the content of the program.	Texts used in the classroom and T's attitude toward them.
13. How do you find this room suits your teaching needs?	Length of time in it. Possibility for changes in arrangement.	T's attitudes toward the adequacy of the physical setting.
14. We would like to have the names of the children according to their seating arrangement.	How T arrived at seating arrangement. The activities the children get up from their seats for. Criteria for the selection of reading groups; their permanency.	The seating chart is needed for the observers to orient themselves to the classroom and familiarize themselves with the children's names.
Also, the names of the children in the reading groups; the class officers; monitors; buddies or	Responsibility of the monitorial positions. Time allotted for jobs. Rights and privileges	Information on the grouping of children, and job responsibilities. T's attitudes about seating of

LEAD QUESTION	POSSIBLE FOLLOW-UP QUESTIONS	RATIONALE
helpers.	attached to positions. How chosen.	children, reading groups, and giving children responsibilities. T's attitude toward children.

SECOND TEACHER INTERVIEW

LEAD QUESTION	POSSIBLE FOLLOW-UP QUESTIONS	RATIONALE
1. In our first interview you told me many things about your class and program. I would like to go into these a little more.		
Also, since the observers had the opportunity to be with your class, do you have any comments about those days?	Were these typical or atypical days?	Information on T's and children's reactions to observers.
What were the children's reactions to the observers?		
2. The observers were particularly interested in knowing what ——— are like.		Specific information on particular children. T's attitudes toward these children.
3. Which children are best liked in the class? Which ones are least liked?		T's perception of the most liked and least liked children. (Compare with sociometric information from the Children's Questionnaire.)
4. How do the children get along as a group? How long have they been together?	Cooperativeness. Competitiveness. Intensity of feeling.	T's perception of relationships among the children.
What friendships have developed among the children?	Permanency of the relationship. Visiting after school. Sitting together.	T's attitude toward the children's socialization.
What is their influence on the rest of the children?		
5. How do the children feel about school?		
What do they like about it? What don't they like?		T's perception of the children's attitudes toward education and herself.

LEAD QUESTION	POSSIBLE FOLLOW-UP QUESTIONS	RATIONALE
6. You mentioned in our first interview what rules you have and how you have worked out your routines.		
Could you tell me what kinds of things you do when the children are not doing what they're supposed to?	Children making too much noise. Children not paying attention. Children telling on one another. Children fighting.	Information on T's control techniques and T's attitudes toward her role as an authority.
Which of these things occur most frequently with these children?		
What ways do you have to show the children you are pleased with their work? with their behavior?		
7. How much opportunity do the children have to talk together?		T's attitude toward the children's needs to socialize. T's goals and expectations for the children. T's approach toward the learning process; her curriculum and techniques for dealing with the subject matter.
8. Let's go back to your program. What kinds of things do you think these children should be getting out of school?		
What kinds of activities are a part of your curriculum?		
Broadly, what goes into the content of these activities?	Specifically, social studies, reading, arithmetic.	
How do you expect to accomplish this?	With the children you have, is there any way of teaching them that you feel works best? Role of discussion, trips, dramatics. Use of groupings. Use of concrete materials. Use of children's interests.	T's attitudes toward the place of creative activities in the curriculum.

LEAD QUESTION	POSSIBLE FOLLOW-UP QUESTIONS	RATIONALE
	Use of workbooks, drill, buddy system.	
	Use of music, art, creative writing, dramatic play.	
Apart from "pure subject matter," what other things are you trying to teach these children?	Use of the subject matter to develop the children's ability to get along together.	T's social values and her attitude toward her role in implementing the children's social relationships.
9. What kinds of things do you think these children should be getting out of school?		T's expectations for children.
10. How is your program planned?	Board of Education directives (Curriculum Bulletins). Administrative policy. Individual initiative.	Information regarding T's autonomy or lack of it in planning her program.
11. What are some of the special things about this school that make it a good working situation?		T's attitude toward working in this particular setting.
12. Could you tell me how you chose to go into teaching and what you see as your future in the field?		T's motivation for teaching and expectations for herself in the field.
How long have you been teaching? All at this school?		Information on T's experience.
13. What age level do you like best to work with? Why?		T's attitude toward children, and particularly her group of children.
How do you like teaching children of this ability and background?		
14. How well prepared do you feel you were for teaching these children?	Where did you get your training?	T's attitude about her preparation for teaching.
15. What do you think these children will go on to do?	What meaning do you think school has for deprived children?	T's attitude toward her group of children and her expectations for them.
	or	
	What do you feel about the adequacy of this school for bright children?	

A P P E N D I X

III

Child Interview*

---

* Developed by Sylvia Knopf Polgar. Section B was given first when fifth-grade children were interviewed to eliminate possible influencing of answers by questions about behavior in Section A.

A. 1. Suppose tomorrow someone told you it was up to you (that you had your choice) as to whether you wanted to go to school any more? What would you do? (Prompt: Would you still go,)
   2. Why?
   3. Do you think you'd miss anything if you didn't go? (Prompt: What else do you learn in school?)
   4. How does school teach you about taking care of yourself?
   5. How does school teach you about getting along? (With other children)
   6. How does school teach you about behavior?

B. 1. If you could choose all by yourself, which child in class would you like best to sit next to?
   2. Who would you choose next? (Who would be your second choice?)
   3. What children in class don't you particularly like? (To sit next to)
   4. How come? (What do they do that you don't particularly like?)
   5. What kind of things do people in your class do that you'd like to do if you could?
   6. Who, for example? (Who does that?)
   7. What kind of things do children in your class do that annoy you most?
   8. Which child in class do most children like?

C. 1. What do you think you'd like to be when you grow up?
   2. Do you think school will help you? (To be a _____)
   3. (If answer "yes") In what way? (If answer "no") How would you learn? To do that or be a _____?
   4. What work (subject) in school do you like best?
   5. How are you at arithmetic? Are you very good, medium good, or not so good? How about reading? Are you very good, medium good, or not so good?
   6. What happens when you can't do an arithmetic example?
   7. What happens when you can't read something?
   8. What does your teacher do? (Does your teacher help you? How?)
   9. What about most children, are they good at arithmetic? Are most of them better than you or not as good as you?
   10. What about reading, are they good at it? Are they better than you or not as good as you?

D. 1. What kind of things do children do that make your teacher particularly happy?
   2. What does she do then? (Does she do anything special?)
   3. What kind of things do children do that your teacher doesn't particularly like?
   4. What does she do then? (Does she do anything special?)
   5. What would you like to do in school that you don't do now?

253

INDEX

academic activities, 73–74, 119, 132, 153, 155, 160–163, 167, 176, 184, 191–193, 196
Academic Freedom, Committee on, 46
acceptance, self, 213
accreditation, 148
achievement, importance of, 66, 73–74, 80, 118–119, 136–138, 141, 149, 155, 164, 167, 195–196, 209, 213
adaptation, individual, 17–18
adjustments, equation of, 26, 161, 215
administrative procedures, 5, 13, 22–23, 87, 151, 165–167
admissions, discriminatory, 5
adult life, 17, 60, 117, 120, 148, 161, 165, 176–179, 200, 211
affirmation, technique of, 70
Africa, 78
after-school activities, 12, 97, 118, 147
age-mates, 32, 116
aggressiveness, spectrum of, 162, 167, 213
amiability, quality of, 48
analysis, problems of, 11, 18, 21, 45
Anderson, R. C., cited, 89
anger, 154
animals, love for, 79, 192
anthropologists, social, 14, 201
anti-white resentments, 154
apathy, 181, 209

aristocracy, 146
arithmetic, problems in, 24, 38, 43, 69, 103, 121, 134, 158, 160, 162–163, 169, 180, 186–192
articulation, lack of, 162
art sessions, 52, 191–193; see also drawing sessions
aspirations, see goals
attendance, necessity for, 25
attention, class, 139
attitudes, 7, 13, 15–16, 49, 53, 59–60, 88, 117–118, 136, 148, 158, 190, 194, 200; anti-white, 154; children's, 18, 170; established, 203; humanistic, 26; negative, 141; positive, 140; school, 9; teacher's, 120, 136, 151, 176, 196, 202, 205, 207; work, 182, 185
authoritarianism, 89, 117, 129–130, 165–166, 212
autonomy, quality of, 90, 103, 110
awareness, social, 24
Axtell, W. B., cited, 22

backgrounds, 12, 204, 212; children's, 26, 80, 140, 142; demographic, 149; home, 143; poor, 206–207
Bank Street College of Education, 149
Bany, M. A., cited, 86, 88, 118
Becker, H. S., cited, 148

255